Elizabeth Pilar Challinor

Bargaining in the Development Market-Place

Elizabeth Pilar Challinor

Bargaining in the Development Market-Place

Insights from Cape Verde

LIT

Cover picture taken by author

Printed with support of
Foundation for Science and Technology (FCT)
Centre for the Study of Social Anthropology (CEAS)

CEAS
CENTRO DE ESTUDOS DE ANTROPOLOGIA SOCIAL

FCT Fundação para a Ciência e a Tecnologia
MINISTÉRIO DA CIÊNCIA, TECNOLOGIA E ENSINO SUPERIOR Portugal

Bibliographic information published by the Deutsche Nationalbibliothek
The Deutsche Nationalbibliothek lists this publication in the Deutsche Nationalbibliografie; detailed bibliographic data are available in the Internet at http://dnb.d-nb.de.

ISBN 978-3-8258-1410-6

A catalogue record for this book is available from the British Library

Auslieferung/Verlagskontakt:
Fresnostr. 2 48159 Münster
Tel. +49 (0)251–62 03 20 Fax +49 (0)251–23 19 72
e-Mail: lit@lit-verlag.de http://www.lit-verlag.de

Distributed in the UK by: Global Book Marketing, 99B Wallis Rd, London, E9 5LN
Phone: +44 (0) 20 8533 5800 – Fax: +44 (0) 1600 775 663
http://www.centralbooks.co.uk/acatalog/search.html

Distributed in North America by:

Transaction Publishers
New Brunswick (U.S.A.) and London (U.K.)

Transaction Publishers
Rutgers University
35 Berrue Circle
Piscataway, NJ 08854

Phone: +1 (732) 445 - 2280
Fax: + 1 (732) 445 - 3138
for orders (U. S. only):
toll free (888) 999 - 6778
e-mail:
orders@transactionspub.com

In memory of

Bernardino Lopes Alfonso
and
Carlos Alberto Gonçalves

Preface

This book is the outcome of a doctorate dissertation that has been restructured and enriched with new field data. I would like to thank the anthropology staff that taught me, at Sussex University, for the stimulating academic environment of my student days. I am grateful, in particular, to my supervisor - Jock Stirrat, as well as to Katy Gardner, Ralph Grillo, Richard Wilson, Ann Whitehead and Jon Mitchell. I also benefited from the enthusiasm of my peers, especially; Joanne Moore, Martha Hannon, Katja Jobes, Harriet Stanley, Fiona Samuels, Bruno Riccio, Branwen Gruffydd-Jones, Peter Luetchford and Ruba Salih.

I wish to thank Clara Carvalho - for encouraging me to publish my work – and José Francisco Portela, for their critical commentaries on an earlier version of the book. I am indebted to Marina Temudo for her constant support as well as for her insightful comments. I am also grateful to the critical eye of Kesha Fykes on drafts of chapters four and five as well as for her encouragement. A very special thank you goes to Jim Igoe for his enthusiasm and persistent interest in my work; helping to clarify my ideas in the innumerable emails that we exchanged and reading and critiquing book summaries and earlier versions of chapters four and five. I also wish to thank my long-standing friend, Cláudia Pazos Alonso, for her unwavering support. I also acknowledge with thanks the help and encouragement from Timothy Sieber, Ramon Sarró, Manuela Raminhos, Rui Silva, Andreia Soares, Ana Sequeira and Cidália Santos. I also thank Veit Hopf from Lit Verlag for his support.

By dedicating this book to the memory of two Cape Verdean friends - Beto and Berne - whom I greatly miss, I wish to remember, with affection and admiration, the devotion with which they always committed themselves to their work.

I am deeply grateful to all of the people in and from Cape Verde who, in some way or another, had to bear the brunt of my fieldwork. Although the list is countless, I should like to thank, in particular, the help from Alexandre Vera-Cruz for putting me in contact with friends and family on my first trip to Cape Verde. I am grateful to Enrique Borges, José Enrique (Torritcha) and Maria Teresa, as well as to Mariza and Tober for their help. I thank Clara Barros and Filomena Oliveira who provided me with invaluable logistical and emotional support in reconciling fieldwork with childcare. Filomena was also a safe sounding board for my thoughts and Clara always ready to help me find additional data at a distance! I am also grateful to Pedro and to Celestino for their help and hospitality as well as to Orlando Sanches for his assistance. I am truly indebted to Titina and Luisinha whose friendship I have treasured over the years, for their support and enthusiasm. I am grateful to Isabel, Gunda, Zinha, Nana, Nena, Cristina and Rosa for their generosity. I wish to thank Humberto Lopes as well as Marina, Jorge and Tibursio for their sharing of local knowledge and Monique Widmer for her friendship and support. I am also grateful to José Silva and Danny Spínola for correcting my Creole quotations. A warm thank you is also due to Amadeu and to Filipe Silva, as well as to the rest of the local field staff and the expatriate staff of ACDI; to Edgar Pinto, David Carvalho, and the NLTPS seminar participants; to Mário Moniz and to all of the NGO personnel and government officials and technicians who gave me their time.

The support from my family during the fieldwork and writing process has been invaluable. I thank my mother and Mike for coming out to Cape Verde and looking after Luís during part of my fieldwork and my mother, nearly a decade earlier, for coming out and looking after Hannah, who took her first steps with her in Santo Antão! I am grateful to both my father and mother for helping out in different ways during the writing process, as well as for their wisdom and encouragement. I thank Avó Maria Cândida for her support. My husband, Júlio, has been a rock throughout the whole process: spending a summer in Cape Verde, looking after the children and being mother and father to them at home, in Portugal, during my absence. His good humour and deep-seated optimism has helped to keep me going. Hannah has supported me all the way and Hannah, Carmen and Luís helped me to start each day afresh.

Acknowledgments

I am grateful to the Portuguese Foundation for Science and Technology (FCT) for providing the finance that enabled me to carry out this research. I also gratefully acknowledge the financial contributions from FCT and CEAS – Centre for the Study of Social Anthropology – towards the publication of this book.

Table of Contents

List of Tables

List of Abbreviations

ACDI	Agricultural Cooperative Development International
AIMO	High Intensity Manual Labour (Alta Intensidade de mão de obra)
CBTA	Community-Based Technical Assistance
CBWF	Community-Based Workfronts
COS	Community Organizers
CRWT	Contour Rock Wall Terrace
CSO	Civil Society Organizations
CWF	Classical Workfronts
DGASP	General Directorate for Agriculture, Siviculture and Animal Husbandry
DGCSFER	General Directorate for Soil Conservation, Forestry and Rural Engineering
EMPA	Public Food Marketing Enterprise
FAIMO	Labour Intensive Workfronts (Frentes de Alta Intensidade de mão de obra)
FFP	Food for Peace Project
GOCV	The Government of Cape Verde
INERF	National Institute for Rural Engineering and Forestry
MAAA	Ministry of Agriculture, Food and Envirnment
MCE	Ministry of Economic Co-ordination
MDRP	Ministry of Rural Development and Fishing
MIT	Ministry of Infra-structures and Transport
MOP	Ministry of Public Works
MPAAR	Ministry of Fisheries, Agriculture and Rural Extension
MPD	Movement for Democracy
NES	National Extension Service
NGO	Non-Governmental Organization
NGOD	Non-Governmental Organization for Development
NLTPS	National Long Term Perspective Study
OASIS	Umbrella Organization of the Associations of Santiago Island (Organização de Associações dos Agricultores, Avicultores Pecuários de Santiago)
OMCV	Organization of Cape Verdean Women
PAICV	African Party for the Independence of Cape Verde
PAIGC	African Party for the Independence of Guinea-Bissau and Cape Verde
RAP	Rural Assistance Programme
RE/F	Rural Engineering and Forestry
REW	Rural Engineering Works
SWC	Soil and Water Conservation
TARs	Watershed Auxiliary Technicians (Técnicos Auxiliares das Ribeiras)
UNDP	United Nations Development Programme
UNICEF	United Nations Children's Fund
WARD	Watershed and Applied Research Development Project
WDP	Watershed Development Project
WMP	Watershed Management Project

Chapter One

Theorizing the 'Shifting Middle Ground'

1.1. Introduction

The islands of Cape Verde, situated opposite Senegal, in the middle passage of the Atlantic Ocean between Africa, Europe and America, were part of the Portuguese colonial empire up until their independence in 1975. Since then, the backbone of the country's economy has been sustained by external resources: a combination of foreign aid and remittances from the Cape Verdean diaspora. With its arid climate and only ten per cent of its surface area (4,033 sq km) potentially arable, Cape Verde produces less than twenty per cent of is food requirements – the rest is imported. The country also imports fuel and manufactured goods and despite its exports of textiles, footwear, bananas, and tinned tuna, it always has a large trade deficit.

Today, the population of Cape Verde, less than half a million, is smaller than the number of Cape Verdeans resident abroad. Many poor families depend upon remittances from relatives abroad and/or upon externally funded social assistance programmes for their survival. Nevertheless, Cape Verde's economic growth over the last decade has been accompanied by a reduction in the percentage of the population living in poverty. Tourism and other services have played a significant role in boosting the economy. Although in 2006 the United Nations still classified Cape Verde as a Least Developed Country, this was not reflected in its GNI per capita, which, in 2005 (U.S. $1870) was already amongst the highest in Africa (DAC database). The United Nations officially reclassified Cape Verde as a middle income country in 2008. This new 'middle status' will accelerate existing reductions in aid which are likely to impact upon poorer sections of Cape Verdean society. Economic growth has also been accompanied by higher rates of unemployment and greater disparities in income distribution (Challinor 2007).

Cape Verde is a country looking inwards, in search of socio-economic stability and cultural authenticity whilst at the same time looking outwards - open to the myriad influences from around the world. What it means to be Cape Verdean is hotly disputed: not only between the different islands of African and European influence but also amongst and between emigrant communities in different parts of the world. What constitutes authentic Cape Verdean traditions is an on-going, often generational, debate. The answers to Cape Verde's development problems are also disputed between pro-market campaigners and advocates of poverty alleviation programmes: a battle often fought along political lines. To live in Cape Verde, whether in the geographical location of the archipelago or in the imaginary transnation of its diaspora, involves engaging, in one way or another, with some of these issues. Whether the issue is the authenticity of a particular genre of music, the economic viability of an enterprise or the identity of the nation, Cape Verdeans are acutely aware of the influences of globalization, although they may not all necessarily use this term. To be Cape Verdean is to look outwards to the world and inwards to the homeland at the same time.

The local language, Crioulo, spoken differently in the leeward and windward islands, constitutes a unifying aspect of Cape Verdean identity, although the official language of the archipelago is still Portuguese. In their daily lives, many Cape Verdeans constantly move to and fro between both languages: the use of Portuguese is mostly reserved for public formal occasions whilst Crioulo is spoken in every day encounters. In rural areas, sections of the population either do not speak, or are less comfortable with Portuguese.

Cape Verde has been particularly attractive to scholars interested in migration studies. Each island has its own history of migration: Cape Verdeans from the island of Brava, for example, have mostly migrated to America whilst those from the island of Santo Antão have tended to migrate to European countries, especially Italy and Holland. That the diaspora outnumbers the Cape Verdean resident population provides a radical example of how processes of globalization can result in the 'deterritorialization' (Appadurai 1990) of a nation. Cape Verdeans often describe their nation as 'not quite Africa' and 'not quite Europe'. This challenges dominant conceptions of a world polarised between Western and Non-Western nations. Although Cape Verde is situated in the middle of the 'Black Atlantic', Gilroy (1993) has overlooked its significance in his critique of African cultural nationalisms. The purpose of this study is to bring Cape Verde to the limelight. Not only is it illustrative of many of the issues discussed by Gilroy, but it is also highly relevant for development studies. The book draws on the Cape Verdean ethnography to set current development issues within the domain of existing debates in Anthropology, African, Cultural and Postcolonial studies.

That Cape Verde was uninhabited, when the islands were settled by the Portuguese, provides a rare opportunity to identify a clear beginning in the analysis of the relationship between global and local processes. The islands' Creole society, their history of slavery and migration and their structural dependence upon foreign aid offer a wealth of case material for enquiring into the on-going effects of globalization.

1.2. A division of the world

Scholars in the social sciences have tried to make sense of globalization through the use of dichotomies, such as centre/periphery, traditional/modern, domination/resistance. Whilst there are evidently other forms of organizing perceptions of the world, the language of everyday life is also frequently shot through with opposites. We talk about the differences between 'us' and 'them', town and country, developed and undeveloped regions and nations. We argue over the relations between government and civil society, state and the private sector, economic profit and social welfare. These oppositional categories are a form of conceptual shorthand which allows us to engage with the issues that concern us, without getting too bogged down in detail. The anti-globalization movement is a good example of this. Protests against how the 'global' harms the 'local' do not invite us to examine the pockets of strategic accommodation between these two polar ends. The way in which we interpret the world is the essence of political struggle; our use of oppositional categories in everyday language is consequently likely to overlook the pockets of empirical reality which do not fit in to our world view.

It is these pockets of diversity and complexity which are the focus of this study, for which I have coined the term a 'shifting middle ground'. This concept provides a fresh perspective on the categories with which we investigate the world. The concept of a 'middle ground' provides us with a close-up lens: it enables us to capture the nuanced intersections between polar ends. The concept of a 'shifting middle ground' equips us with a zoom: it allows us to capture the fluid, shifting nature of these intersections and to vary our focal length accordingly.

To essentialize events through the use of binary oppositions is not the only way in which we apprehend the world. Three and four –based concepts, for example, are also very common in the Jewish- Christian culture[1]. Yet, whatever forms of categorization are used, there is always the risk of simplifying reality. The concept of a 'shifting middle ground' may serve as a reminder that in our attempts to achieve integration and generalization, we should bear in mind that reality is always more complex than our categorizations will allow for. No sooner do we think that we have grasped the meaning of something, than we find that it has slipped out of our hands. For the purposes of this study, let us return to consider the frequent use of dualisms.

Bourdieu's theory of practice accounts for the generation of oppositional categories by stating that it is a means of making sense out of the world: 'a vision of the world is a division of the world' (1990:210). However, a 'division of the world' is not only a cognitive enterprise but also a political project which has

[1] My thanks to José Portela for turning my attention to this.

subjugated alternative visions of the world. Mignolo argues that colonial discourse has imposed historical dichotomies upon the world through the invention of 'colonial differences' (2000:337). He consequently proposes a 'postcolonial theorizing' that thinks 'from the borders and the perspectives of subalternity' (2000:110):

> The subaltern reason is what arises as a response to the need of rethinking and reconceptualizing the stories that have been told and the conceptualization that has been put into place to divide the world between Christians and pagans, civilized and barbarians, modern and premodern, and developed and underdeveloped regions and people, all global designs mapping the colonial difference (2000:98).

Mignolo's thesis on 'border thinking' raises critical questions regarding the validity of the concept of a 'shifting middle ground'. In my positing of the concept as a tool of analysis, I cannot claim to be thinking from the 'borders' and acknowledge the danger of proposing yet another abstract, universal category, or, in the words of Mignolo, of producing a '(master) empty signifier that will house the entire diversity of particulars' (2000:66). There is also a degree of irony in the positing of a 'universal' tool of analysis for deconstructing universal categories. This is where I am obliged to mark out the incompleteness of my position, which, rather than thinking from the 'borders', engages with postcolonial theories as an 'academic commodity' (Mignolo 2000:100) and, as such, does not claim to subsume subaltern reason. Having acknowledged these limitations, I shall attempt to demonstrate there is still some validity in the use of the concept of a 'shifting middle ground', not only in terms of the Cape Verdean ethnography, but also in the fields of the anthropology of development and development practice. In particular, I should like to think that it serves as a bridge –imperfect as it may be – between postcolonial theorizing and development practice.

As scholarly debates on the nature of globalization intensify, the analytical validity of dichotomous tools of analysis has been called into question. Both the literature on the anthropology of development and on postcolonialism, express similar misgivings regarding the adequacy of dualisms such as domination/resistance, modern/traditional and state/civil society for studying local/global relations. Before turning to the Cape Verdean ethnography, the following pages examine some of the main arguments in these fields, in the light of the concept of a 'shifting middle ground'.

1.3. Locating the 'middle ground'

What does taking the 'middle ground' help to understand better about the dualism of domination and resistance? Let us briefly examine evolving approaches towards our understanding of domination. The growing disillusionment with totalizing frames of analysis has led researchers to turn their attention to the micro-processes of the periphery. Hannerz, for example, argues that one of the problems with the concept of 'core-periphery relations' is that it reduces the periphery to a 'defence-less victim' (1992:256). Gledhill argues that focusing on resistance to domination helps to bring to light aspects of human agency which could otherwise be overlooked (1994:80). He cites the case of Scott's analysis of 'the weapons of the weak' (1985). Scott's study was a groundbreaker for the political sciences because he chose to study the local level. Equipped with a close-up lens, he exposed the nuances of the 'everyday peasant resistance' of Malayan villagers to the introduction of double-cropping and mechanization which had transformed production relations to the extent that it had become a threat to peasant livelihoods (1985:305). If Scott had gone looking for more visible forms of resistance such as demonstrations and direct confrontations then this 'middle ground' – characterized by 'foot dragging' resistance - would have been obscured. Scott distinguishes between different levels and types of resistance, namely: 'formal – informal, individual – collective, public – anonymous, those that challenge the system of domination – those that aim at marginal gains' (1985:299). The last example given by Scott raises an important question: can we be sure that 'resistance' tells the whole story? What happens if we add a zoom to our close-up lens? Scott concludes that the degree of repression is likely to determine the options of resistance available to peasants (1985:299); but it could also be the case that the concept of 'resistance' is unable to account for all of the options taken by the peasants. Adding a zoom to our close-up lens allows us to, paradoxically, broaden our horizons and embrace the possibility of locating a 'shifting middle ground' where strategies of resistance intersect with strategies of productive cooptation. Escobar raises a similar point in his discussion of a project in Colombia aimed at protecting the biodiversity of the Pacific Coast region:

> ...the project has had to accept the communities as important interlocutors, and several black leaders have been able to insert themselves into the project staff. These professionals/activists are aware of the risks involved in participating in such an enterprise, yet they believe that the project presents a space of struggle they cannot afford to ignore. Are these activists merely assisting capital in the semiotic conquest of nature and communities? Are they contributing to the superficial greening of economics and communities? Or, on the contrary, or simultaneously, can they engage in cultural resistance *and articulate their own productive strategies?* (1995:205, my emphasis).

The idea that strategies of resistance intermingle with strategies of productive cooptation is central to the argument of this book. Mbembe's concept of the 'postcolony' sheds further light upon this issue which bears similarities to my use of the concept of a 'shifting middle ground'. Mbembe argues that the binary categories used in standard analyses of domination obscure our understanding of postcolonial relations which are best characterized as 'convivial' since the dominant and the dominated have to 'share the same living space'. Mbembe describes the fluid nature of the 'postcolony' as made up of several public spaces each with its own logic which becomes entangled, in certain contexts, with other logics. The postcolonial subject has consequently learnt to bargain in a 'conceptual marketplace' (2001:103-104).

Mbembe's ideas on 'conviviality' and conceptual bargaining also broach the issue of how best to understand the impact of processes of globalization upon the 'local' level. Robertson maintains the need to transcend the debate about global homogenization versus heterogenization by 'spelling out the ways in which homogenizing and heterogenizing tendencies are mutually implicative' for which he uses the term 'glocalization' (Robertson 1995:27). One of the problems with this concept is that it may lead us towards painting an over-integrated picture of the intersections between the 'global' and the 'local'. Appadurai's ideas on disjunctive flows are helpful here:

> The various flows we see – of objects, persons, images, and discourses – are not coeval, convergent, isomorphic, or spatially consistent. They are in what I have elsewhere called relations of disjuncture. By this I mean that the paths or vectors taken by these kinds of things have different speeds, axes, points of origin and termination, and varied relationships to institutional structures in different regions, nations or societies. (2002:274).

Appadurai goes on to argue that these disjunctures produce global problems which take on profoundly local forms. For example, media flows across national borders transmit images of material welfare which simultaneously raise and frustrate local expectations (2002, 274); however, not even media flows are unidirectional from the 'centre' to the 'periphery'. Indigenous peoples have also used the media to internationalize their struggles which has transmitted images of 'authentic' locals to the West. The disjunctures between these often idealized images and the reality of the everyday lives of indigenous peoples are referred to by Conklin and Graham (1995) in their analysis of the encounters between Amazonian Indians and western environmentalists. The relevance of their study to my discussion is that they also use the concept of a 'shifting middle ground' to analyse the arenas of interaction between these two social groups. Conklin and Graham draw on White's definition of a 'middle ground' as a 'mutually comprehensible world characterized by new systems of meaning and exchange' ([1991, ix] 1995:695). And yet as they develop their argument we see that these relations of mutual accommodation are forged within an unstable, unequal political space, since their maintenance depends upon meeting idealized western expectations of Indian 'authenticity'. If their actions fail to correspond to these expectations and the media gets wind of these disjunctures then they run the risk of diminishing the strength of the international support for their struggles (1995:704). Conklin and Graham envisage a 'shifting middle ground' as a political space of unequal transnational alliances which produces essentializing discourses that are maintained through media flows and western contacts with a handful of 'indigenous cultural mediators' (1995:703). This provides a more nuanced analysis of relations of domination between the 'north' and the 'south' which are often interpreted in terms of standard dichotomies such as submission versus resistance. Yet it tells us very little about the relations of the 'indigenous cultural mediators' with their own native communities. This constitutes another level of enquiry which may easily be overlooked by enthusiastic celebrations of the current proliferation of translocal alliances.

Relevant here is Ferguson's study of African politics in which he posits a 'worldly, well-connected and opportunistic' grassroots (2004:394). Ferguson argues that our uncritical use of the state/civil society opposition has blinded us to the transnational nature of political resistance in an increasingly globalized world. He elucidates the fundamental similarities between changing approaches towards 'state' and 'civil society' in development thinking, by demonstrating how they have reproduced, in a largely uncritical manner, the state/civil society opposition. The 'nation-building' approach, which characterized development interventions in the newly-independent African countries, championed the state as the main protagonist of development, whilst the 'local' - home to 'tribalism' - was seen as a threat to national unity. The growing dissatisfaction of the performance of the state eventually resulted in a reversal of these popularity ratings whereby the 'local' became the new focus of attention - now home to the exciting promises of 'civil society' to claim back space from the state to develop its own dynamic and creative potentials. Ferguson holds that both approaches share the same assumption regarding the relationship between state and society: that the state operates on a higher level than society somewhere 'up there' whilst the 'local' is situated down 'below'. The problem with this 'vertical topography of power' is that it ignores the transnationalized context within which both the 'top' and the 'bottom' operate; for example, the imposition of policies upon African states by international agencies and the linking of 'local' struggles to global issues such as that of the environment and human rights. In the case of the latter, the state's customary appeal to 'higher', 'national' interests is undermined by the transnational power base of 'local' organisations which equips them with the trump card of 'universalist principles':

> In this optic, it might make sense to think of the new organizations that have sprung up in recent years not as challengers pressing up against the state from below but as horizontal contemporaries of the organs of the state – sometimes rivals, sometimes servants, sometimes watchdogs, sometimes parasites, but in every case operating on the same level, and in the same global space (2004:11).

What are the consequences of this 'transnational topography of power' for our understanding of the nature of political resistance? Whilst making it clear that this new horizontal paradigm does not replace, but rather co-exists with the older vertical model, Ferguson suggests that it requires us to throw out received ideas of 'locality, authenticity and bottom-up struggle' (2004:11). He is neither in favour of taking the older vertical paradigm for granted nor of disregarding it altogether; rather, he is advocating that its naturalization be treated as a 'precarious achievement' and as an 'ethnographic problem' (2004:17). In other words, whilst the social scientist is obliged to subject his or her use of analytical categories to rigorous scrutiny, it is equally important to study the social life of these same categories in their ethnographic context.

Ferguson's deconstruction of traditional notions of the 'authenticity' of the grassroots illustrates the pertinence of distinguishing between 'grassroots' as a category of analysis and 'grassroots' as a normative discourse that reproduces reified conceptions of the 'authentic' and the 'inauthentic'. It is important to distinguish between binary categories as normative discourses subject to interpretation and analysis and binary categories as tools of analysis because the former destabilize the latter. Yet we cannot discard dualistic tools of analysis altogether. Essentialised conceptions of the 'other' do not go away once we have identified them as such. Whilst the close-up lens of the 'middle ground' elucidates the nuanced intersections between simplistic dualisms the latter remain starkly visible. Indeed, it is the task of the social analyst to expose the ways in which social actors simultaneously construct and deconstruct reified ideas about the world.

Notions of authenticity continue to shape the field of development action. The significance of the 'local' or the 'grassroots' as the most worthy site of intervention has sustained the proliferation of non-governmental organisations (NGOs) throughout the last few decades. Consider the following affirmation:

> The approach of the voluntary organisations to Third World poverty is now the new orthodoxy. Big is no longer beautiful. Even among those official agencies which are quite incapable of reforming themselves there is a tacit acknowledgement that the only chance of sustained development is to work from the grassroots up, not from a bureaucratic apparatus down (Gill 1988:169).

In the wake of increasing donor concerns to reach the 'grassroots', 'authenticity' has become a valuable 'commodity' which some local actors are more successful at selling than others in the 'conceptual marketplace' (Mbembe 2001). The enormous increase of local community, association and NGO leaders in Africa over the past few decades is evidence of a newly emerging institutional and discursive space which is characterized by its own internal logics of inequality. We need to know more about the unequal 'bargaining powers' of different social actors and about what structures the options available to them.

1.4 The blind spots of the 'middle ground'

The concept of a 'shifting middle ground' does not only describe a transactional space between politically differentiated social actors; it also opens up an analytical space which helps to raise important questions regarding the use of universal categories in both everyday language and in the social sciences. Bourdieu's theory of practice (1977) offers useful insights here. The concept of a middle ground can be compared to that of a blind spot: an area where our view may be obstructed and our understanding diminished or impartial. Bourdieu accounts for the existence of 'blind spots' in his theory of practice (1977). He argues that the generation of oppositional categories is an elementary feature of social life: it is a means of making sense of the world by dividing it into opposing entities. The outcome is a simplification of reality: 'no more logic is mobilised than is required by the needs of practice' (1977:110). The price to pay for this 'economy of logic' is a lack of precision: we overlook the bits of the everyday world around us which do not fit into our worldview. The logic of practice is a 'logic of suggestion and ambiguity' that is characterized by 'indeterminacy' and 'fuzziness' because it 'presupposes a loss of rigour for the sake of greater simplicity and generality' (1977:110, 112-113).

According to Bourdieu, the social analyst occupies a privileged position because he or she is able to accumulate far more information than can be done by any single informant; however, this privileged position is also prone to its own blind spots since it fails to take into account the distorting effects of external observation. People in everyday life are not trying to frame their thoughts and actions into a consistent system: they are more concerned with meeting their everyday practical interests. The social analyst's ability to identify underlying patterns and connections in our collective social life does so at the expense of capturing the transitional, strategic logic of these everyday interests. In other words, it is the very quest for greater understanding that turns out to be our Achilles' heel: it produces its own brand of blind spot. All we can do, as every seasoned driver knows, is to adjust our side mirror accordingly, so that the size of our blind spot is reduced to a minimum.

Anthropological approaches towards the study of identity politics have become fine tuned into the transitional dimension of the 'shifting middle ground'. It has become commonplace to assert that identity is unstable, mobile, situational, relational and so forth. Yet this is not the case in the field of development which reproduces universal categories of identification. Let us take the example of stakeholder analysis: a common practice in the design of development projects that is part of the process of labelling described by Escobar (1995 109-110) in which people are represented as 'cases' in need of development assistance.

The social development division of the Department for International Development in the UK has produced a 'Guidance note on how to do stakeholder analysis of aid projects and programmes' (1995). It describes stakeholders as individuals, groups or institutions that have interests in a project or programme. The guidance note also distinguishes between primary and secondary stakeholders: the latter include those who are affected in a positive or negative manner by the development intervention ('winners and losers') and the former constitute the intermediaries in the process of aid delivery. The aims of conducting a stakeholder analysis are to identify the different interests of all of the stakeholders in relation to the issues the project is intended to address, and once the project has started, to identify stakeholder interests in relation to the project. This in turn will help to identify conflicts of interest between the different stakeholders which will provide an indication of the project's chances of success. The identification of stakeholder interests is concerned above all with minimising the risks in project implementation and securing the participation of direct stakeholders. Stakeholder analysis usually involves filling in tables with brief statements of stakeholders' interests, expectations, strategies and so forth (see Haug, Anderson and Grude 2004).

What would taking the 'middle ground' help us to understand better about stakeholder analysis? Firstly, it would take us beyond the rigid and fixed category of the 'stakeholder'. Peoples' interests or stakes are fluid, shifting and context specific. The convergence of interests in one context may disappear in another. Conflicts of interest do not only arise *between* different categories of stakeholder but also *within* the same categories. Groups and individuals may also have contradictory interests so that they are simultaneously 'winners' and 'losers' of a given project. The prescriptive identification of stakeholder interests is likely to overlook the transitional logic of these everyday interests. This brings me to the second point: taking a 'middle ground' may help development practitioners to go beyond what Hailey calls 'formulaic approaches to participative decision-making' (2001:88). Based on research carried out on South Asian NGOs, Hailey emphasizes the importance of 'informal', 'non-formulaic' and 'highly personal modes of interaction' between local communities and NGO staff (2001: 89):

> The NGOs in the research sample all invested considerable resources in building credibility and trust in the local communities with whom they worked. Respondents and researchers were at pains to point out that this process was not based on a set of formal tools or participative techniques designed to elicit local needs. Trust and respect were based on regular contact, personal ties and shared values. During the start-up phase NGO staff invested considerable time, emotion and energy building up relationships of trust and shared understanding between themselves and local people (2001:90).

As already stated above, mutual understandings are likely to co-exist with misunderstandings and disagreements not only between NGO staff and local communities but also between different members of the same community. The 'myth' of the homogeneous community has already been widely debunked (see, for example, Guijt and Shah, 1998); it is precisely this awareness of the existence of conflicting interests within a given community that has made stakeholder analysis so popular. And yet, one of the potential blind spots of 'stakeholder analysis' is to be found in its inability to attend to the fragmentation and instability of stakeholder categories.

Relevant here is the discussion by Swartz et al of the concept of a 'political field' ([1966] 2002). The authors maintain that the study of politics involves centring our attention on processes instead of on groups or locations within which these processes occur. This is because the field of political activity cuts across group and spatial boundaries, in other words: 'the political field can expand and contract' (Swartz, Turner and Tuden, [1966] in 2002:107). Taking the 'middle ground' in stakeholder analysis alerts the practitioner to the fluid, cross-cutting nature of 'stakeholder interests' and consequently to the limitations of working with fixed, stable categories. These limitations do not only highlight the relevance of deconstructing rigid categories, they also turn our attention to the fluidity of power relations which has also become an issue in post-colonial studies.

1.5. Engaging with post-colonial theories

The underlying concern of postcolonialism has been to contest the structural continuity of unequal power relations between the West and non-Western worlds. Post-colonial studies have frequently dismissed 'development' as a form of neo-colonialism. Their influence upon the anthropology of development is evident in the work of authors such as Rahnema (1990, 1997), Sachs (1992), Hobart (1993), Escobar (1991, 1995), Crush (1995) and Kothari and Minogue (2002). A parallel concern, in both post-colonial studies and the anthropology of development, is whether such a structural mapping of power adequately captures the ambiguous, contradictory nature of imperial-subaltern power relations. Arce and Long, for example, argue that poverty and inequality cannot be adequately understood in terms of the broader relations of inequality between regions and nations. There is no substitute for analysing local power struggles over meanings and resources (2000:159).

The notion of the passive victim, evoked by structural mappings of power, also implies a rigid separation between the experiences of domination and subordination. In the 'Rhetoric of English India', Suleri challenges this by proposing that we pay more attention to the issue of 'exchange' and 'intimacy' between coloniser and colonised. She invites us to re-interpret colonial aggression as a sign of terror, rather than as a sign of confident control. This terror is masked by claims regarding the 'unreadability of the colonized subcontinent' (1992:6). We may imagine a local official exclaiming 'it is impossible to understand these people!' Emphasizing the precariousness of colonial power, Suleri argues that such claims serve as a smoke screen for the colonial fear of its own cultural ignorance. The colonizing subject fails to see how the intimacies between ruler and ruled produce a counter-culture that blurs the dividing line between 'self' and 'other', powerful and powerless. In other words, the idea of the impenetrable 'otherness' of the colonized subject helps to keep the unsettling reality of these 'imperial intimacies' at bay. Yet, the need to maintain an appearance of being in control also produces 'an anxious impulse to insist that colonized peoples can indeed be rendered interpretable within the language of the colonizer' (1992:7). The subsequent literalisms and misrepresentations of the 'other' have since constituted the critical focus of colonial cultural studies. However, Suleri argues that their construction of the 'other' as a universal category has gained such a self-explanatory force that it has become a comfortable false arrival which has precluded the need to investigate the nuances and specificities of each colonial encounter. The endeavour to put right the colonizer's cultural misrepresentations of the colonized subject has created a fallacious representation of an absolute, intransigent 'other' thus rendering 'otherness' indistinguishable from the 'exotic' (1992:12-13). In seeking to debunk the myth of the totality of imperial domination, colonial cultural studies have given utmost priority to the perspective of the dominated subject as 'other', paying scant attention to the shared worlds of complicity and guilt between rulers and ruled. In rejecting the static dualisms of colonizer/colonized, domination/subordination, Suleri claims that "the stories of colonialism – in which heterogeneous cultures are yoked by violence – offer nuances of trauma that cannot be neatly partitioned between colonizer and colonized" (1992:5).

At the heart of stories of 'colonial exchange' lies the precariousness of imperial power; both colonizer and colonized are implicated in a mutual relationship of powerlessness (1992:3). Although Suleri is writing about 'English India', her observations coincide with those of Mbembe in his writings on the African postcolony (2001). Mbembe argues that ruler and ruled are linked by an 'intimate tyranny' which invalidates standard interpretations of postcolonial relations of power in terms of domination versus resistance (2001:128,103). Just as Suleri emphasizes the importance of stories of 'colonial exchange', Mbembe draws our attention to the 'logic of conviviality' between officialdom and the people. Ordinary citizens participate in rituals which reaffirm the tyranny of official power in intimate ways: they wear the party uniform, hang portraits of their president in their homes, fill the streets to dance and applaud their ruler as he passes them by in procession. However, postcolonial subjects are able to distance themselves from these dramatizations of their subordination by taking recourse to humour: faced with the conspicuousness of official lies and of the impertinence of the elites, the body 'breaks into laughter' thus emptying officialdom of its meaning and power. Relations in the African postcolony, like those of 'English India', are relations of powerlessness. The masses handle the incontestability of state power by playing with it whenever they can, thus assuming multiple identities; however, this only serves to erode the legitimacy and not the material base of state power. State power, on the other hand, feeds off public manifestations of its apparent legitimacy such as 'applause' and 'flattery' and is consequently nonetheless deflated by the ludic ambiguity with which its supposedly dominated subjects engage in official rituals and rites (2001:128-129, 111). For both Suleri and Mbembe, postcolonial relations are best captured by the idioms of 'conviviality' and 'exchange' rather than that of postcolonial power, too easily associated with totalizing and reifying conceptions of the nature of domination. Nonetheless, theorizing a middle ground does not wipe out its polar ends. As Mbembe observes, the endurance of state power is not threatened by conviviality. The question of where the structural continuity of power relations fits in with this approach requires further investigation; there is a danger of placing too much emphasis on the role of agency. It is consequently fitting to return to the polar end of domination in the light of Mignolo's thesis on 'border thinking'. In the same way that Suleri takes issue with the universal category of the 'other', Mignolo disputes the 'abstract universalism of ONE local history' (2000:92), commonly evoked in critiques of Eurocentrism. Drawing our attention to the existence of multiple, diverse local histories, Mignolo maintains that it is our awareness of the 'locus of enunciation', rather than adhering to the myth of a deterritorialized, disembodied practice of universal theorizing, that provides the key to the decolonization of knowledge production. Mignolo is not advocating an essentialist return to the 'roots' of indigenous knowledge, but rather, a radical re-conceptualization of the geo-historical 'routes' of knowledge production. Modern reason is a product of 'coloniality': its separation of scientific knowledge (epistemology) from human meaning and understanding (hermeneutics) marginalised other forms of knowledge, relegated to the disempowering status of objects of study (2000:13). Thus the 'knower', purportedly detached and unaffected by the 'known', was able to produce the myth of a universal reason which obscured the particular socio-cultural and political conditions of its production. He recommends Freire's ideas on dialogical thinking (1972) – 'thinking *with* instead of thinking *for* or *about* people' – as a way of contributing towards public policy (2000:265, 11). In this respect, 'border thinking' provides a link between postcolonial theorizing and development.

1.6. Development theory and practice

In theories of 'modernization', the social organisation of any given society was characterised in terms of two polar types: the traditional and the modern. Societal change was perceived, in a somewhat simplistic manner, to entail the shifting from one state to the other. A range of different aspects of society were categorised into two opposed lists and it was presumed that there was a logical connection between all of the elements in each list. Thus, for example, traditional society was perceived to be rural, agricultural and particularistic whereas modern society was urban, industrial and universalistic (Robertson 1984:28). Peasants were seen as an obstacle to the project of national development owing to the 'traditional' characteristics that were ascribed to them. Rogers, for example, identified what he called the 'ten elements in the subculture of peasantry' namely: mutual distrust in interpersonal relations, a lack of innovativeness, fatalism, low aspirational levels, lack of deferred gratification, limited time-perspective, familism, dependency upon government authority, localiteness and a lack of empathy (Rogers 1969:115). Some of these characteristics could easily be applied to infants. Indeed the imperative to become 'modern' appears in many ways to be a moral injunction for peasants to 'grow up' and become responsible 'adults'. Consider the following claim made by Rogers in relation to deferred gratification:

> For whatever precise reason, deferred gratification seems uncharacteristic of peasants. Thus, in terms of the Aesop fable, subsistence farmers behave more like the grasshopper than the ant. And this lack of deferred gratification tends to maintain their position of hungry grasshoppers rather than well-provisioned ants. For upward social mobility certainly depends in part on the ability to postpone immediate gratification for the sake of long-range ends (Rogers 1969:122).

Rogers established a correlation between the economic behaviour of peasants and the extent of 'modernization' of their villages which, he argued, could be placed on a continuum between the polar types of 'pure folklike isolation' and 'modern urbanism'. The degree to which peasants exhibited efficiency, market orientation and economic rationality - the kind of economic behaviour attributed to 'modern man' – depended upon where their communities were situated on the continuum (Rogers 1969:118). That many peasants failed to exhibit this desired economic behaviour became, as Robertson states, one of the major obstacles identified by advocates of 'modernization theories' (Robertson 1984:30). Changing the mentality of peasants was thus considered to be the key to changing their behaviour.

It could be argued that the influence of postcolonial theorizing is evident in the emergence of 'people-centred' approaches to development. For example, Chamber's renowned volume entitled 'Rural Development: Putting the Last First' (1983) which has acquired canonical status, appears to parallel Mignolo's approach of 'thinking from subaltern experiences'. What is striking, in the quotation below, is the way in which the category of 'urban based professional' becomes the new 'obstacle' to development, whilst 'local' or 'rural' categories are celebrated as the most 'authentic' development agents. Not only is 'local knowledge' no longer backward and fatalistic, but it is now represented as superior to 'modern scientific knowledge'. The need to change the mentality of the 'backward', 'irrational' peasant is transformed into the need to change the mentality of the 'arrogant', 'insensitive' professional.

> At its ugliest...professional training inculcates an arrogance in which superior knowledge and superior status are assumed. Professionals then see the rural poor as ignorant, backward and primitive, and as people who have only themselves to blame for their poverty....
>
> For originators and bearers of modern scientific knowledge, it requires a major effort to recognise that rural people's knowledge exists at all, let alone to see that it is often superior....
>
> [O]ne first step is for outsider professionals, the bearers of modern scientific knowledge, to step down off their pedestals, and sit down, listen and learn (Chambers 1983:6, 98, 101).

Proponents of 'people-centred' approaches to development have referred to this change of approach in terms which evoke a complete break with older approaches to development, such as: 'reversals', 'paradigm shifts' (Chambers 1983, 1993), 'redefining development' (Clark 1991) and 'new orthodoxy' (Gill 1988). In development jargon, it has characteristically been referred to as a shift from 'top-down' to 'bottom-up' development. Yet not only are people-centred approaches re-working the same oppositional categories as those of modernization theories but with the same intent to change mentalities. These approaches also reproduce the rural/urban opposition characteristic of modernization theories; the difference lies in the way that the 'rural space' is celebrated as the most 'deserving', 'authentic' site of development. Lipton, for example, claims that the most important class conflict in developing countries is between the rural and urban classes and argues that the latter are more powerful and articulate enabling them to 'win' most of the rounds of the struggle with the countryside' (1984:152).

A closer examination of both of these approaches reveals that they are still situated within an ethnocentric paradigm (Henkel and Stirrat 2001). The institutionalization of 'Putting the Last First' has, somewhat ironically, contributed towards the consolidation of stereotyped stakeholder categories of the 'other'. Rather than giving voice to the voiceless, it has, to recall Suleri's argument, gained such a self- explanatory force that the 'Last' has become a new prescriptive label, ruling out the need for further investigation.

In order to overcome the creation of prescriptive labels, Long proposes the adoption of an actor oriented perspective (2001). He exemplifies the problems caused by rigid stakeholder categories through an analysis of the interface between service providers and street children in Mexico City. Long describes a research project (Turnbull 1998 in Long 2001:85-88) whose initial aim was to identify the most suitable organizations for helping street children reintegrate into mainstream society. However, it soon became evident that there were already plenty of organizations equipped to meet the basic needs of these children who appeared to prefer the streets. The research aims of the project consequently had to be modified. The project had initially reproduced the same stereotyped stakeholder categories that informed the work of these organizations, portraying the street children as helpless victims of '[p]overty, social injustice and family dysfunction' (2001:85). The question of how they actually managed to survive on their own in the streets had not been addressed. Given that the children often refused outside help, the project supervisor decided that it was important to listen to what the children had to say for themselves (putting the last first); so that they could meet their real needs and readjust the help programmes accordingly. The researchers consequently drew up a series of exercises aimed at encouraging the children to talk about how they spent their time on the streets, what services were available and what their ideal hostel would be like. The children never really showed much interest in participating in these discussions and often failed to turn up to the meetings. This led the research supervisor to search for 'a more dialogical and interactive method, in which knowledge is perceived as the joint product of the ongoing relations between the researcher and actor, and not as something the researcher obtains from his/her informant' (2001:86). This new approach, which paralleled Mignolo's (and Freire's) call to think *with* subaltern peoples rather than *for* or *about* them, was able to bring to light the agency of street children, transforming dominant conceptions of their 'lack of power' into a new awareness of their 'particular use of it based on a different appreciation of the situations they encountered' (2001:87). The inability of these help programmes to build upon the children's capacity to fend for themselves was due to their ignorance of the children's 'lifeworlds, knowledge and social practices'. Long argues that the organizations were more likely to be sympathetic if the children corresponded to the stereotyped image of a helpless victim in search of 'personal salvation from the evils and degeneracy of street life' rather than if they came together as a group claiming their rights (2001:88). Thinking *for* or *about* subaltern peoples – even with the best of intentions – is likely to result in paternalism. Interface analysis challenges us to go beyond the 'performance' of planned interventions to engage in dialogical conversations that do not follow a set script: 'to learn lessons from the "autonomous" settings in which people cope with their own problems, irrespective of whether or not the foci of concern or parameters of action can be linked with outside intervention (2001:90).

Whilst paternalism is usually associated with the delivery of social welfare, market driven approaches to development are often represented, in the liberal view, as being informed by a neutral practice of universal, economic theorizing. This could be seen, in terms of Mignolo's 'border thinking', as a product of 'coloniality' that separates economic knowledge from human meaning on the grounds that the former is value free. The following section challenges the assumption of value neutrality that underpins the economic liberal view by revealing its implicit moral position.

1.7. Social welfare and market driven development

Wilk argues that neo-classical economics is based on a representation of the economic market as obeying natural laws. The foundation of modern Western economics as a discipline is usually traced back to Adam Smith who set himself the task of a natural scientist: to lay bare the workings of a gigantic machine - the economy (Wilk 1996:45-6). Wilk's discussion of the intellectual history of the effort to develop the science of economics reveals the origins of the assumption of value neutrality, demonstrating how early economists searched for a secular measure of value, in order to detach economic philosophy from theology (1996:46). Yet this approach also resulted in the creation of a moral position: namely, that it is 'immoral' to deny or interfere with the natural workings of the market.

The 'immorality' of intervention owes much to the influential theory of economic equilibrium, invented by David Ricardo (1772-1823) who formulated a series of assumptions, summarised by Wilk as follows:

> ...(1) most property is privately owned, (2) labor time is the ultimate source of value, (3) economic actors have freedom of choice, (4) the economic human is a rational maximizer of economic gain...and (5) all things being equal is the natural state of the economy. Equilibrium...represents an ideal state of balance between supply and demand, values and prices, input and output. Equilibrium is the "natural" state of an economy that is allowed to operate without interference. The idea of equilibrium rests ultimately on the belief that there are natural laws of the economy that are just like the natural laws of physics.
>
> Ricardo saw all these assumptions as "natural" states of being (not descriptions of the real world) and viewed his deductions as scientific statements of mechanical laws, but we can see his axioms as social philosophy. *They describe a set of values about the way things should be.* But by stating these principles as plausible lawlike generalities of human behaviour, Ricardo *tucked the moral philosophy away under the cover of fact* (Wilk 1996:48, my emphasis).

The drive to expose the 'values' which Wilks claims were 'tucked away' beneath the theory of equilibrium accounts for the emergence of an explicitly ethical approach towards development. The failure to treat human beings as qualitatively different from other inputs in a productive machine, such as capital or raw material (Goulet 1995:20) constitutes one of the major criticisms that advocates of 'people-centered' approaches have made of economic theory. Seers argued that a ‘universally acceptable aim’ of development was ‘the realisation of the potential of human personality’ (1972:123). This ‘human’ approach towards development was also promoted by Korten and Carner in their adoption of the concept of ‘people-centered’ development:

> A major failing of conventional development models, both socialist and capitalist, is that they become so production-centered that the needs of the productive system have assumed precedence over the needs of people (1984:201).

Archer criticizes the ‘market-driven’ approach for having ‘Darwinian consequences for the least well-endowed’. He argues that the theory of the market not only indicates that the least skilful players will fail but that they *should fail* in order to prevent the reduction of economic efficiency (1994:29). In neo-liberal economics, people are meant to serve the market, rather than the other way round. By this logic, people who do not have value or add value to the market are seen as disposable. However, because of the putative divide between ethics and efficiency, this displacement of disposable humans is not seen as a market problem but as a social problem to be dealt with by the state (usually by re-defining these people as lawbreakers) and/or by NGOs (usually by defining these people as ‘at risk’). In other words, the market comes first. The community realm is relegated to the ‘inferior’ sphere of emotions, tolerable to the extent exemplified in the saying, that, if you aren’t a socialist by your twenties, then you don’t have a heart, but if you’re not a capitalist by your thirties, then you don’t have a head! However, part and parcel of having a head is to be prone to blind spots.

Relevant here is the work of Grassi – an economist troubled by the blind spots of her discipline – which draws attention to the limitations of the methodological tools of classical economics for capturing the complexity of economic life at the micro level. Determined to overcome these limitations without ‘betraying’ her disciplinary roots (2003:306), Grassi analyses the integration of Cape Verde into the world economy ‘from below,’ by focusing on the lives of local women, engaged in networks of informal transnational commerce. She argues that, like elsewhere in Africa, this itinerant trade – known as ‘rabidancia’ in Cape Verde - is structural to the local economy and consequently cannot be consigned to the sphere of unproductive subsistence activities (2003:78). It is easy to see how this may happen since, as Grassi points out, many of the characteristics of these micro-enterprises are overlooked by traditional economic indicators. The rate of return, for example, loses its significance in the informal sector since the profit generated is often used to satisfy immediate needs. Grassi concludes that a more accurate indicator of the economic success of these micro-enterprises is to evaluate their impact upon the living standards of both the entrepreneurs and the communities to which they belong (2003:261). The role of the community in sustaining these enterprises is also elucidated in Grassi's study through a description of the solidarity groups which provide mutual, rotating support for member entrepreneurs and of the processes through which their professional 'know how' is transmitted from woman to woman (2003:260-262).

The founder of the Grameen Bank of Bangladesh, Muhammad Yunus, raises similar concerns, in his description of the difficulties he encountered in convincing the economists of the Bangladesh Central Bank of the economic viability of Grameen's housing programme, which aimed at providing credit for leak-proof roofs. The programme was originally rejected by the Central Bank because the poor structures of the houses in question did not 'satisfy the structural definition of a house' and would subsequently add nothing to the 'housing stock of the country' (Yunus 2003:128). The Grameen Bank consequently submitted a second application in which the terminology 'housing loans' was substituted for 'shelter loans', in the hope that the bank would be unable to disqualify the proposal for want of a definition or statistic for 'shelter stock'. Once again the proposal was rejected because the economists argued that these shelter loans were 'consumption items' which the Grameen borrowers could not afford to take out, given that they were not 'income-generation' or 'productive activities' (Yunus 2003:129). A third application was submitted in which the Grameen bank referred to 'factory loans' justified as follows:

> We explained that the majority of our borrowers were women and that they worked from the home. "Our borrowers look after their children while they work and they earn money from their work," I explained. "Most of this activity is performed in their own homes. Since their homes are places of work, we choose to call them factories. Furthermore, the monsoon plagues them for five months out of the year. During that time they can't work because they don't have sturdy roofs over their heads. To continue to work and generate income, they need protection from the rain. That is why we want to offer them factory loans. True, this 'factory' will double as a house, but more important, it will have a direct impact on their income generating ability as it will allow them to work throughout the year with some comfort" (Yunus 2003:129).

What is fascinating about this account is the way in which the Grameen bank altered its terminology – from social welfare to productivity – in its attempt to convince the economists of the viability of its proposal. Whether they were called shelters or factories, these houses were situated at the putative interface between the community and market realms. Yunus goes on to highlight one of the blind spots of mainstream economic theories, which, by producing a 'theoretical dichotomy between entrepreneurs and laborers', fail to acknowledge the creativity of the majority of the population of Third World Countries in creating their own jobs. Yunus considers the 'informal sector' to be a 'catchall category' that sets these self-employed people apart as a symptom of underdevelopment and prefers to focus on their ingenuity through the use of the term the 'people's economy' (2003:150).

According to Gudeman, dominant definitions of the economy, as the transaction of goods and services in markets, tend to neglect the other side of the coin: that the economy is constituted through social relationships. Whilst the neo-liberal view would have us believe that social relationships are of little importance to the modern economy, Gudeman argues that '[e]conomic growth depends on community and culture' since 'markets never exist 'outside' a cultural and social context (2001:94). Gudeman makes it clear that he is not positing a homogenous, harmonious model of 'community'; rather, he is arguing that in the community sphere, mutuality is valued for itself, whereas in the market sphere, it acquires an instrumental status: valued for something else (2001:140). Since we cannot put a price on mutuality, Gudeman expresses misgivings in relation to the engineering of social relations. Commenting upon the successful initiatives of the Grameen Bank in Bangladesh, for example, Gudeman questions the appropriateness of community building for the sole purpose of wealth creation, whereby people and communities become transformed into means rather than ends (2001:139-140). Yet, it could also be argued that, in some contexts, mutuality initially valued for the sake of something else (wealth creation) may eventually also become valued for itself. Yunus tells the story of a poor Mexican woman, in inner-city Chicago, where the five-woman group idea of the Grameen initiative was implemented, to grant credit for income generation activities by the Women's Self-Employment Project (WSEP). When asked whether she felt it would have been easier to get a loan without being obliged to form a group, the woman replied as follows:

> In the fifteen years I have been here, I never had a friend. I didn't even know anybody. I was all alone. Now I have many friends. My four friends in the group are like my own sisters. Even if the WSEP did not give us money, I would not leave the group (Yunus 2003:188).

The Woman's loyalty to the group, does, nonetheless, bear witness to Gudeman's thesis regarding the importance of social relationships to the economy. Yet this is easily overlooked in the global shift towards the market and private initiative which relegates social relations to an 'inferior' community sphere of 'traditional' ties that hamper market initiative. This is the approach adopted by De Soto whose influential work exemplifies the power of the putative divide between the market and community realms.

De Soto (2000) proposes that non-western countries have failed to reap the benefits of capitalism because the majority of their populations are excluded from the economy, sitting on 'dead' capital. Their lack of access to legal property rights prevents them from using their assets, such as their own homes, as collateral to qualify for credit to finance income generation activities. It is not a matter of 'lack of entrepreneurship', but rather a question of lack of 'easy access' to 'property mechanisms' (2000:46). This argument is all the more convincing, because it appears to reject the kinds of 'cultural arguments', discussed above, characteristic of Modernization theories, to account for the failure of capitalism to take root beyond the West. (2000:240):

> Much behaviour that is today attributed to cultural heritage is not the inevitable result of people's ethnic or idiosyncratic traits but of their rational evaluation of the relative costs and benefits of entering the legal property system.

De Soto claims that if the legal barriers to the titling of the most humble of properties are removed, then the benefits for the poor of entering the legal system outweigh the costs. Once a poor person's home has a legal title, it can take on a parallel life that releases its latent potential for financial investment: 'Formal property…invites you to go beyond viewing the house as mere shelter – and thus a dead asset – and to see it as live capital' (2000:48).Yet, the language that De Soto uses to describe how the benefits of this process have already been reaped in the West reproduces the implicit assumptions of Modernization theories regarding the nature of local social relationships. De Soto claims that acquiring legal rights to assets will free people, from 'time-consuming' 'restrictive' 'local arrangements', 'primitive economic activities' and 'burdensome parochial politicking inherent to closed societies' (2000:53,184). Mitchell's (2007) critique of De Soto's proposals which have resulted in the implementation of numerous titling programmes, challenges his view of the existence of a boundary that separates the market from non-market worlds. Instead of the existence of a thin dividing line that those excluded from capitalism need help to cross over, Mitchell talks of a 'broad terrain' of power struggles over redistribution and control. He identifies a major historical blind spot in De Soto's analysis of the emergence of formal property rights in the West: the crucial role played by dispossession and eviction. Mitchell reveals how these titling programmes may result in the loss of claims made through local property arrangements for poor, vulnerable groups. Moreover, De Soto's insistence upon the benefits of transforming one's house from a 'shelter' to 'live capital' (2000:48) glosses over the issue of 'risk'. Mitchell points out that legalization increases the value of property not because it releases 'dead capital' but because it encourages speculative investment. The increase in the cost of land and housing does not benefit the poor. Poor people who depend upon their houses for 'shelter' cannot afford to risk losing them by defaulting on a loan. When this occurs, they are usually obliged to sell their properties at minimal prices at times when demand is low. Local forms of collateral, such as the production and storing of grain or keeping animals are therefore a safer option than the prospect of losing their own dwellings. Only the wealthy can afford to take such a risk. Mitchell's case study material, from urban and rural Egypt, corroborates the mounting evidence he cites from elsewhere that it is the wealthy, and not the poor, who benefit from these programmes. Their success is dependent upon being able to exercise the power of eviction when a borrower defaults on a loan. Poor property owners are thus less secure than they were before. The prospect of making the poor homeless is not a 'market' concern; De Soto is more interested in 'making people accountable' to the market. In order for them to be 'taken seriously' people must have property 'to lose' which De Soto designates as a sign of 'commitment'. Although he claims that the 'largest beneficiary will be the poor' (2000:201), De Soto has nothing to say about helping those who fail to honour their commitments. They appear to have become disposable, since, De Soto explains, in the West, citizens who fail to act honourably jeopardize their reputations as trustworthy individuals (2000:54-55). Thus the failure to pay back a loan is associated with deficits in the character and behaviour of individual entrepreneurs rather than in the structural vulnerability of the poor. The risks and ethics of engagement are placed squarely on their shoulders whilst the rationality and efficiency of the proposals is guaranteed by the law. Yet, Mitchell argues that the speculative investment that follows titling programmes redirects capital away from productive activities and consequently aggravates wider problems, caused by the lack of investment in activities that generate employment.

Many of the issues discussed above are relevant to the case of Cape Verde. The glossing over of risk, for example, is evident in discourses regarding both the fatalism of peasant mentalities and the imperatives of market growth. The following section provides an overview of each chapter.

1.8. Book overview

The Cape Verdean ethnography analysed in this study derives from eleven months' fieldwork carried out mostly on the island of Santiago between 1996 and 1997 and from a shorter three month period in 2005 and one month period in 2007. The names of all individuals have been changed.

Chapter Two discusses the history of Cape Verde in the light of conflicting debates on the cultural effects of globalization. Is globalization a steam roller over local cultures and traditions or do the interconnections between local and global processes open doors for the emergence of new hybrid cultures? The history of Cape Verde offers a fascinating case study for exploring both of these perspectives. The text consequently moves to and fro between structuralist perspectives of the exploitative nature of capitalism and intercultural perspectives that celebrate hybridity. The chapter focuses in particular on the work of Paul Gilroy in order to elucidate the pertinence of his concept of a 'Black Atlantic' culture for interrogating notions of cultural authenticity (1993). Although Gilroy limits his cultural-historical reach to that of Anglo-Saxon transnationalism, his critique of Afro-centric reconstructions of 'authentic' African traditions, unsullied by colonial contact, applies well to the historical case of Cape Verde as a product of the intercontinental slave trade.

Chapter Three takes the reader forward into contemporary Cape Verde through an examination of the nitty-gritty of debates concerning Cape Verde's future economic and socio-political development. The chapter focuses on the micro processes of knowledge production in a week long seminar, organised within the ambit of a national long term perspective study (NLTPS) on Cape Verde, coordinated by the United Nations Development Programme (UNDP) as part of a wider regional project entitled 'African Futures'. Many documents were produced throughout the study; the purpose of analysing a single event in such depth is to invite the reader to find out what happens beyond the printed words. The tendency of radical critiques of development discourse to isolate the analysis of documents from the social conditions of their production obscures more than it reveals about the nature of the generation of development knowledge. This chapter illustrates the limitations of studying local meanings and practices of development as the product of global processes without paying attention to micro-processes of politics and power.

Chapter Four elucidates the fluidity of stakeholder categories by examining processes of 'othering' in normative discourses of identification in Cape Verde which reproduce the binary categories of opposing theories of development. Constructions of the 'other' as an obstacle to development are characteristic of both Modernization theories and 'People-centred' approaches to development. In the former it is the 'backward' peasant who must learn from the town how to become modernized and in the latter it is the 'corrupt' civil servant and 'arrogant' development professional that needs to leave the tarmac roads in order to learn from the innate wisdom of 'authentic locals'. The ethnography illustrates how these mirror images of town and country gloss over the complexities of 'local realities' by locating a 'shifting middle ground' in the mobility and fragility of these relations of difference. Yet these mirror images still inform practice, serving as powerful legitimating discourses for changing the mentality of the 'other'. The Chapter focuses on monetised food for work programmes which have become a paradigmatic symbol of the rural population's dependence upon the state and describes how their continued existence and inefficiency were attributed to the 'laziness' and 'dependence' of the workers. I also discuss factors which affected the poor performance of workers and look at how these factors were addressed by a donor programme which promoted community-based initiatives that were both efficient and productive, thus challenging the normative discourses of 'idle' workers. The chapter then analyses discourses of identification in rural Cape Verde that compare urban based professionals with locally based extensionists trained by the donor program. Discourses regarding urban based professionals portrayed them as uncommitted 'outsiders' whilst local extensionists were constructed as 'authentic' 'insiders'. The discussion moves on to analyse ethnographic case material which breaks down these differences between 'self' and 'other'. Concrete examples of the effects of these discourses on practice are given by looking at how the social construction of 'authentic' locals became a straight jacket that imposed populist ideals upon individuals. The chapter also includes a case study analysis of power relations at the community level that reveals how categorizations constitute lucrative development labels. I describe how a local association president manipulated populist notions of 'authenticity' in order to preserve his position of power and to enjoy privileged access to resources. The chapter concludes with a discussion of how authenticity has become an increasingly valuable commodity in the 'development encounter'.

Chapter Five elucidates the relevance of the concept of a 'shifting middle ground' to describe the different ways in which social actors with different agendas and differential access to material and symbolic capital collaborate and compete with each other as they negotiate the paradoxes created through aid delivery and development interventions. The chapter brings to light a fundamental tension in the transnational donor imperative to alleviate poverty through market-driven interventions. It analyses the contradictions and tensions generated by the attempt to reconcile the pursuit of profit with the delivery of social welfare. The case material derives from the donor programme referred to above, which involved the privatization of soil and water conservation work (SWC) carried out in monetised food for work programmes. The donor programme helped local residents to form associations so that they could contract directly with the government to carry out SWC in their communities. The Chapter is divided into two parts. The first part examines these tensions across a range of programme beneficiary associations. The second part of the chapter adopts a close-up lens: a comparative case study analysis of two associations that examines in more detail how people actually negotiate the paradoxes of aid delivery in the light of Mbembe (2001) and Bourdieu (1977).

Chapter Six examines the differential capacities of social actors to further their own agendas within a political field which cuts across the state/civil society divide. The NGO sector is often taken to represent 'civil society' in opposition to the 'state'. The former is usually associated with the 'grassroots' and the fight for social justice whilst the latter connotes bureaucracy, power and authority. The close-up lens of the 'middle ground' focuses on the shifting spaces between 'civil society' and the 'state' and consequently destabilizes dominant perceptions associated with this historical dualism.

I describe how the legitimacy to represent 'civil society' became a new political currency in Cape Verde and analyse the differentiated 'bargaining powers' (Mbembe 2000) of local organisations and NGOs in the light of Mbembe's concept of the 'postcolony' and Bourdieu's theory of practice (1977). I follow the 'entangled logics' of local debates of how to define what constitutes an NGO in three interrelated public spaces and demonstrate how the official agendas of these public meetings served as a smokescreen for local power struggles; the social and political capital of urban based NGO leaders enabling them to make the 'rules of the game' serve their interests more effectively than the presidents of rural associations many of whom were mired in 'doxa'. Bourdieu describes the experience of 'doxa' as taking the social world for granted: the dominant worldview is seen as self-evident and undisputed. Any awareness of the possibility for antagonistic views is moulded within the boundaries of what Bourdieu calls the 'field of opinion' which delimits the scope of any questioning that takes place. The official agenda of the public meetings between government and NGOs analysed in this chapter constitutes the 'field of opinion' that concealed the cross-cutting alliances between NGO leaders and the government. To theorize the 'intimacies' and 'complicities' of these alliances, requires recognition of the persistence of unequal power relations, within and across the multiple public spaces that make up the 'middle ground'. The existence of internal relations of inequality within the NGO sector also challenges received ideas of a homogeneously harmonized and emancipatory civil society. The chapter addresses the issues of how to deal with the problematic concept of 'authenticity' - traditionally associated with civil society and the 'grassroots'- and how to account for the experience of doxa without denying the capacity for agency.

Chapter Seven provides a synthesis of the discussions and the book concludes with a postscript interview with a seminar participant (who comments upon his reading of chapter three) thus giving him the opportunity to speak back.

Chapter Two

'Structural Hybridities': Learning from the History of Cape Verde*

2.1 Introduction

Readers unfamiliar with Cape Verde will be pleasantly surprised to discover just how compelling a case study this archipelago is of the interconnections between local and global processes. This small island state is situated in the Atlantic Ocean, approximately four hundred and fifty miles west of Senegal. Although the islands occupy a 'middle ground' between Africa, America, Europe and the Caribbean they are often omitted from world maps produced in the West: the kind of illustrative maps that appear on posters, calendars and in general text books. This omission suggests that Cape Verde belongs to what we may call the 'periphery'. Indeed, much of the history of Cape Verde could be interpreted in the light of structuralist perspectives of the expansion of capitalism and its systematic exploitation of the ′periphery'. For example, Barrows (1991) analyses Cape Verde's incorporation into the Portuguese mercantile world and its role in the establishment of the Atlantic slave trade in the light of Frank's dependency theory (1967). Frank argued that development and underdevelopment were not separate phenomena since the expansion of capitalism in the 'core' depended on the simultaneous underdevelopment of the 'periphery' whose economic surplus was exploited, through a hierarchical chain of metropolises and satellites. Cape Verde was Portugal's satellite: the islands were settled in order to meet external interests and very little was done to develop their economy and infrastructure. This perspective helps us to understand the exploitative nature of colonial relations; however, it provides little leeway for interpreting the interconnections between local and global processes as anything other than relations of domination and submission. Relevant here is Gilroy's concept of the 'Black Atlantic' (1993) which offers an alternative, complementary perspective.

Whilst the number of researchers interested in Cape Verde is steadily increasing, few have explored the significance of the Cape Verde islands for Gilroy's (1993) 'Black Atlantic': a stimulating enquiry into the relationship between race, nation and culture. What is interesting about Gilroy's approach is that he is also in search of a 'middle ground' – and applies various intermediate concepts between the local and the global which bear similarities to my concept of a 'shifting middle ground'.

---

* An earlier version of this chapter, entitled "A History of Cape Verde: Centre/Periphery Relations and Transnational Cultural Flows" was presented at the International Conference on Cape Verdean Migration and Diaspora in the Centro de Estudos de Antropologia Social – ISCTE, Lisbon, 6-8 April 2005.

Gilroy looks at how experiences of racial subordination and migration become repossessed in a Western strand of black identity politics that creates its own 'blind spot': the inability to recognize the potential for cultural creation within historical relations of subordination. His study of what he calls the 'Black Atlantic' emphasizes the opportunities for political dissent and cultural production which arose in the slave ships that sailed from Africa to the West. Gilroy refuses to reduce the African slaves that crossed the Atlantic to mere commodities on the grounds that they should also be envisaged as individuals 'engaged in various struggles towards emancipation, autonomy and citizenship' (1993:16). He adopts the image of ships crossing the Atlantic – some of which stopped by in the Cape Verde islands – as the main organising symbol of his work. These ships were living micro-systems of cultural, linguistic and political hybridity (1993:4). In other words, there is no need to deny the Africans that were taken as slaves any possibility of resistance and creation in order to condemn slavery. And yet celebrations of hybridity may also be manipulated in order to gloss over the harsh realities of colonial oppression; it may be more helpful to think in terms of the paradoxical middle ground of 'structural hybridities'.

In this chapter, I shall attempt to locate this 'middle ground' by discussing the history of Cape Verde from the two perspectives outlined above, namely: a structuralist perspective which places Cape Verde within the world-system of capitalist expansion (Frank 1967, Wallerstein 1974) and an intercultural perspective (Gilroy 1993) which celebrates agency and transnational cultural flows (Appadurai 1990). These two perspectives reflect conflicting standpoints in the debate on globalization.

2.2. Understanding globalization

'Globalization' - a term which has been coined to refer to the increasing interconnected nature of the world - is both celebrated and bemoaned by academics and non-academics alike. It is beyond the scope of this chapter to provide a comprehensive discussion of this debate which has produced a vast literature covering a range of themes. (See 'The Globalization Reader' edited by Lechner and Boli (2000) and the volume edited by Kothari and Minogue which provides a useful discussion of how the globalization debate articulates with development issues). The aim of this chapter is to discuss the history of Cape Verde within the conflicting debates on the cultural effects of globalization. Scholars who celebrate the effects of 'globalization' point to the increase in cultural diversity around the world as different cultures are brought into contact. Appadurai (1990), for example, examines the 'third cultures' which develop as a result of transnational cultural flows. Critics of globalization, on the other hand, portray it as an undesirable process of standardization in which heterogeneous cultures become incorporated into a dominant culture. This is the perspective that is adopted in the critical studies of 'development discourse' which argue that the world-wide dominance of 'the Western discourse of progress' is one of the pernicious effects of processes of globalization (Escobar 1984, 1991, 1995; Sachs 1992; Rist 1997).

These studies are influenced by the theories of Frank (1967) and Wallerstein (1974) which interpret the interconnections between the different parts of the world from a Marxist perspective. They draw attention to the way in which the South was exploited and underdeveloped by the expansion of capitalism. Studies of how the 'development encounter' (Escobar 1995) facilitates the exploitation of the South tend to focus almost exclusively on the homogenizing effects of globalization: local cultures disappear (Sachs 1992:4), minds become 'colonized' (Shrestha 1995:266) and indigenous knowledge is 'lost' (Hobart 1993). This notion of the imposition of Western cultural categories almost inevitably leads to calls for the 'decolonization of the mind' and a retreat into the 'authentic' and 'indigenous' which characterize the black political discourses analysed by Gilroy (1993). Gilroy claims that the pursuit of autonomy has led some black intellectuals and artists to turn away from the promises of modernity and to embrace the idea of a pure, invariant tradition:

> ...the idea of tradition is often...the culmination, or centre-piece, of a rhetorical gesture that asserts the legitimacy of a black political culture locked in a defensive posture against the unjust powers of white supremacy. This gesture sets tradition and modernity against each other as simple polar alternatives as starkly differentiated and oppositional as the signs black and white...It is interesting that in this understanding of the position of blacks in the modern, western world, the door to tradition remains wedged open not by the memory of modern racial slavery but in spite of it. Slavery is the site of black victimage and thus of tradition's intended erasure. When the emphasis shifts towards the elements of invariant tradition that heroically survive slavery, any desire to remember slavery itself becomes something of an obstacle. It seems as if the complexity of slavery and its location within modernity has to be actively forgotten if a clear orientation to tradition and thus to the present circumstances of blacks is to be acquired (Gilroy 1993:188-89)

The idea of an 'autonomous´ 'primeval' community, interrupted by the onslaught of slavery, colonialism or capitalism, is also challenged by Gupta and Ferguson who argue that that 'the community' was formed 'out of the interconnected space that always already existed' (1997:36). In other words, whilst processes of globalization may have multiplied and intensified in the last century, particularly in the fields of travel and communication technology, these interconnections are not in themselves new. In this chapter I shall demonstrate how the history of Cape Verde provides a striking example of the way in which its Creole population (read 'primeval community') is a 'local' product of a previous 'global' situation. My account of Cape Verdean history consequently begins when the islands were sighted by sailors, in the mid-fifteenth century.

2.3. Beginnings: The discovery and settlement of Cape Verde

Most historians seem to agree that unlike continental Africa, the Cape Verde islands were uninhabited when they were sighted by Genoan sailors in the mid-fifteenth century and claimed for the Portuguese Crown (Lobban 1995). The archipelago was named after the Green Cape in Western Senegal due to its location. The first island to be settled, Santiago, is also the largest and is part of the leeward islands together with Brava, Fogo and Maio. São Vicente, the last to be settled much later on in the eighteenth century, is part of the windward islands which include; Santo Antão, Santa Luzia, São Nicolau, Sal and Boa Vista (Moran 1982:65).

The geo-strategic location of the archipelago on the trade winds route was the Crown's main motive for encouraging settlement because it facilitated access to Brazil and to the Asian colonies. Although slaves were also taken from the West African coast to create a plantation society, the strategic location of the islands was always more important to the Portuguese. This eventually turned Cape Verde into a logistical maritime support base and an entrepôt in the flourishing slave trade between West Africa, Europe and the Americas (Moran, 1982:64-5). The island of Santiago was the control point for taxing slaves en route as well as for breaking slaves in on the plantations (Bigman 1993:73).

Following the discovery of the islands, the Crown issued two extensive land grants (capitanias) to one of the original discoverers of the islands, António de Noli, and to the administrator of Madeira, Diogo Gomes. One of the duties of these grantees, or 'capitães', was to recruit settlers; however, this did not prove to be easy. The archipelago offered few incentives to Europeans. It was far away from Portugal, in a hot, dry, tropical zone which early European settlers had already discovered was unsuitable for growing the products characteristic of their diets, such as, wheat, barley, olives and vines (Correia e Silva 1995:19). In order to encourage settlement, Dom Afonso V consequently granted Santiago residents exclusive rights in 1466 over the slave trade in neighbouring parts of the Guinea Coast (Carreira, [1977] 1982:7-10).

The commercial privileges granted to the early settlers in 1466 proved to be short lived. Once the settlement of the islands had been established the Portuguese Crown decided that these privileges were causing it to lose too much wealth. So in 1472 the Crown forbade the resale of slaves for transport elsewhere. Since the Portuguese authorities did not command enough human resources to exploit the economic potential of the archipelago directly, they decided to lease out monopolies in slave trading and in the produce and trade of other goods to external parties, mostly based in Lisbon. A few large and medium rural proprietors in Cape Verde were also granted special privileges, whilst the majority of the population was left with next to nothing (Carreira 1982:7-11, Lobban 1995:17).

Relations between the Cape Verdean ruling classes and the Portuguese elites provide an example of the hierarchical chain of dependency through which the economic surplus of the 'periphery' was exploited by the 'core' (Frank 1967). Lobban argues that it was the external power base in Portugal, with its own economic interests, that provided the ruling classes in Cape Verde with their security: the constant threat of force from Portugal guaranteed the continuation of the colonial administration on Cape Verdean soil for five centuries (1995:73).

The 1472 restrictions on foreign trade marked a turning point in the economy of Cape Verde. They created a demand for locally produced goods for export resulting in the establishment of plantations (Correia e Silva 1995:31). The two original land grants referred to above consequently evolved into feudal land holdings granted to noble families, called 'morgadios' and 'capelas'[2] (Carreira 1982:5). These holdings were farmed on Santiago Island by slaves taken from the West African coast to produce sugar cane, cotton and coffee for export. Slaves were also made to weave the cotton into strips of cloth, which were used as a substitute for coins, and to gather the plant dyes that grew in the islands, (orchill, indigo and urzella). These dyes were both exported and used locally in the production of cloths (Lobban 1995:25).

My account of Cape Verdean history presented in this section illustrates how the Cape Verdean economy was subject to the dominance of the economic imperialism of the West. The Cape Verdean elite were incorporated into the system and did little to establish a more diverse, independent form of economic activity. The internal use of slaves in the Cape Verdean economy was geared towards external interests, at the expense of developing the internal potentials of the islands. Given that the islands were uninhabited at the time of settlement, the most striking aspect of this period is not so much that Cape Verde was subjugated to the West, but rather that Cape Verde was in a sense created by Portugal. In the words of an ex-minister whom I interviewed: 'Cape Verde is a colonial creation; a necessity for colonial interests...We, the Cape Verdean people, did not ask to be born!'

The limitations of interpreting the history of Cape Verde from a structural perspective are outlined by Hannerz who challenges the assumption that economic dependency automatically leads to cultural dependency:

> [I]n the social sciences, understandings of globalization have usually involved a view of asymmetry; key conceptual pairs have been center (or core) and periphery, metropolis and satellite...

[2] The capelas were church owned land holdings (Lobban, 1995:23).

> Asymmetries are present in the global social organization of meaning as well. *But what kind of asymmetries are they? How closely aligned are the asymmetries of culture with those of economy, politics, or military might? How do center/periphery relationships in the world affect structures of meaning and cultural expression?* (1992:218-9, my emphasis).

To study the history of Cape Verde by focusing exclusively on the structural asymmetries referred to above could easily blind us to the issue of agency. Wolf also points out that the principle aim of both Frank (1969) and Wallerstein (1974) was 'to understand how the core subjugated the periphery, and not to study the reactions of the micro-populations habitually investigated by anthropologists' (1982:23). Gilroy's Black Atlantic, on the other hand, invites us to subvert the image of the African 'victim', by pointing to the opportunities that existed for cultural production and resistance which arose in the slave ships that sailed from Africa to the West. In the following section, I shall continue my account of Cape Verdean history by demonstrating how changes in the social structure of Cape Verdean society provided opportunities for political dissent and cultural productivity. I shall focus in particular on the activities of the 'micro-population' of mulattoes and freed slaves.

2.3.1. Smuggling networks and resisting peasants

The social structure of early Cape Verdean society was largely determined by patterns of land use and land tenure. In Santiago and Fogo, lands were allotted to Europeans before any slaves had become freed men so that no black man could aspire to own a farm (Carreira 1982:20).

Most of the early setters came to Santiago from Portugal where the dominant pattern of land tenure was 'latifundia' sustained by primogeniture. The establishment of plantations consequently assured the continuation of the 'latifundia' system since the 'morgadios' and 'capelas' were inalienable and indivisible (Moran 1982:66). Some small land holdings were nevertheless granted to settlers and farmers under the Portuguese law of 'sesmarias' (1375), which stipulated that if the land was not used within five years it would be granted to someone else. No such conditions were placed on the large landowners who held on to their land through thick and thin.

The rigid division between whites and blacks in Cape Verdean society soon began to crumble for a variety of reasons. There were very few European women on the islands so that sexual relations between white men and slave women became common practice. This produced a new generation of mulattoes or crioulos many of whom were eventually freed from slavery by their paternal masters (Langworthy and Finan 1997:55). The principal was also established of granting freedom to well behaved slaves on holy days which gave their Catholic masters the promise of rewards in the after life as well as material benefits. Slaves were released without receiving any goods, food or money, thus forcing them to become sharecroppers, often on the land of their former masters who had now relinquished any moral obligation to take care of them (Meintel 1984a:85).

Despite the 1472 restrictions which resulted in the leasing out of large monopolies, these freed slaves were often sent out as middlemen - known as lançados - to trade on the Guinean coast. For although the monopolies leased out by the Crown placed severe restrictions on foreign trade, the Crown never had the power to enforce inspection and was consequently unable to prevent the development of a powerful and extensive smuggling network which eventually became institutionalized (Carreira 1982:7-11, Lobban 1995:17).

An analysis of the role of the lançados in the smuggling network provides an example of the opportunities for political dissent that were created despite the existence of the Crown monopolies. Lobban argues that an exploration of the lançados' role contributes towards an understanding of the history of power relations in Cape Verde:

> Much of the islands' history can be seen as a tug-of-war between those with ties to the formal powers in Lisbon and those with the practical, commercial links to the coast...
> ...there was a tension between the interests of the state (whether feudal or republican) or the capitão representatives, on the one hand, and the interests of the intercoastal merchants, represented by the lançados who were the gatekeepers of commerce at the point of production, on the other (1995:73-4).

These illegal commercial activities operating though inter-class 'alliances' between small rural landowners, the clergy, treasury officials, crioulos and freed slaves also provided the necessary opportunities for socio-economic advancement amidst the lower classes. So although skin colour had initially defined everyone's position on the social scale this changed as an intermediate class, consisting of blacks and crioulos, who had been freed in different ways, rose in society (Carreira 1982:24).

The inter-class alliances of this smuggling network are consistent with Mbembe's (2001) thesis of the conviviality of postcolonial relations, discussed in Chapter One. The dominant Portuguese landowners 'shared the same living space' as the dominated Crioulos; all of which learnt to bargain in a conceptual, economic and linguistic market-place.

The lançados played an important part in the development of the Crioulo language, since they needed a lingua franca for their commercial activities

(Lobban 1995:74). Cape Verdean Creole was born out of the necessity for dialogue between the African slaves and their European masters and consists of a blend of Portuguese and African languages[3]. Although it evolved as a result of the unequal encounter between 'the core' and 'the periphery', the Crioulo language has now become a hallmark of Cape Verdean identity. This provides the kind of example that Gilroy (1993) is looking for, in his discussion of the contributions that the history of slavery and colonialism can make towards theorising black identity.

Another example of political dissent in Cape Verde comes from the popular mythology regarding the peasants from the hinterlands of Santiago - the ‘badius’. The term ‘badiu’ is now commonly used to distinguish Santiago born Cape Verdeans from Cape Verdeans who originate from the other islands of the archipelago:

> As the etymology of their name suggests, the *badius* of Cape Verde are wanderers and runaways. Essentially, they form the core of the peasant population in the interior of São Tiago and are descended, in most cases from runaway slaves. They have retained a certain degree of African-based cultural distinctiveness in their customs, folklore, religious practices...Living in remote regions and maintaining a social distance from the rest of the population during the years of colonial rule, the *badius* were less assimilated to Portuguese culture than the rest of the Cape Verdean population. They were viewed as the primary representatives of an African heritage, and, as such, they have historically been denigrated by colonial authorities and looked down upon by other Cape Verdeans. The few known instances of slave and peasant rebellion in Cape Verde tended to occur in the *badiu* populations, giving them a certain notoriety in popular mythology that has engendered both disdain and admiration (Lobban 1995:74).

Meintel argues that in the popular imagination of the Leeward (Barlavento) islands - which had far less African influence – there was an ambivalent attitude towards the badius. On the one hand they were seen as 'mythical, knife-wielding savages', on the other hand, badius were often the central characters of anecdotes in which the Portuguese were portrayed as losers:

> Badius...represented something both opposite to and opposed to ‘Portuguese-ness’, something disdained and yet on occasion, admired. While they were normally seen as ‘other’, as different from normal, civilized

[3] There are also variations of Crioulo spoken in the different islands which in broad terms can be distinguished between ‘badiu’ spoken in the leeward islands and ‘sampajudu’ spoken in the windward islands. The former has far more African influences than the latter.

> Cape Verdeans, they could also serve, on the symbolic level, as representatives of Cape Verdeans (1984a:142).

The political dissent and cultural productivity of the badius and lançados discussed in this section demonstrates how 'micro-populations' (Wolf 1982) are active agents. They are not totally constrained by the exploitative structures of the 'world system' (Gardner and Lewis 1996:59); however, this is not to reject a structuralist perspective altogether. Mitchell argues that 'the heralding of subject positions 'at the margins' too often neglects the actual marginalization of subjects' (1996:220-1). The lançados and badius were active agents operating within an oppressive system.

Many of the badius were conscripted for labour migration to São Tomé e Príncipe. Lobban suggests that by resisting assimilation the badius were more likely to be conscripted due to the threat that they posed to the colonial authorities (1995:74). Barrows argues that this form of neo-slavery was a direct result of the legacy of the slave trade with the failure of the authorities to establish agricultural systems based on free peasant labour. This, according to Barrows, established the roots of Cape Verde's 'underdevelopment' (1991:34). The following sections analyse some of the effects of the oppressive nature of Portuguese colonial rule.

2.3.2. Out of the frying pan: from slaves to sharecroppers and tenants

In the seventeenth century Cape Verde's dominant role as an intermediary in the slave trade began to fall into decline. Innovations in sea travel enabled ships to make direct links between the West African coast and the Americas, facilitating the avoidance of Cape Verde altogether. Competition in the slave trade was also growing from other European powers and it was becoming increasingly difficult to import slaves. Aided by the confusion caused by frequent pirate attacks, slaves had also begun to run away to the remote areas of Santiago or to other islands, where they formed their own isolated communities. Landlords consequently found themselves with an increasing labour shortage on their plantations and so they began to recruit freed slaves as tenants on their lands (Carreira 1982:24).

Yet despite the legal abolition of slavery in the mid-nineteenth century, the transition from plantation agriculture to small holder subsistence agriculture continued to lock the majority of the population into exploitative relations with their landlords. Competition over the use of scarce land forced peasants to accept rental or sharecropping contracts for survival. Given that there was a surplus of candidates for working the land, rents were high. This in turn served as a disincentive to increasing the productive value of the land because any improvements would only cause the landlords to increase the rent. (Moran

1982:67, Furtado 1993:53). Crop failures were frequent, since tenants worked on rainfed lands, cultivating mainly maize and beans which were unsuitable for the cyclical aridity of the islands. No attempts were made by Portuguese colonial policy to substitute these crops with others, more adapted to local conditions, (such as sorghum or millet). Maize cultivation was also a major cause of soil erosion (Langworthy and Finan 1997:9). Neither were any serious preventative measures taken by the colonial government to mitigate the effects of drought and crop failure. In years when harvests were good, staples were exported instead of being stored in Cape Verde (Bigman 1993:81). From a structural viewpoint, those who managed to escape from the frying pan discovered themselves jumping into the fire.

2.3.3. Into the fire: drought, famine and migration

From 1719 to 1946 fourteen major droughts assailed every island of the Cape Verdean archipelago, with the number rising to twenty for the island of Santiago. The percentage of the registered population that suffered famine-related deaths in 1773, 1830 and 1863 was 44%, 42% and 40% respectively: figures that were common right up until the twentieth century. Even as late as 1950 mortality rates often reached fifteen per cent (Langworthy and Finan 1997:61, Moran 1982:71).

One of the ways in which the Portuguese authorities 'coped' with these drought related crises was to ship Cape Verdeans to work on the coffee plantations in São Tomé e Príncipe - a Portuguese colony which was short on manpower particularly after the legal abolition of slavery. For many, São Tomé e Príncipe offered the only escape from the imminent threat of starvation; nonetheless, it was a very unpopular destination. Although the government claimed that Cape Verdeans were recruited as freely contracted labourers, in reality, recruitment was a form of forced migration. Driven by famine and the false propaganda of the state recruiting agencies, Cape Verdeans were shipped across like animals. Upon arrival, they were treated like near slaves, forced to renew their contracts against their will, given miserable wages and subjected to corporal punishment (Carreira 1982:101-176). Those who managed to return home arrived broken by poverty and tropical diseases. As São Tomé became more and more unpopular, the Portuguese authorities adopted various methods to discourage migration elsewhere. For example, at the beginning of the twentieth century, they began to charge a high fee for the acquisition of a passport to emigrate to America. In times of famine those who could not afford to pay were consequently redirected to São Tomé which was their only hope of escaping the imminent threat of starvation in Cape Verde (Carreira [1977] 1982:101-176).

Another way in which the authorities responded to the famine was to set up state construction projects. According to Meintel, the earliest reference to these schemes can be found in 1864 which testifies to the building of basic infrastructure, mostly roads, by paying hungry peasants for their labour with small amounts of money to buy food ([Barcelos, 1912 VI:241], Meintel 1984a:63). Situated where the most famine victims were to be found, these construction projects were rarely planned in advance of the outbreak of famine and were often abandoned and left incomplete once the famine was over. Using only the simplest of tools, workers were subjected to the dangers of falling rocks and dynamite blasts (Meintel 1984a:63, Bigman 1993:83).

The colonial two-fold policy of forced migration and state construction projects was clearly inadequate to prevent the large number of famine related deaths that frequently took their toll on the archipelago's population. Whilst it is true that Portugal itself was suffering from economic decline, most scholars conclude that the colonial authorities lacked the political will to implement more effective famine prevention and relief measures (Bigman 1993, Meintel 1984a, Lobban 1995).

A combination of drought, famine, population growth and an imbalanced distribution of the land, drove Cape Verdeans to emigrate in increasingly large numbers, in particular to the United States and Europe, in search of better social and economic conditions (Carreira 1982:18). The United States was the most common destination for the first wave of Cape Verdean emigrants. They were recruited on the American whaling ships that fished in the waters near the islands of Brava and Fogo as helmsmen, harpooners and later as pilots and captains. When the whaling industry collapsed, many of these emigrants had acquired their own boats and moved into maritime commerce (Meintel 1981:238).

The nature and effects of the migration of Cape Verdeans to America are discussed below from a dual perspective which takes into account both structuralist and intercultural approaches. The weaving together of these oppositional standpoints has led me to take some liberties with the use of illustrative snapshots of the history of Cape Verde at the expense of chronological order.

2.4. A 'peripheral' society at the core of a transnational social world

Appadurai argues that it has now become a truism that the world we live in is characterized by ‘objects in motion’ which include ‘ideas and ideologies, people and goods, images and messages, technologies and techniques’ (2002:274). The history of Cape Verdean migration to America provides excellent examples of these ‘objects in motion’, described by Greenfield (1976) in an article that pre-dates both Gilroy and Appadurai in its evocation of their concepts of a ‘Black Atlantic’ and a ‘transnation’.

Greenfield's analysis of the involvement of Cape Verdean emigrants in America in maritime commerce, during the mid nineteenth century, indicates how the ships that crisscrossed the 'Black Atlantic' served as a means of economic emancipation. By the beginning of the twentieth century, the Cape Verdeans owned a fairly large fleet and divided their time sailing between America and the West Coast of Africa. They would leave New England in the autumn to spend the winter engaged in the North Atlantic trade between Cape Verde and the African coast and set sail for New Bedford or Providence in the spring, laden with freight and with more Cape Verdean passengers. Greenfield argues that this maritime commerce enabled the Cape Verdeans to maintain close contact not only with the islands but also with Cape Verdean emigrants in other port cities in Europe and Africa. He points out that although their social world was separated by oceans it still remained Cape Verdean because it was connected by their ships. Greenfield goes on to evoke Appadurai's use of the concept of a 'transnation' when he claims that it would be no exaggeration to say that all of these dispersed locations constituted the geographical extremes of a 'single socio-economic universe' (1976:5-6).

Many Cape Verdeans also emigrated to work in the cranberry and blueberry industries in south-eastern New England and Cape Cod. Lobban claims that approximately twenty five per cent of the immigrants arriving in the United States from Cape Verde during the period 1900-1920 listed Plymouth County in the heart of the cranberry district as their intended destination. He goes on to point out that although the economic success of the cranberry industries became almost totally dependent upon Cape Verdean immigrant labour, hardly any Cape Verdeans became owners of the bogs (1995:64). Writing in the early eighties, Meintel interpreted this Cape Verdean response to external labour needs from a world-system perspective:

> While the reasons for migration seem obvious (a dry and erratic climate, a high birth rate, etc.) these factors only become "causes" when capitalist development elsewhere created new labour needs; e.g.; on São Tomé's plantations, deserted by the former slaves, and in the United States, under the impact of industrialization. Portuguese colonial policy was an important factor in making Cabo Verde a labour reserve of potential emigrants (1984b:120).

The anthropologist Meillassoux (1981:118) also applied this kind of neo-Marxist, structural analysis to the study of labour migration in Africa. He argued that it was not in the interests of the capitalist core for the periphery to 'catch up' since the maintenance of a domestic mode of production was vital for capitalist accumulation. Value could be extracted from the periphery at low costs, since, in the case of migrant labour, it was the periphery that bore the economic and social burden of its reproduction. In order to achieve a systematic supply of cheap labour, the periphery had to be kept as a labour reserve and could not be allowed to develop capitalist relations of production.

Writing in the early 1980s, Meintel argued that one of the cultural repercussions of this labour migration in Cape Verde was the fostering of an ideology of cultural dependence (1984b:120). In her 1970s study of the influences of migration to America upon the Cape Verdean island of Brava, Meintel examined the changes that occurred in the sponsoring of local feasts. These used to be the responsibility of the landowning class, but were then taken over by American migrants who spent up to a year's salary in order to provide large quantities of imported food and drink. Another example of cultural dependency, offered by Meintel, is the way remittances were spent by local people to buy prestige goods. Meintel argued that these patterns of conspicuous consumption were contested in public outcries by the elite of the need to combat Cape Verde's cultural dependency (1984b:108-10). The implied assumption here is that Cape Verdeans had internalised foreign models which compromised their own cultural identity. Lesourd also cites the example of a former Minister of Culture in Cape Verde who lamented the decline of the nation's cultural identity (cited in Lesourd 1995:265n34). And yet, as Gilroy (1993:103) and others have pointed out, the concept of 'consumption' is highly problematic because it is associated with passivity, and consequently obscures the agency and creative imagination of the 'consumer'. In the words of Featherstone: 'demand and cultural consumption are not merely dictated by supply, but they must be understood within a social framework' (1995:24).

The increasing interest in the socio-cultural dimensions of globalization over the past few decades has led writers to address the limitations of adopting structuralist frameworks for understanding the impact of global processes upon the local. Jameson suggests that it is probable that cultural studies of globalization will reveal more difference and differentiation than economic studies which are more likely to represent globalization as a 'picture of standardization on an unparalleled new scale' (1998:56-7). These studies have helped to elucidate the limitations of the concept of 'cultural dependency' which appears to lament the passing of an earlier 'autonomous', 'untarnished' culture. Appadurai, for example, argues that 'groups unsullied by contact with a larger world have probably never existed' (1988, cited in Featherstone 1995:24). This brings us back to Gilroy's critique of the idea of a 'pure', 'invariant tradition' (1993). Whether we see the influences of migration to America upon Cape Verdean society as an 'intrusion' upon the local culture is likely to depend upon our standpoint. As Featherstone points out, the origins of every culture are plural and creole. Whether we celebrate pluralism or advocate particularity consequently depends on what we choose or are able to see (1995:124).

Relevant here is Gilroy's criticism of totalizing conceptions of black identity that characterize the Africentrism of blacks in the United States and Great

Britain. Africentrism, according to Gilroy, dismisses slavery and colonialism as mere 'interruptions' in Africa's history and does not recognize the impact that they had upon Africa's traditions. Black identity is thus conceived as being anchored in authentic roots rather than as a process of constant change and mediation (Gilroy 1993:19). If it makes no sense to conceive of black identity in terms of the 'purity' of its roots, neither is it simply a case of celebrating hybridity. It may make mores sense to think in terms of 'structural hybridities'. This is evident in the case of Cape Verdeans who emigrated to America. Faced with a binary racial classification system they were forced to develop new strategies of ethnic identity projection. These occupied a 'shifting middle ground' between their historical roots in Cape Verde and their contemporary routes into American society.

2.4.1.. Strategies of ethnic identity projection in America

The majority of Cape Verdeans who emigrated to America were from rural areas and had had minimal contact with Portuguese or other outsiders, so that for them, the question of identity had remained implicit rather than a felt concern of everyday life. Confronted with the challenge of making a place for themselves in American society, they soon discovered that the issue of identity was of utmost importance as they were expected to fit into one of two categories: black or white. Moreover, an individual with the slightest trace of African ancestry was classified as black irrespective of his or her appearance or socio-economic position (Meintel 1981:240-1).

Such a simple system of binary racial classification was bound to split the Cape Verdean community which was such a diverse group. The physical attributes of its members ranged from those who were highly Negroid in appearance to individuals who could pass as white: even within the same family there were individuals who represented both extremes of the colour continuum, as well as other types of physical differences. There were those who had acquired a college education whilst others had not managed to complete primary school, and some who had achieved a degree of socio-economic success whilst others were branded as failures by American standards. Neither were there any community-wide institutions or groups to which all Cape Verdeans belonged, where they could meet to try and reach an agreement upon the most favourable strategy to adopt (Greenfield 1976:9). It is therefore hardly surprising that a range of responses emerged to the challenge of having to represent themselves in the most favourable light possible within American society.

Greenfield has identified four major strategies of ethnic identity projection amidst the Cape Verdean immigrant community which he has labelled as: Cape Verdean Portuguese, Cape Verdean Black, Cape Verdean African and Cape Verdean American (1976:10).

The Cape Verdean Portuguese Strategy was the first one to develop and dates back to the first immigrants. They were aware of the inferior position of black people in America and so when faced with the problem of identity - in their limited interactions with non-Cape Verdeans - they sought to share the white identity of the Portuguese from Madeira, the Azores and the Continent (Greenfield, 1976:8). In order to pursue this strategy, the Cape Verdeans spoke Portuguese instead of Crioulo in public, tried to join Portuguese clubs and avoided social relations with Americans of colour. However, the Portuguese were unwilling to share their identity with any dark skinned Cape Verdeans whom they considered to be African, due to their colour and to other cultural differences. Not only did they fear being associated with the inferior Negro status that had been ascribed to many Cape Verdeans, but they also found themselves in competition with them for jobs and other benefits. The Portuguese consequently excluded them from their social clubs. Nevertheless, despite the hostility of the Portuguese, in their absence Cape Verdeans were still able to present themselves as Portuguese Americans to society at large (Greenfield 1976:8).

Following the outbreak of the Second World War, many young Cape Verdean men were recruited into the army where they suffered, some of them for the first time, the humiliation of being classified as ‘niggers’ and treated as inferior beings (Greefield, 1976:8). Consequently, after the war there was an increased interest by Cape Verdeans to have themselves defined as Portuguese and once again this strategy was met with opposition by the Portuguese Americans who wished to protect their position in society (Greenfield 1976:10).

Those whose phenotype enabled them to pass as white were able to successfully adopt a Portuguese identity; however, at the cost of disowning any friends and family of dark complexion whilst having to disguise their own personal histories. Meintel summarises the consequences for those who attempted to adopt such a strategy:

> Pursuit of a non-Black identity has usually involved denial or reinterpretation of certain Cape Verdean cultural items and historical experience. Crioulo was passed off as Portuguese, African-inspired musical forms largely forgotten, the experience of slavery denied. The body of course, did not escape criticism and modification. A darker child was a disappointment, Afro hair styles, anathema. To the extent that traits considered racially indicative could be controlled...they were (1981:251).

The Cape Verdean Black strategy developed as a result of the American civil rights movement of the 1950s and 1960s, which tried to improve the socio-economic and political opportunities for black people in America. Many Cape Verdeans who were frustrated by their attempts to overcome the 'colour obstacle' chose to turn it to their advantage by joining in the efforts of the movement to publicly advocate the improvement of opportunities for black people. In order to share a common identity with other blacks they rejected their Cape Verdean heritage and defined themselves as Black Americans. Many moved out of their Cape Verdean neighbourhoods into the black ghetto of New Bedford as a sign of their solidarity with other blacks. They also adopted Afro-American clothing and hair styles, learnt to speak Black English, changed their diets to eat soul food and married Black Americans (Greenfield 1976:11). This strategy entailed encountering the wrath of Cape Verdean friends and family who accused them of being traitors. Neither could they be sure of being accepted by the black American community. If they chose to adopt a black identity without foregoing their Cape Verdean cultural heritage they risked rejection as the following extract from Meintel's interview with a Cape Verdean college student, who chose to adopt a black identity demonstrates:

> Meintel: “Why are the black kids so resentful when you show anything Cape Verdean - remember when you spoke Crioulo in front of that guy, and he wouldn't speak to you after that?”
>
> Student: “It's because they figure that it weakens their force - the more people they can get behind them the better, right? I believe that the only thing Cape Verdeans share with the black people is the sociological aspect, in America...the same social problems, and that's the only place where I think they should unite... they're trying to deculture everyone of colour, so that they'll be more unified...Like they say we should wear dashikis - but they don't wear them in Cape Verde...” (1981:249-50).

Cape Verdeans who opted for a black identity were also open to criticisms of opportunism by the American black community, since adopting a black identity entitled them to benefit from various poverty and social programmes. There were also Cape Verdeans who found themselves living amongst black Americans through no choice of their own. One of the reasons was that a major urban renewal programme of the mid 1960s had torn down some of the older Cape Verdean residences and relocated their poorest occupants in what seemed to the project personnel to be the most appropriate place: together with other black communities. Consequently, some of the poorest Cape Verdeans were forced to accept the black identity that was foisted upon them out of fear that they may lose the social assistance they had received (Greenfield 1976:11-12).

The binary racial classification system of America was not only problematic for the Cape Verdean diaspora. According to Du Bois (1989), the black internalization of an American identity created an uneasy ‘double consciousness’ for members of the American black community who encountered difficulties in reconciling the African with the American aspects of their identity. Gilroy claims that this unease is due to the over integrated conceptions of culture which present immutable ethnic differences between 'whites' and 'blacks', which have arisen as a result of the spread of cultural nationalism. Diaspora blacks drew upon the idea of 'rootedness' as an indication of cultural authenticity, perceived to be necessary for the political project of nation building (1993:112).

The liberation struggle in Cape Verde, which emerged as part of the independence movement in Africa in the 1960s, gave new legitimacy to the projection of a Cape Verdean black identity in America. Its leader, Amílcar Cabral, believed that Cape Verde had been cut off from its African heritage through Portuguese rule and saw the future of the islands in an alliance with the Portuguese colony of Guinea-Bissau. He consequently founded the African Party for the Independence of Portuguese Guinea and the Cape Verde Islands (PAIGC) in 1956 (Davidson 1989:72). By 1972 this initially small and clandestine party had grown in numbers and in strength and it began to recruit supporters in America. Cape Verdean Americans could now share a common cause with other blacks without having to reject their cultural heritage, since the struggle for an improved black identity could be linked symbolically with the independence movement in Africa (Greenfield, 1976:12). They tried to re-educate other Cape Verdean Americans stressing the heritage of slavery and colonialism and the positive value of their cultural practices (Meintel 1981:251-2).

Those Cape Verdeans who refused to see themselves as black or African took strong opposition to this Cape Verdean African strategy as well as to the PAIGC and were horrified when the party became the legitimate government as a result of Cape Verdean independence in 1975:

> In their view, the unification of the islands with the continent by means of political fiat after all these centuries denied the very thing that they believed most deeply and had worked to project as the basis of their identity: that they were a mixed people of combined European and African heritage who had produced something unique that was neither African nor European. To have their homeland a part of an African nation made them African whether they liked it or not. Therefore they opposed the Cape Verdean African strategy even though they were not necessarily united on an alternative position (Greenfield 1976:13).

In order to free themselves from the stigma of being associated with Black Americans, advocates of a Cape Verdean American Strategy rejected the rigid black-white distinction and sought to gain the recognition from Americans of Cape Verdeans as a distinct ethnic group (Greenfield 1976:13-14). One of the challenges they faced was to try and control the content to be projected as their unique Cape Verdean culture, which they achieved by creating a protective boundary with strictures on behaviour supported by a gossip network. However, for some this became too claustrophobic and stultifying, and for others their geographical or social mobility left them beyond the shelter of the community's protective boundaries: their attempt to project a distinct ethnic identity in the wider society failed to make them visible as a separate group. Cape Verdeans were in fact only recognized as a separate category in the census of 1980, after years of effort by advocates of the Cape Verdean American strategy (Meintel 1981:246-53).

Nevertheless, in areas where they were numerous Cape Verdeans managed to make themselves visible and came to be viewed as a 'special case' that did not fit the binary racial classifications of America. Their strategy came under criticism from American blacks who interpreted their claims to cultural distinctiveness as a form of racism. The advent of Cape Verdean Independence, however, seemed to give new legitimacy to their claims of cultural distinctiveness for the general public. This change is reflected in the fact that Cape Verdeans were finally granted facilities to provide their children with a bilingual English-Crioulo education, years after numerous bilingual programmes had been established for the Portuguese speaking immigrant community (Meintel 1981:246-53).

In their attempts to project what they considered to be the most favourable identity for themselves, Cape Verdeans were contested from all quarters: blacks accusing them of being racist and white and whites accusing them of being traitors and black. Meintel cites the case of 'Johnny' (pseudonym), a stevedore living in Providence, to demonstrate the dilemmas and contradictions faced by an individual who chose to adopt a Black identity:

> To the dismay of his family who berated him for "denying your Cape Verdean culture", John had come to look at himself as Black. Lunching on the job one day, Johnny met up with a Cape Verdean friend and began conversing with him in Crioulo. One of his co-workers reacted by saying "You're not really black, then you're Portuguese" and began referring to him as "the Portagee". Some weeks after that an Azorean joined the work group and when told that John was Portuguese, responded with "No, he's a black African" (Meintel 1981:248).

In some circumstances, Cape Verdeans were able to turn their ambiguous identity to their own advantage by purposefully engaging in shifts of identity - on occasions they might stress their Cape Verdean-ness, whilst on others they would take on a black identity - to suit their needs at any given moment (Meintel 1981:251). Nevertheless, as we have already seen, there was rarely any guarantee that the identity they chose to project in any given situation would be accepted by their audience.

Despite the internal divisions within the Cape Verdean immigrant community described above, many of its members believed that they still could or should share a common identity in order to bind their community together in an unfamiliar environment. Equally important, for the creation of a new shared identity, were events 'back at home' in Cape Verde. As Cape Verdeans became aware that the future of the islands was an important factor in whichever identity they chose to project, they began to try to have a voice in the socio-economic and political future of their homeland (Greenfield 1976:14). They may have been living in America, but, the boundaries of their social world were clearly not defined by America's coastline. The significance and impact of transnational connections upon the struggle for Cape Verdean independence is discussed in the following section.

2.5. The birth of a nation

The Cape Verdean liberation struggle provides a fascinating case study of the interconnections between different localities. The 'deterritorialization' (Appadurai 1990) of the struggle took place in the seemingly disparate locations of Portuguese Guinea and America. The leader of the struggle, Amílcar Cabral, was born to Cape Verdean parents in Portuguese Guinea in 1924. He returned to Cape Verde in 1933 and after a few years in Santiago, Cabral moved with his mother to São Vicente. Here, he was able to attend the only secondary school that existed, not only in the archipelago, but in the whole of the Portuguese Empire in Africa: Liceu Gil Eanes (Chabal 1983:29, Foy 1988:135). Many Cape Verdeans educated at Gil Eanes were recruited as teachers, administrators and petty officials in other Portuguese colonies, to take up posts which the native Portuguese did not want (Lobban 1995:60, Foy 1988:135-6). This placed the Cape Verdeans in an ambivalent position as both colonisers and colonised (Meintel 1981:236) which created the same kind of 'double consciousness', referred to above, identified by Du Bois in American blacks. Nevertheless, these colonial assimilation and education policies eventually backfired, since Gil Eanes also produced many of the protagonists of the liberation struggle (Lobban 1995:60, Foy 1988:135-6).

Amílcar Cabral drew on the idea of 'rootedness' in the liberation struggle against Portuguese colonialism. The creation of a party that united the people of Guinea and Cape Verde was not a mere strategic matter of joining forces to overthrow colonial rule. The historical and cultural ties between the two countries constituted, for Cabral, the foundations for his political project of unity (Vicente Lopes 1996:638). Cabral coined the term the 're-africanization of the spirits', as a counter-attack on Portuguese colonial assimilation policies (Chabal 1983).

The PAIGC had considered the possibility of a peaceful route to decolonisation and had initiated its struggle by organising groups of militants in the main urban centres of Guinea as well as by engaging in trade union activities. However, by 1959 the colonial authorities began to suspect that the PAIGV was behind trade union strikes, which according to Chabal, accounts for the Pidjiguiti massacre of 3 August 1959. Dock and harbour workers were wounded and killed when they were fired upon in reaction to their strike for higher wages. This marked a turning point for the PAIGV which decided to abandon the policy of nationalist agitation in the towns to take up armed struggle in the countryside (Chabal 1983:56).

The war never extended to Cape Verde for two main reasons. Firstly, the location and the geographical characteristics of the islands rendered them unsuitable for the requirements of guerrilla warfare. Secondly, there was no guarantee that the population would be able to support the fighters: the socio-economic living conditions of the majority were too poor and neither was there enough political mobilization (Chabal 1983:104).

After more than eleven years of armed struggle in Guinea, on 25 April 1974, a peaceful military coup overthrew the fascist regime in Portugal which resulted in a cease-fire in Guinea. Following a period of intense negotiations between the new Portuguese government and the PAIGC, an agreement was finally reached on the 26 August 1974, making Portugal the eighty fifth country to recognise Guinea's independence. The right of Cape Verde to independence was also recognised in this agreement pending elections to be held in the following year (Chabal 1983:143, 153; Vicente Lopes 1996:306, 315). This delay was due to the lack of political mobilization on the islands: there had been no real opposition movement to colonial rule within the archipelago with the legitimacy to take over power immediately from the Portuguese. The tragic assassination of Cabral in the previous year – the circumstances of which are still clothed in mystery – had also made some party members decide that the declaration of independence should be made separately in order to guarantee the consolidation of the Cape Verdean nation before embarking upon unity with Guinea Bissau (ex-combatant cited in Vicente Lopes 1996, 642).

The independence of Cape Verde had proved to be a sensitive issue in the negotiations, due in part to foreign interests in the geo-strategic position of the archipelago. The identity of Cape Verde, as an African country, was also disputed. In an interview given later on, the head of the Portuguese negotiating team, Mario Soares, later to become the president of Portugal, expressed his conviction that Cape Verde was not really part of Africa:

> In all sincerity, I was always convinced that Cape Verde would gain more by becoming an autonomous region, more associated with Portugal, than as it is, an African country. Cape Verde is not quite Africa; it is an archipelago open to the crossing of African cultures and the South Atlantic (cited in Vicente Lopes 1996:321, my translation).

Cape Verde's poor resource base had frequently been evoked, particularly by the older generations of Cape Verdeans, as a reason for remaining linked to

Portugal (see Davidson 1989, 46) - an argument that has re-appeared in reaction to the funding opportunities generated by the creation of the European Union. As we have already seen, some sections of the Cape Verdean diaspora in America were also keen to associate Cape Verde with Portugal. They were against the PAIGC becoming the legitimate government of Cape Verde because of the effect this had upon their ethnic identity projections: automatically conferring an African identity upon them when they considered themselves to be Portuguese. In a desperate attempt to safeguard Cape Verde from Africa, the Cape Verdean Juridical Congress in America made a unilateral declaration of the independence of the Republic of Cape Verde in 1975, in a hotel in Boston (Lobban 1995:105). Although this declaration failed to prevent the PAIGC from coming to power, the Cape Verdean diaspora in America was still able to exert some pressure on the new government. In the PAIGC's attempt to fulfil its promise of carrying out agrarian reform, for instance, the new independent government soon realized that it could not ignore the interests of absentee landlords abroad, particularly of those in America. The land had an enormous psychological significance for these landlords: it was not only symbolic of their wealth and socio-economic status but also of their desire to come back to the homeland. The American emigrant community was too large and powerful for the government to upset its members, whose remittances were one of the main cornerstones of the national economy. The government consequently decided that the limits fixed on absentee landlordship would have to include the usual size of American emigrant holdings (Bigman 1993:120-1).

The PAIGC remained the ruling party of both Guinea Bissau and Cape Verde until 1980 when a coup carried out by João Nuno Vieira in Guinea Bissau put an end to Cabral's project of unity. The reaction from the leadership of the Cape Verdean branch of the PAIGC was to choose a new name for the party - the African Party for the Independence of Cape Verde, PAICV, thus formally severing the link between the two countries (Lobban 1995:112-15).

2.6. Roots and routes

The significance of the Cape Verdean emigrant community becomes evident when we consider that the resident population of Cape Verde is now smaller than that of its diaspora. In 1998 the population of the archipelago amounted to 415 000 whilst the number of CapeVerdeans overseas came to a total of 500 000. The United States alone was home to 300 000, 55 000 were living in Portugal, 35 000 in Angola, 25 000 in Senegal and 15 000 in France (Economist Intelligence Unit Limited 1998:54-60). The affective attachment of the diaspora to Cape Verde, as seen in the examples from America, illustrates how the 'global' can re-create the 'local':

> ...globalization, defined in its most general sense as the compression of the world as a whole, involves the linking of localities. But it also involves the "invention" of locality, in the same general sense as the idea of the invention of tradition (Hobsbawm and Ranger, 1983), as well as its "imagination" (cf. Anderson 1983). There is indeed something like an "ideology of home" which has in fact come into being partly in response to the constant repetition and global diffusion of the claim that we now live in a condition of homelessness or rootlessness; as if in prior periods of history the vast majority of people lived in "secure" and homogenized "locales" (Robertson 1995:35).

Critiques of the neo-imperialism of the 'development encounter' (Escobar 1995, Sachs 1992, Crush 1995) also construct 'ideologies of home' based on a local/global opposition. For example, the notion that 'local' cultures and 'indigenous' knowledge are rapidly disappearing due to the homogenization of the world leads Sachs to predict a 'looming vision of horror - modern man all alone for ever in the world' (1992:102). But who is this modern man? Gilroy draws our attention to Morrison's claim that the intensity of the slave experience marks out blacks as the 'first truly modern people' because they had to handle difficulties in the nineteenth century which only appeared in European everyday life in the twentieth century; namely, the 'postmodern problems of dissolution, the loss of and the need to reconstruct certain kinds of stability' (Morrison in Gilroy 1993:221). The experience of modernity is not only about the loss but also about the re-invention of a sense of place and identity. The experience of tradition is not only about the preservation but also about the re-construction of place and identity. In other words, experiences of tradition and modernity are mutually implicative rather than opposed to each other. The intersections between 'tradition' and 'modernity' are fluid and shifting because there is no fixed line that can be drawn between the past and the present. Where, for example, do the past end and the present begin for Cape Verde? If we are to agree with Morrison that 'modern life begins with slavery' (cited in Gilroy 1993, 221) then Cape Verde has never been anything other than modern. The desire to preserve a distinctive 'Cape Verdeanness' must draw an arbitrary line between 'past' and 'present': in other words, it occupies a shifting middle ground. Gilroy's concept of a 'Black Atlantic' culture invites us to counterbalance an ethnic and nationalistic focus on 'roots' with a transnational focus on 'routes'. The author's deconstruction of over-integrated projects of cultural ethnicity and cultural nationalism occupies a 'middle ground' between essentialist and anti-essentialist conceptions of black political culture. His celebration of hybridity challenges the essentialism of Africentric perspectives which advocate a return to authentic roots, unsullied by colonial contact, by elucidating the internal differentiation of black culture; however, this does not lead him to adopt a pluralist stance which deconstructs blackness altogether. To argue that there is no such thing as a unitary black community, because it is internally divided by class, gender, economics, political consciousness and so forth, is to turn a blind eye to the persistence of racialised forms of oppression (1993:32). Gilroy locates a 'middle ground' at the intersection between 'roots' and 'routes' for which he has coined the term a '*changing* same' (1993:99-101). The different strategies of ethnic identity projection of Cape Verdeans in America, discussed above, provide a good example of this. The new identities that they projected in response to racialised forms of identification could be labelled as 'structural hybridities'.

Gilroy's approach does not imply that we have to abandon all of the insights generated from structuralist perspectives of the relationship between the local and the global. Mitchell warns against the 'abstract celebration of agency' which can easily lead us to disregard the oppressive effects of global socio-economic forces (1996:220-1). A number of authors have pointed out that Gilroy's deconstruction of Afro-centrism pays insufficient attention to the significance of its growing popularity in the West, amidst Black grassroots communities in Britain (Anthias 1998, Christian 2001) and in the United States (Chrisman 1997). These authors argue that Gilroy's attempt to transcend racial categories leads him to overlook the creative potential within Afro-centrism for fighting against the effects of the interlocking of racism with socio-economic exclusion. Anthias (1998) makes the additional point that processes of hybridisation cannot only be studied in relation to their empowering and emancipatory effects but must also be investigated in terms of their internal relations of subordination and inequality. Cautioning against the over-celebratory use of the concept of 'disaspora', Anthias claims that it turns our attention away from the ways in which trans-ethnic relations are also embedded in local power relations.

The growing popularity of Afrocentrism, referred to above, is not necessarily an indication of the hardening of racial boundaries. There is a danger that Gilroy's critique may homogenize Afro-centrism by failing to attend to the nuance and complexity of people's ideas about race. In his thought provoking enquiry into the relationship between race, nature and culture, Wade challenges dominant perceptions of racial discourses which presume that they are automatically essentialist, deterministic and evocative of permanence and fixity (2002). Without denying the importance of anthropological insights into the social construction of race, Wade points out that they have often led us to overlook the 'shifting middle ground' between nature and culture in racial discourses:

> A key feature of a racial discourse is not simply that it naturalises, or biologises, but rather that it allows strategic equivocation between nature and culture. It is a discourse that, for example, allows room for culturalisation – "Oh well," white English people might say of a woman of Afro-Caribbean parents, raised in the UK, "she was brought up here in England, so we hardly see her as one of them" – but also leaves open the door for re-naturalisation in particular circumstances – "Well, after all, she *is* one of them" (Wade 2002:14-15).

Wade also emphasizes the importance of scrutinizing our use of analytical categories such as nature and biology in our thinking about 'race' and racism. He argues that current perceptions regarding the social construction of race in the social sciences may produce caricatures of the discipline of biology that ignore variants within the field which address the intersections between human biology and social processes. Stereotyped ideas about the determinism of biology-the-discipline are then conflated with popular views of biological determinism thus reproducing the rigid dichotomy between nature and culture. Any references to biology in social investigations of racial discourses are consequently left unexamined since they are automatically assumed to evoke fixity, permanence and determinism. Wade suggests that there may be more flexibility in the way people outside the academia think about biology than social scientists have commonly assumed (2002:112-115). His arguments provide a cautionary note against giving too much weight to the opposition between roots and routes in celebratory uses of the concept of diaspora.

Despite its limitations, what insights may be gained from Gilroy's approach for our understanding of the interconnections between local and global processes? Transcending nationalistic perspectives elucidates the limitations of world systems and dependency theories for interpreting local/global relations; for as Gilroy points out, structures of domination are no longer co-extensive with the borders of nation states. Political struggles have consequently also become increasingly transnational. Ecological movements, for example, have played an important role in tying to bring ethics into politics by linking the issue of sustainability with that of justice (1993:7). Development has also been couched in terms of cultural nationalism by dividing the world up into 'civilized' and 'uncivilized' nations and the Africentrism analysed in the 'Black Atlantic' provides a good example of the ways in which resistance to the Eurocentrism in development may be expressed through a celebration of the indigenous. The political struggle for a more just, inclusive development is also fought out in the 'developed' world where the experience of racism often interlocks with socio-economic exclusion, as the experiences of some of the Cape Verdeans in America illustrate. Transcending nationalistic perspectives equally involves deconstructing Eurocentric conceptions of the need to protect the 'purity' and 'authenticity' of the West from the 'illegitimate intrusions' of black culture (Gilroy 1993:7). Gilroy's insistence upon the need to embrace hybridity, by tuning into the diaspora conversations which have developed over the centuries within the Black Atlantic, warns us that neither claims of the 'civilizing' mission of development nor of the outright rejection of 'intermixture' with the 'modern' accurately portray the nature of the relationships between meanings and practices at local and global levels.

2.7. Learning from Cape Verdean history

Cape Verde is not the only postcolonial nation created out of capitalism and slavery. In his analysis of the 'Black Atlantic' Gilroy has not only omitted Cape Verde but also the French Caribbean. Whilst these omissions are understandable – all studies must establish boundaries – it is nonetheless ironic that, in his attempt to transcend nationalistic perspectives, Gilroy should limit himself to the Anglo-Saxon examples without a few lines acknowledging the existence of other transnational realities from, for example, the lusophone or francophone worlds. Despite his endeavour to defend against cultural nationalism, this exclusive focus suggests that Gilroy has not managed to free himself completely: is there a case for arguing that this testifies to the power of categories upon us even as we try to deconstruct them?

In this chapter, I have provided the reader with what can only be a snapshot of the rich and complex history of Cape Verde, in order to draw attention to the value of the archipelago as a case study for exploring the nature of the interconnections between local and global processes, in the light of the concept of a 'shifting middle ground'.

To study the history of Cape Verde, as a product of the intercontinental slave trade, reveals the structural asymmetries of colonialism; however, it also limits our understanding of the nature of colonial power relations. Relevant here is Cooper's excellent article that calls for a rethinking of the history of colonial Africa. He points out that recognizing the superior power of the Europeans in the 'colonial encounter' should not blind us to the impact of African agency upon the shaping of the encounter. The dichotomies such as domination/resistance, colonizer/colonized and Western/non-Western are too blunt a tool for capturing the fluidity of power relations (1994:1517, 1529). Like Gilroy, he also takes issue with the idea that a 'truly African history' is only to be found in pre-colonial times. To study Cape Verde as a product of colonialism challenges Afro-centric reconstructions of 'authentic' African traditions unsullied by colonial contact. The reality of Portuguese colonialism cannot be dissociated from the history of the Cape Verdean nation: there are no 'authentic' Cape Verdean traditions to be found prior to colonial contact. Cape Verde thus presents an alternative perspective on African traditions – one which sees them as having evolved within, and in some instances despite, the oppressive nature of colonial rule. In this chapter I have focused on the role of the 'lançados' in the smuggling networks which defied the colonial restrictions on foreign trade, the development of the Crioulo language and the refusal of the 'badius' to become assimilated to Portuguese culture. These are only some of the examples of the possibilities that arose for political dissent and for economic and cultural production. I am cautious of using the concept 'resistance', because, as Cooper argues, it 'can be expanded so broadly that it denies any other kind of life to the people doing the resisting' (1994:1532). Enquiries into the ways in which Africans 'resisted' colonial rule must be careful not to reproduce the very dichotomies that they challenged at the outset. The special status of Cape Verdeans within the Portuguese empire as both colonised and coloniser, referred to earlier, serves as a stark reminder of the limitations of these dualisms for the study of colonial African history. Mbembe's thesis (2001) regarding the convivial nature of relations between coloniser and colonised, renders the special status of Cape Verdeans illustrative of the nature of the African 'colonial encounter'.

Acknowledging that the history of the Cape Verdean nation is inseparable from Portuguese colonialism automatically situates Cape Verde at the core of a transnational world. The archipelago served as an entrepôt in the Atlantic slave trade, and, following the abolishment of slavery, as a pool of cheap migrant labour. The military struggle for Cape Verdean independence did not take place on Cape Verdean soil and the political struggle was extended to other nations, including America. Right from the beginning, Cape Verde, as a nation, has always looked outwards. To study Cape Verde, as the core of an intercultural, transnational social world offers a wealth of material for investigating the cultural effects of globalization and, more specifically, the relationship between processes of continuity and processes of change. The influence of the Cape Verdean diaspora upon the socio-economic and cultural life of the archipelago and the influence of events in the archipelago upon its diaspora have only been touched upon in this chapter. Nevertheless, they also provide an indication of the limitations of notions of 'authentic' cultures and traditions. To problematise the concept of 'authenticity' does not require us to deny its significance for Cape Verdean traditions and for a national identity. However, it does remind us that the line drawn between the past and the present, in discourses which regret the 'decline' of a Cape Verdean identity or lament the 'cultural dependency' of the Cape Verdean people, is not set in stone. If the line between the past and the present were to be drawn differently then what are perceived as 'intrusions' upon CapeVerdean culture may equally be seen as contributions towards the ever-changing mosaic of Cape Verdean culture.

Chapter Three

Participation, Conflict and Consensus*

3.1. Introduction

In the previous chapter we saw how Cape Verde was subjected, throughout its history, to the dominance of Western economic imperialism. Following the independence of the archipelago, the extent of Cape Verde's dependence upon foreign aid could be interpreted as a continuation of these centre/periphery relations. However, we also saw that the adoption of this kind of structural perspective will only provide us with a partial understanding of the significance of events at the micro level. If we establish a correlation between centre/periphery relations - that connect different parts of the world at an economic and political level - and micro processes of cultural production then we are more prone to 'see' 'cultural dependency' and 'colonised' minds. If, on the other hand, we allow ourselves to become immersed in the local context of social practice, then we are more likely to discover internal meanings and connections, the logics of which cannot be reduced to a mere reflection of global structural asymmetries. This requires us to adopt a close-up lens and pay attention to detail, to be on the look out for the seemingly insignificant; this is where ethnographic fieldwork plays an important role. In this chapter, the reader is invited to plunge into an ethnographic analysis of micro processes of knowledge production in order to get a fuller picture of the meaning of events at the local level. Whilst a macro analysis of Cape Verde's dependence upon foreign aid may support a structural perspective, these micro processes reveal a more complex picture.

The chapter analyses contemporary debates concerning Cape Verde's economic and socio-political development, within the context of a seminar in which participants were invited to critically assess alternative hypothetical scenarios of the development of Cape Verde in the year 2020. Readers may legitimately question the relevance of such a narrow empirical base of that of a single seminar. However, the point of the analysis is to demonstrate how the contents and dynamics of the seminar, which are disregarded in the resultant official documentation, provide the key to a deeper understanding of local processes of knowledge production. Given that seminars, workshops and meetings are core activities in the development field, a detailed analysis of the seminar dynamics

* An earlier version of this chapter, entitled "Public Participation and the Production of Consensus: Reflections from the Case of Cape Verde" was presented at the International Conference on Public Participation and Information Technologies at the Department of Urban Studies and Planning, MIT, Massachussets, co-organized with Citidep on 10-12 November 2003.

will also provide a means of examining the kinds of communication processes through which a large amount of development knowledge is generated.

The seminar was part of a wider national study on Cape Verde carried out within the ambit of a regional project entitled 'African Futures', coordinated by the United Nations Development Programme (UNDP). The Cape Verdean study had already identified the long term objectives of 'sustainable development', 'durable economic growth' and 'human development': concepts the reader is undoubtedly familiar with and which radical critics of development would dismiss as part of the meaningless jargon characteristic of development discourses. It is not difficult to see how this choice of objectives can be interpreted as an indication of minds 'colonised' by the dominant development paradigm. However, if we limit our investigation to a textual analysis of the documents produced within the ambit of the study, then we will know very little about what happened beyond the printed words.

Many of the documents produced in the development world are the product of informal discussions, formal meetings, seminars and workshops. Yet these documents have been studied by radical critics of development (Escobar 1995; Sachs 1992; Crush 1995; Ranhema 1990) without paying attention to their conditions of production. To read a text without any knowledge of the local social dynamics involved in its production is to assume that the coherence and unity displayed in the text reflect consensual interests and meanings. The plurality of opinions and conflicts of interest that contributed towards shaping the final version of the text - words that have been omitted being equally important as those that appear in the text - are consequently hidden from view. The voices that have inevitably been silenced along the way are excluded from the analysis. To analyse a document, not only as a written text but also as social practice, is to be aware that since documents misrepresent the conditions of their own production, they may only create the illusion of consensus. Participatory methodologies have now become commonplace, due to the widely held view that they guard against external impositions and give voice to those who may otherwise not be heard. Nonetheless, just as the contents of documents should not be taken at face value, neither should the purported effects of adopting these methodologies be taken for granted. The degree to which the use of participatory methodologies renders communication processes more or less democratic has been questioned in the development literature; the answer is always context specific. The following section sets the scene through a brief discussion of Cape Verde's economic and socio-political climate following its independence from Portugal.

3.2. Cape Verde after independence: an overview

When the PAIGC came into power in 1975, the main economic experience of its party leaders was limited to models of state-run enterprises, such as those operating in the countries which had provided support to the PAIGC during the liberation struggle (Lobban 1995:127). The PAIGC had retained close ties with the social democratic and socialist governments of these countries (Foy 1988:112) and it is consequently not surprising that the party should have opted for a planned economy. However, it was not only the influence of socialism that informed this decision. The restraints imposed by the country's economic geography - lack of natural resources, limited potential for increased agricultural production, the infra-structural difficulties of establishing an economy of scale in an archipelago (Sanches 1996:10) - and the consequent dependence of the Cape Verdean economy upon foreign aid contributed towards the PAIGC's decision to centralise the economy. The main objective during the first Republic was to retain as much control as possible over the aid process. In the words of a former PAIGC state official whom I interviewed: 'We needed to be in command because we did not want to be led by the North. We wanted to manipulate our dependency which is why there was much more control'.

The African Party for the Independence of Cape Verde (PAICV) took on this name, as we have seen in the previous chapter, in 1980, following the severing of its formal links with the African Party for the Independence of Portuguese Guinea and the Cape Verde Islands (PAIGC). The PAICV remained in power in Cape Verde until 1991 when the Movement for Democracy (MPD) won the first multi-party elections of the country and was then re-elected in 1995. (Although the PAICV has since returned to office, the ethnographic material analysed in this book comes from fieldwork conducted in the wake of the re-election of the MPD).

The change in political system in 1991 accelerated the re-structuring of the economy, initiated by the PAICV in 1988 when a legislative package was created in order to open up the economy to national and foreign private capital (Sanches 1996:24). The peaceful transition to democracy in 1991 provided the guarantee of political stability that investors were looking for. The MPD government consequently began to privatise state companies and to encourage external investment in areas such as small high labour intensive industries, the recuperation of marine and air services, export production, off shore banking and tourism (Dow 1995:7). The government's objective of liberalising the economy was also supported by international donors such as the United States Agency for International Development (USAID) which within the ambit of a project entitled 'Export Development Services' helped to create a centre for the promotion of investments and exports. This centre, called PROMEX, provided a range of services to foreign and national investors. The African Development Bank also provided financial support, within the ambit of its 'Institutional Support' project, for the creation of an institute for the promotion and development of small and medium sized national businesses operating in the following sectors: light industry, commerce and services (Sanches 1996:24).

Critics of the MPD have argued that the government has been over zealous in its attempt to liberalise the economy. Furtado claims that liberalism has attained hegemonic proportions in Cape Verde with the concomitant risks of an excessive privatisation of the public sector and the instilling of citizens with the principle of 'every man for himself' (1995:100). The former PAIGC official, referred to above, told me that the MPD had begun by investing too much in the private sector and had destroyed everything that promoted participation and solidarity simply because it had belonged to the PAICV. The official went on to add that the MPD was now promoting participation again - probably due to the influence of northern donors.

Regardless of the political party in power, the most pressing challenge for Cape Verde, ever since independence, has been to convince the international donor community of the viability of investing in the country. This concern reflects a wider debate on the 'viability' of small states in general (Benedict 1967; Selwyn 1975, 1980). Although there is no universally agreed definition of what constitutes a small state, the demographic threshold of 1.5 million inhabitants appears to be the most commonly used. With Cape Verde's population of 415,000 (Economist Intelligence Unit Ltd 1998:54) distributed amongst nine islands, the country was not only classified as a small state but also as a 'small island developing country'. This category has been recognized by the United Nations as needing special attention due to its particular handicaps arising from the interplay of factors such as: smallness; remoteness; geographical dispersion; transport and communication constraints and vulnerability to natural disasters (UN, 1994). Cape Verde was also classified together with the small states of the South Pacific as a MIRAB economy - Migration, Remittances, Aid, Bureaucracy (Bertram and Watters 1985). This has led some authors to question the long-term 'viability' of an economy so dependent upon the outside world (Lesourd 1995). As Foy points out, the amount of wealth produced inside Cape Verde - the Gross Domestic Product (GDP) – has been negligible in comparison with the Gross National Product (GNP), which represents the amount of funds used by the government or consumed by the population. The difference has been made up of the remittances from the Cape Verdean emigrant population and foreign aid (Foy, 1988:108).

During the period of my fieldwork, foreign aid constituted an average of around forty per cent of the GDP, amounting to approximately two hundred dollars per capita per year. Food aid contributed to around seventy-five per cent of grain supplies and sixty per cent of supplies of milk and vegetable oil (Sanches 1996:11, Duarte and Mertz 1996:vii). Foreign aid also funded the state construction projects referred to in the previous chapter which had been set up to assist drought victims in the colonial period and had now evolved into a form of social security system for the unemployed. Known as 'AIMO' or 'FAIMO' - high intensity manual labour workfronts (Frentes de Alta Intensidade de Mão de Obra) – the name usually connoted inefficiency, laziness and dependence and had become a paradigmatic symbol of Cape Verde's dependence upon foreign aid. The primary sector - agriculture, livestock and fishing - amounted to an average of less than fifteen per cent of the GDP and the contribution of industry averaged at around nineteen per cent. According to Sanches, the tertiary sector - commerce, transport and public services – which came to an average of just over fifty nine per cent of the GDP, offered the most potential for strengthening the Cape Verdean economy (1996:12).

The nature of Cape Verdean politics needs to be understood in the light of the country's socio-political history. According to Teixeira and Monteiro, there had been no effective organised opposition to the PAICV throughout its rule which accounts for a lot of what happened following the advent of democracy. Teixeira and Monteiro claim that critical voices had been silenced through fear of accusations of dissent and of being seen as traitors to the cause of independence. The activism of the PAIGC, the weakness of civil society and the fact that the state was the principal employer meant that anybody who wanted to have an active role in political affairs had to join the PAIGC or its organizations (Teixeira and Monteiro 1996:9). Since the PAICV and the MPD were the only political parties to contest the 1991 elections, Cape Verdean society became polarized into competing political positions. These were manipulated by the politicians through the use of simple binaries such as: good versus bad, democracy versus totalitarianism and liberalism versus statism (Furtado 1995:97). The MPD's re-election in 1995, with over a two-third majority in parliament, denied the three new parties that had also contested the elections the chance to contribute towards opening up Cape Verdean politics and the polarization of the socio-political field became even more entrenched. Evidence of this polarization will be evident in the case material below.

3.3. The National Long Term Perspective Study

In April 1996 I made a short trip to Cape Verde to prepare for my anthropological fieldwork. I left two weeks later, laden with documents which had been produced in 1995 as part of the first phase of a national long term perspective study (NLTPS) on Cape Verde. The documents - given to me by the director of a technical team assigned to the project - had been compiled from a series of questionnaires, round tables and interviews, conducted by civil servants on nearly all of the islands, in order to collect qualitative data from different social groups regarding their aspirations for the future of Cape Verde. These were then grouped together and labelled in the documents as the 'main national aspirations'.

The NLTPS study, coordinated by the United Nations Development Programme (UNDP) was part of a regional project called 'African Futures'. The Cape Verdean project, entitled 'Cape Verde 2020', was financed by the Dutch

government. The aim of the project, as described in the NLTPS phase one report, was to assist African countries in the formulation of national long term development strategies which founded on the aspirations of the people, aimed at achieving 'sustainable human development' (MCE 1995a:1-3).
Towards the end of 1996 the project was reaching the end of the second phase which was to create a data base. This entailed analysing past and present national development strategies and results, in order to identify the critical issues for the future of Cape Verde. These would feed into the third stage of the study to create alternative future scenarios for appraisal, one of which would serve as the source for producing a collective vision for Cape Verde in the year 2020. The fourth and final stage of the study was to use the vision as a basis from which to formulate new national development strategies (MCE 1995a:2).

The documents produced by national consultants during the second phase of the project included studies on: demography (Monteiro 1996); institutional development (Teixeira and Monteiro 1996); women in the context of sustainable human development (Salústio 1996); the international dimension of development (Sanches 1996); culture and development (Veiga 1995); the national productive system (Pires 1995); decentralization and regional development (Cardoso Mendes 1995); education and health (Carvalho et al 1995) and policies for territorial management (Pereira Silva 1995).

When I began my fieldwork in Cape Verde in August 1996, I discovered that the NLTPS technical team was preparing a week long seminar in order to produce inputs for the final phases of the NLTPS study and obtained permission from the director to attend as an observer[4].

3.3.1. The National Long Term Perspective Seminar

The individuals invited to participate in the NLTPS seminar were comprised of the urban elite: civil servants, private consultants, politicians, lawyers, agronomists, economists and sociologists. All of the participants were resident in Santiago island - the majority in the capital, Praia - although many originated from other islands. Participants were taken in two small buses from Praia to the other end of the island of Santiago to the municipality of Tarrafal. Here the seminar was to take place in a tourist compound called 'Green Bay' which was equipped with seminar rooms and was situated on the beach of Tarrafal. Many of the seminars and workshops organized by international donors took place here. Breakfast, lunch and dinner in an open air restaurant overlooking the

[4] The seminar was a relatively small event in comparison to the whole of the NLTPS study. My analysis of the dynamics of the seminar is in no way intended as a critique of the whole study.

beach as well as accommodation were all provided in the compound and paid for by the NLTPS project[5].

Tarrafal beach was the main tourist attraction of Santiago Island and it was very common for Cape Verdeans to go there for week-ends and short holidays. The team director justified his choice of location to me by explaining that if the seminar were to take place in Praia, it would be very difficult to secure the attendance and concentration of participants whose work commitments would be constantly knocking at the seminar door.

A French speaking UNDP consultant from the regional project 'African futures' was also present to give assistance in the clarification of concepts related to the methodology of the seminar, as well as to provide inputs for discussion. She was part of the 'army of specialists' referred to by Sampson (1996:123), in his study of an aid project in Albania. The role of the specialist is to communicate the precise meaning of the development jargon frequently used in projects (referred to by Sampson as 'project-speak'). In the seminar, participants were expected to toe the 'development line' by accepting the terminology and methodology of the exercise which dictated the contents of their discussions and reproduced the dominant Western paradigm of national planning. Are we to conclude that the seminar participants were reduced to passive recipients of a foreign agenda? The methodology of the seminar undoubtedly illustrates the potential for domination inherent in purportedly democratic participatory methodologies which, in the name of consensus, may silence divergent ideas and conflicting interests. Rather than deepening the process of participation, the emphasis on consensus-building characteristic of these methodologies can transform it into a 'performance' which excludes anything that will prevent the show from going on. Considerations of power and politics are consequently swept under the methodological carpet, for, as Cleaver argues, they are construed as divisive and obstructive (2001:36); however, the methodology does not always run the show. In her discussion of participatory techniques Kothari argues that individuals and social groups are able to subvert the methodology and gain control both of their 'performance' and of the information they choose to conceal or disclose (2001:142). The dynamics of the seminar provide a good example of this. I shall demonstrate how, by instigating a process of knowledge elimination, the pursuit of consensus finally backfired. Participants refused to allow the contents of their discussions to be subordinated to the methodology and they became active agents in the construction of alternative agendas. In other words, they knew how to bargain in the 'conceptual market-place' (Mbembe 2001) of development.

[5] I was unable to find accommodation at this hotel, but the technical team kindly included me for both lunch and dinner so that I would not be excluded from the informal dynamics of the seminar.

3.3.1.1. What should Cape Verde do?

Twenty-four people attended the seminar, out of which eight were women (including a foreign consultant). The seminar took place in a large room in which tables were set out in the form of a rectangle so that participants were all facing each other. I had come expecting to hear lengthy discussions over the documents produced during the second phase of the NLTPS study. Instead participants were invited to engage in a highly structured form of debate with a number of support documents to assist them.

Each participant received a glossary of the main concepts to be used, a description of the different stages of the methodology of the NLTPS study and a support document entitled 'Seminar for the construction of scenarios and formulation of strategies'. This document contained lists extrapolated from the NLTPS study data base that consisted of a wide range of the socio-economic and political characteristics of Cape Verde, classified under the following headings: Main Actors; Main Strengths; Main Weaknesses; Main Tendencies; Main Opportunities; Main Threats; Significant Events for the Future; Critical Uncertainties.

The first few days were taken up with analysing and discussing these lists. This was the stage in which there was the most freedom for participants to express their views. They were invited to suggest amendments to any of the items, as well as to add any items to the lists that they felt were missing. The average number of items on each list was sixty, plus an extra twenty to forty items added through discussion. This proved to be a very time consuming process and by the end of the second day the technical team came under pressure to put a leash on the debates. The methodology then narrowed down the focus of discussion by eliminating topics through the means of a voting system.

Participants had to choose the ten most important items in each list. Once each participant's choice had been recorded, then all of the items that had not been voted for were disregarded and participants then had 30 points each to distribute at their will amongst the remaining items. The rationale behind this second round was to give people the chance to re-consider their choices. Participants were told that they could allocate thirty points to a single item if they so wished. The top ten scoring items of the plenary for each list were then selected.

Gender relations in Cape Verde constituted one of the issues raised before the second round of voting took place. A female participant, who was a lawyer by profession, felt that this was an important issue that was missing in the lists and she proposed an addition to the list of the main threats to Cape Verde, formulated as follows: 'The survival of patriarchal, traditional values of Cape Verdean men and women excludes women from positions of power'. She then included this item in her personal top ten choices. In the second round, few people allocated points to her item. However, the lawyer gave it twenty-five out of her thirty points, thus boosting it to fourth place in the top ten threats to Cape Verde. Her attempt to put gender relations squarely on the agenda was nonetheless foiled by the methodology of the seminar which obliged participants to focus on the top ten items in the list of critical uncertainties, given in Table 3.1. The italic letters represent amendments or additions to the lists made by participants.

Table 3.1: Top ten voted critical uncertainties of Cape Verde

Score	List Four: Critical Uncertainties.
1	Evolution of external aid
2	Capacity for a dynamic insertion into the global economy
3	Capacity to combat social exclusion, unemployment and poverty
4	*Results of laws and reforms (e.g. Will the educational reform correspond to people's needs?)*
5	Evolution of the attitude of civil society towards the problematic of development
6	Evolution of the capacity to manage the national economy
7	Evolution of the economy of the country
8	Evolution of the African situation
9	Evolution of the problematic of unemployment
10	*The capacity to implement laws (e.g. The external investment law has not attracted as much investment as hoped for.)*

The difference in wording between items six and seven in the table above is minimal. Both items refer to the same critical uncertainty: the evolution of Cape Verde's economy. Had the technical team chosen to conflate these two items then another item would have been included in the top ten. It is interesting to note that the issue of desertification which did not get voted into the top ten also appeared in the original list of critical uncertainties in two similar phrases: 'the rhythm of desertification' and 'the evolution of the process of desertification' which received nine and fifteen votes respectively, making a total of twenty four votes. The capacity to implement laws which is the last item on the top ten list of critical uncertainties had received two votes less than this. Desertification which is a critical issue for Cape Verde was consequently omitted from the list. Item ten, 'the capacity to implement laws', could also have been conflated with the fourth item, 'the results of laws and reforms'; this would have produced a single item with a total of sixty nine points. Item number two on the list – the capacity for a dynamic insertion into the global economy - had a lower total of sixty eight points. And so I could go on shuffling around the positions not only with this list but with all the other lists that also had items which could have been conflated.

The point I am making here is that the top ten scoring items of each list may not have all been representative of the majority vote. The technical team justified the similarity of some of the phrases on the grounds that the nuanced differences could reflect different sensibilities. Whilst this rationale appears to make sense in terms of the promotion of inclusive participatory processes, the combination of nuanced qualitative phrases with a win or lose voting system had the opposite effect: not only were the nuanced differences of a given item ignored but the item itself was denied its majority vote through a distortion in the results. For all its emphasis on participation, the methodology did not allow much space for questioning any in-built assumptions because the results of the voting procedures had to be respected. This limited the range of issues to be discussed at the onset and also conditioned the way in which these issues were dealt with.

The wide range of issues proposed for discussion throughout the seminar was subordinated by the methodology to a single interest: that of the Cape Verdean nation, treated as though it were a business enterprise. The reader may have noted that the methodology, used to identify the strengths, weaknesses, opportunities and threats for the development of Cape Verde, was transferred from the field of firm management. This methodology, informally known as 'SWOT' analysis, is intended to help a company to increase its competitiveness in the marketplace. It now constitutes a common practice in the development field which testifies to the continuing influence of the neo-liberal paradigm. Ferguson spells out the consequences of this kind of approach in his analysis of 'development discourse' on Lesotho. By reifying the nation and asking 'What should Lesotho do?' internal conflicts between different groups in society are hidden from view (1990:62). The question 'What should Cape Verde do?' constituted the underlying concern of the NLTPS study. Conflicting aspirations, identified in the first phase of the study, were consequently diluted by the technical team into the consensual long term objectives of 'sustainable development'; 'durable economic growth' and 'human development'. Consider the following aspirations in relation to the FAIMO system - the symbol of Cape Verde's dependence upon aid:

> Maternity leave for women working in FAIMO (MCE 1995b: 115);
> Definitive freedom from FAIMO (MCE 1995b:129);
> The need for more attention to be paid to FAIMO (MCE 1995b:168);
> The extinction of FAIMO together with the creation of conditions for self-employment (MCE 1995b:217);
> Overcome the delays in the payment of FAIMO salaries (MCE 1995b:168, my translations).

These aspirations indicate that there was a conflict of opinion in relation to whether the FAIMO system should be abolished or improved. Yet when this issue was raised during the initial discussions in the seminar, members of the technical team refused to engage in the debate on the grounds that FAIMO would have become an irrelevant detail by the year 2020. The aim of the seminar was to reach a consensus and not to dwell upon divergent ideas.

By following subsequent stages in the methodology foreign aid, insertion into the global economy and poverty were singled out as the most important factors for achieving the long term objectives referred to above. The other items in the list of critical uncertainties were disregarded. The next step was to justify this choice. Discussions followed in order to establish why participants considered the top three items important and what the nature of their uncertainty was.

With regard to item one, the continuation of foreign aid was deemed important by some of the participants because aid generated many projects which were considered necessary for the development of Cape Verde. Other participants challenged this idea, arguing that foreign aid was an obstacle to national production and hence to development, bringing it into direct conflict with the second item on the list - Cape Verde's capacity for a dynamic insertion into the global economy. One participant, for example, questioned whether foreign aid was positive for Africa by emphasizing the benefits it brought for donor countries. ‘Aid’, she claimed, ‘resolves the problem of excess production for Europe. Frozen chicken, for example, is a disincentive to local production. This is not the case for Cape Verde because we don’t have the capacity for local production. But we eat third class rice bought as though it were first class…’

The UNDP consultant referred to the experience of Korea, as an example of a country that had reacted positively to the reduction of foreign aid, by interpreting it as a challenge to develop its own potential. In reaction to her comment there were murmurs from some of the participants sitting close to me about the need to change people's mentalities in Cape Verde first. The 'mentality' of 'lazy' FAIMO workers was frequently construed as an impediment to national development in the discourses of the local elite. This issue is explored in more depth in the following chapter.

Discussions regarding the third item in Table 3.1 - the capacity to combat social exclusion, unemployment and poverty - also treated 'the poor' as an obstacle to national development. Poverty was identified as a structural problem which affected thirty per cent of the population: fourteen per cent of the population was classified as very poor. These figures come from a World Bank study on poverty (1994) and were frequently quoted in many of the meetings and seminars that I attended throughout the period of my fieldwork. There was a degree of confusion surrounding these figures, due to another version of the statistics which circulated that held that the fourteen per cent who were very poor were part of the thirty per cent figure of poor people. Whichever version of the statistics people referred to, the poor became reified as a number and turned into a problem.

One of the questions that was debated was which 'target group' to work with - the fourteen per cent who were very poor or the not-so-poor who had more of a chance of freeing themselves from poverty. An equally pressing concern was whether Cape Verde - as a nation - could afford to go on spending money on 'the poor' - conceived as a single social group. Participants were divided over this. For some integration into the world economy - the second item in Table 1 - was of paramount importance whilst others argued in favor of the fight against poverty. These conflicting views, discussed in more detail below, reflect tensions between 'people-centered' and 'market-driven' approaches to development and constitute the focus of Chapter Five.

With regard to the second item, the UNDP consultant also challenged the participants' concept of integration into the world economy by arguing that Cape Verde was already integrated. The implication here, although the consultant did not say as much, was that foreign aid provided the means of integration into the world economy. Those who had already argued against foreign aid replied that integration had always occurred through dependence - the challenge now was to achieve integration into the world economy through independence. Discussion on this item finished with the conclusion that without integration into the world economy, which was the only means for economic survival, it would be the death of the nation. The choice was between integration and marginalization.

3.3.1.2. Hypothetical scenarios of Cape Verde in 2020

In the next stage of the methodology, foreign aid, insertion into the global economy and poverty were used to serve as the bases for the elaboration of a range of future hypothetical scenarios for Cape Verde. The scenarios considered to be the most realistic were then selected for discussion. These are given in abbreviated form in Table 3.2.

Table 3.2: Hypothetical scenarios of Cape Verde in 2020

Scenario	Foreign Aid	Dynamic insertion into global economy	Combat poverty
A	-	+	-
B	+	+	-
C	-	+	+
D	+	-	+
E	+	-	-

Scenario D for example, reveals an increase in foreign aid, inability to insert Cape Verde into the global economy and an increased ability to fight poverty. Scenario E was finally eliminated on the grounds that it reflected Cape Verde's present situation and was therefore not worth considering.

The plenary was then divided into four groups and each group was given a different scenario to work with. The task in hand was explained by the UNDP consultant. The scenario was an image of Cape Verde in the year 2020; each group had to explain through logical steps how Cape Verde had arrived there and to give a description of Cape Verde in 2020. The four groups worked very hard analysing the range of possible explanations to account for their scenario. The team had assigned me to group D which worked until midnight and still met early the next morning to go over the written document. Each group presented its scenario with its corresponding message in the plenary. These presentations were recorded by the technical team, summaries of which are discussed below.

3.3.1.3. Crabs, dragon trees, turtles or dolphins

Scenario A (aid - , integration + , poverty -) was named the Crab and the Oyster. Despite a positive increase in 'economic growth', there had not been sufficient 'social development', hence the depiction of a crab which takes one step forward and two backwards. Two Cape Verdes had emerged within the country: whilst a part of Cape Verde - symbolised by the crab - advanced, the other part was ostracised, closed in its shell like an oyster. Members of this group invented the word - 'badié' - a francophone distortion of the term 'badiu': the name originally given to the peasants of the hinterland of Santiago and now used to refer to all Santiago born Cape Verdeans. 'Badié' was intended to represent the more sophisticated class that had emerged as a result of the social differentiation depicted in this scenario.

Scenario B (aid +, integration +, poverty -) revealed a similar situation to that of scenario A above. Economic growth had failed to benefit the majority of the population because issues of equity and social justice had been ignored, leaving a widening gap between the rich and the poor. In contrast to scenario A above, Cape Verde had managed to secure the continuation of aid. This was interpreted as the result of having succeeded to create and sell a positive image of the country to the outside world.

This scenario was named the stepmother dragon tree. The dragon tree is resistant to aridity and strong winds and was chosen to symbolise the persistence to survive which characterised the history of Cape Verde. The dragon tree has a wide bushy tree top which provides good protection for those underneath it. The group chose to call it a stepmother dragon tree after a popular saying that claimed that Cape Verde had always been a good stepmother: ever since colonial times the authorities had made life easier for foreigners, especially for Europeans, to the detriment of the Cape Verdean born population[6].

[6] As already noted in Chapter Two, Europeans constituted the majority of those who benefited from the Crown monopolies leased out by the colonial government in fifteenth century Cape Verde. See Carreira (1982) and Lobban (1995).

The message that emerged from these two scenarios was essentially the same: that 'economic growth' should not take place at the expense of 'social development'. The coining of the term 'social development' is traced by Marsden back to the 1950s when United Nations reports began to separate the ‘social’ from the ‘economic’ in response to growing concerns that the ‘human factor’ had been sidelined by the pursuit of economic development. ‘Social development' then became equated with the moral commitment to assist the needy which helped to galvanize public support for poverty alleviation programmes (1990:16, 20). Implicit in the two scenarios described above was an ethical message that it was immoral to marginalize 'the poor'. In the next scenario, the underlying message was that it was wrong to deny the market.

Scenario C (aid - , integration + , poverty +) was by far the most challenging of scenarios to work with because it required breaking out of dichotomous models of 'economic' versus 'social' development to demonstrate how the issue of poverty had been largely resolved without jeopardising 'economic growth'. It was an expression of everybody's ultimate dream. The suppression of aid was interpreted as an indication of Cape Verde's liberation from dependence. The scenario was named 'Tuninha' - the Atlantic dolphin. As a highly intelligent creature, the dolphin was considered an appropriate metaphor for a country that had turned inwards to draw upon its own creative intelligence on the route to success.

The message that emerged from scenario C was more specific than the other two: that Cape Verde had a natural vocation for external trade which had to be exploited to the utmost in order to guarantee Cape Verde's future and viability. Areas included tourism, insurances, banking, off-shore services and ‘modern’ services through the use of new information technologies: international conferences on areas such as bio-diversity and renewable energies, distance learning, telecommunications and teleconferences. Integration into the world economy through external trade was conceived as the only means of securing the survival of Cape Verde as a nation. In other words, the emphasis in this scenario was upon the need for Cape Verde as a nation to develop the 'virtues' of modern economic practice.

This scenario raised many questions for a country whose majority of the population was dependent to some degree upon agriculture - despite the ongoing drought - to make a living. Some people claimed that the agricultural potential of the country had yet to be harnessed through the construction of dams, the desalination of water and the use of high technologies, such as drip irrigation. (Scenario C envisaged a green revolution for Cape Verde with the use of these technologies). Others believed that agriculture could never be the backbone of Cape Verde's external trade which they held was to be found in services and tourism. Advocates of both sides were engaged in the debate, already discussed above, concerning the viability of Cape Verde. A Cape Verdean aid worker told me in an interview that he felt that the majority of international aid personnel were too polite to question the 'viability' of Cape Verde in front of Cape Verdeans. I had noted how, in the plenary, the UNDP consultant had congratulated participants for identifying as many as sixty four items in the list of Cape Verde's strengths, whilst she commented, in one of the small group discussions, that in reality most of these items were not viable.

Scenario D (aid +, integration - , poverty +) was named the pace of the turtle, indicating the slow pace forward of a country that experienced no real growth because it was dependent on foreign aid. Should the turtle fall on its back then it would lie helpless waiting for a Good Samaritan to come along and turn it over onto its feet again. The turtle inhabited the surrounding waters of Cape Verde and had become one of the country's national symbols, frequently produced in local handicrafts. The image of the helpless turtle was a visually powerful way of evoking Cape Verde's dependence. The 'humiliation' of having to rely upon the helping hand of a Good Samaritan was a challenge to the participants' sense of national pride. During the small group discussions, for example, a participant in group D had declared that if integrating Cape Verde into the world market in the next thirty years could only be achieved by sacrificing the fight against poverty, *she* would be willing to make that sacrifice. In responding to the 'development' question (Ferguson 1990) 'what should Cape Verde do?' this participant was prepared to personify Cape Verde at the expense of the poor. The participants in the seminar were engaged in the construction of an 'imagined community' in which they saw themselves as agents charged with the kind of modernizing mission identified by Pigg in Nepal that classified people on either side of the 'great divide' between 'progress' and 'backwardness' (1996, 163).

3.3.1.4. Choosing between the stepmother or the Good Samaritan

The next stage in the methodology was to evaluate the scenarios according to their plausibility and desirability. The purpose here was to select a scenario, to serve as the basis for a collectively constructed vision of Cape Verde, and then to elaborate national strategies for the realisation of that vision. Scenarios A and C were unanimously considered to be the worst and best options respectively. The former, the Crab and the Oyster, was rejected for its lack of humanity, increased inequalities, repressive state and poor external image. Although the latter, the dolphin of the Atlantic, was characterised as more painful since it meant relying on inside strengths and was consequently less probable, it was chosen because it was more sustainable and represented an ideal and a challenge for Cape Verde.

Up to this point, the methodology had managed to produce a working consensus. Participants had been able to agree upon the choice of the Atlantic

Dolphin scenario as the basis for the construction of a vision because it represented an ideal which, in very broad terms, it was difficult to take issue with. The debate now centered on a comparison of scenarios D and B. Was it better to depend on outside assistance and reduce poverty or to achieve integration into the world market at the expense of reducing poverty? The consultant then brought up the problem that aid was very conditioned by the fight against poverty. She told the plenary that the new president of the World Bank had chosen poverty as a primary objective. The consultant suggested that unless Cape Verde found new partnerships, such as with China or Indonesia, countries that were not particularly concerned with combating poverty, then Cape Verde had little choice in the matter. She also pointed out that the donor community was probably not interested in helping Cape Verde integrate into the international market. The consultant went on to add that achieving the latter required providing guarantees of social stability for investors. This could only be achieved by having a dictatorial regime to keep the poor masses at bay. Who would want to invest where there was a dictator? The consultant was not in favor of opting for scenario B. A participant commented to me later that he felt that the consultant did not believe that Africa could survive without the Good Samaritan of foreign aid. Despite the consultant's comments, a majority was finally reached which placed the Stepmother (scenario B) in second place, followed by scenarios D and A.
Many of the consultant's contributions were to clarify the concepts which constituted the basic tools of the methodology. That she could not speak Portuguese did not seem to pose major problems during the seminar because many of the Cape Verdeans present spoke French. The seminar was, nevertheless, conducted mainly in Portuguese, Cape Verde's official language. I was also fortunate enough to speak both Portuguese and French and was consequently feeling confident in my ability to follow the seminar; nevertheless, in the subsequent stages, I soon discovered that understanding the literal sense of what was being said was only to uncover the tip of an iceberg. As the seminar progressed, emotions began to fly and I became increasingly perplexed, unable to understand why participants were arguing over what appeared to me to be relatively insignificant differences in terminology. During these moments, participants switched over to speak to each other in Creole. Although one of the problems seemed to be related to the indeterminacy of the translation of certain concepts, it seemed to me that something more significant was at stake.

3.3.1.5. Building a consensus: idealists or realists? Words at war

The next stage was to write the vision. The necessary steps towards making a collective construction of the vision were spelled out by the consultant. She drew attention towards the important distinction to be made between a vision and an aspiration. The consultant described the former as a collective act of faith, a realistic and realizable ambition that took into account the weaknesses and strengths that had been identified a few days before. The vision should retain the inspirational, mobilising components of an aspiration, readjusted in order to render it feasible.

The first attempt at writing up the vision was drawn from the aspirations identified in phase one of the study and from the Atlantic dolphin scenario. It was a very short, snappy, inspirational general text which the team wrote up on a board. I found the text so general that I did not bother to write it down. The gist of the text was that Cape Verde was economically strong and independent, with advanced technologies, a healthy environment and satisfactory levels of social development. There were no qualifications or adjustments written into the text in accordance with the consultant's recommendations described above. As far as I was concerned, the vision presented was no different to an aspiration. This point was voiced by other participants who seemed to be unhappy with the text because it was too 'perfect'. Many heated discussions followed in which participants began to take sides for or against the text. Some participants took issue with the words 'free from dependence' or 'independent' because they felt it was too idealistic to suggest that Cape Verde would be totally free from foreign aid in the year 2020. Other mitigating phrases were suggested such as 'Cape Verde on the road to independence' or 'Cape Verde free from the indispensability of aid'. Discussions were becoming more and more heated as participants became visibly angry with each other. I could not understand why there should be so much fuss over deciding upon the precise wording of a vision which, in very broad terms, everyone was in agreement with.

In short, the first vision was rejected by the plenary and so a new one had to be written. A much longer version was presented by a participant who had been busy writing whilst the storm raged over his head. He began by saying that Cape Verde would not be free from dependence in the year 2020 and that Cape Verde was going to get into debt to pay for its development. He also spoke of the emergence of a new scientific and technological mentality which would replace the magical beliefs and fatalistic mentality of the population. He ended by saying that Cape Verde would be an aesthetically more beautiful country and that development would be based on deeper philosophical conceptions than those used at present. When he had finished reading out his vision many people clapped enthusiastically. The team then asked the participant to reduce his text by summarising the main points on the board. He began, rather reluctantly, with the first point which was increased debt. One of the team members retorted angrily: ‘How can you have increased debt as part of the vision?’ There was certainly nothing inspiring about that! Pandemonium broke out once again.

To calm spirits, the team leader suggested that everyone take a ten minute break. I went outside feeling more perplexed than ever. My interpretation of the problem was that there was an inherent dilemma built into the methodology. Participants were being asked to create a vision which was both inspiring and realistic. The problem here was that a 'realistic' vision was not inspiring enough and an inspiring or idealistic vision was not convincing enough. The problem did not seem to me to be that difficult to resolve and was essentially a matter of playing with words. I tried to communicate my opinions to the person whose vision had been applauded, but he seemed to be too perturbed. Paying little attention to my words he said:

> Cabral's vision of independence was so very close to being an aspiration that there was barely any difference. Few of us believed that independence was possible at that time. We, Cape Verdeans, are afraid to dream because if the vision looked like an aspiration, then we need to understand how we got there.

I then began to understand how making a distinction between an aspiration and a vision was a highly complex, subjective and sensitive matter. It was all very well to make a theoretically conceptual distinction, as the consultant had done above; the problem arose when deciding upon the ingredients. It was not just a matter of what were they to be, but how much and when? To achieve consensus on these kinds of questions was clearly far more difficult than subscribing, for example, to the very broad concept of 'sustainable development' - hence the usefulness of these kinds of terms to create at least an impression of consensus. Nevertheless, there was also something else at stake. As the quotation above suggests, engaging in discussions about the nitty-gritty details that distinguished an aspiration from a vision was also to show ones true colours in terms of ideology and political allegiance. This required addressing issues which could otherwise be ignored through the adoption of such broad concepts as 'sustainable development'. Concrete political decisions would have to be made regarding what should be done. How much debt, for example, should political leaders be prepared to get into? This kind of question was considered inappropriate by the team member above who was more concerned with producing an inspirational text.

After the break, participants continued with their attempt to produce a vision acceptable to everybody. Eventually it looked as though a tenuous consensus had been reached. At this point the team also wanted to produce a slogan to complete the vision which would be used to publicize the results of the NLTPS study. The suggestion put forward by the team extrapolated from the phase one aspirations, was 'Cabo Verde Verde' (Cape Verde, Green). A shower of protestations immediately followed. 'Cabo Verde Verde' in the popular imagination could only signify rain and hence was highly inappropriate given the country's prolonged drought. Others defended the slogan by emphasizing its poetic qualities: it also signified hope. Someone else protested that 'Cabo Verde Verde' was a myth. 'Yes and myths are very powerful', came the reply in defence of the slogan. The conflict between an idealist and realist approach had surfaced once again. Arguments came back and forth but somehow the question remained unresolved and the plenary began to discuss the choice of strategic questions for small group discussions that had to be extrapolated from the vision for the following stage in the methodology.

Five main areas were identified but since there were only four groups one of them had to be eliminated. The choice was between developing elevated technology and transforming Cape Verde into a useful and credible country - the basis for Cape Verde's foreign policy. The plenary looked set for more prolonged discussions. In order to avoid this, there was a vote and elevated technology was consequently eliminated. The four strategic questions were then formulated as follows: how to develop a dynamic and strong productive system; how to develop a sense for aesthetics and a concern for the environment; how to transform Cape Verde into a useful and credible country and lastly, how to promote a social policy geared towards durable human development.

A different strategic question was about to be allocated to each group for discussion when one of the team members suddenly declared in Portuguese that he could not accept the questions that had been chosen, nor could he accept the vision. One of the seminar participants immediately expressed dissatisfaction with the slogan - 'Cabo Verde Verde'. I could see exasperation written on many faces as the realization dawned upon participants that they were back at square one - squabbling over the vision.

Turmoil broke out with people splitting up into little groups of heated discussions in Creole, whilst others left the seminar room. A UNDP expatriate consultant involved with the project who was sitting by my side, turned to me complaining that nobody had heeded his warnings, the day before, when he had said that participants should reach a solid consensus with regard to the contents of the vision. It was then that he explained that the government was showing little interest in this study. He told me how he had spent two hours talking to a top government official who had not made a single reference to the NLTPS project. This expatriate could not understand why. I had already noticed that there was hardly any media coverage of the seminar: unlike the other national seminars that I had attended, the NLTPS seminar had no televised opening or closing ceremonies. A few minutes later, a participant came back into the room muttering that this party politics split was totally out of order. I welcomed these snippets of information with a degree of relief, for they helped me to make more sense out of what was going on.

3.3.2. Local political cleavages

References to the political cleavages in Cape Verde had appeared in the voting lists referred to above. For example, ´the propensity for the politicisation of the public and private spheres` constituted one of the original items of the list of weaknesses which had received a total of three votes. One of the suggested items added to the list of main tendencies during the discussions, that had received a total of four votes, was that the political profile of individuals was overvalued to the detriment of their technical profile.

Informal discussions outside of the seminar context also confirmed that party politics had been influencing the dynamics of the seminar, although of course this is not to say that every participant had 'taken sides'. Some knowledge of participants' own histories would have been useful for me in order to be able to gauge their respective positions. However, as an outsider who was only just beginning fieldwork, I lacked much of this information. I consequently had to rely upon informal conversations in which participants re-interpreted events for me according to their perceptions of each other's political ideologies and allegiances. For example, the team member who had protested against the elimination of elevated technology from the choice of strategic questions expressed his views to me over a few drinks. The impact of the introduction of new information technologies upon the mentality of Cape Verdeans constituted one of the items that had been added to the list of critical uncertainties during the initial discussions and had received a total of five votes. This team member argued that members of the opposition party were out-dated and had no concept of what elevated technology was about. He explained to me that he had joined the team at a later stage of the study in order to keep an eye on things for the government, appearing to suggest that the study was heavily influenced by the opposition party. More informal discussions revealed the reasoning behind the MPD's position: the individual responsible for the regional coordination of all of the NLTPS studies (carried out within the ambit of the 'African Futures' project) was the former Minister of Planning and Cooperation who had been one of the key political figures of the PAIGC/PAICV regime. He had left Cape Verde and was now working for the UNDP based in Abidjan. According to other informants, this ex-minister's involvement with the project was the reason behind the MPD government's lack of interest in the study.

In order to overcome the impasse described above, the methodology had to be adapted to accommodate the lack of an over-all consensus. The technical team consequently decided that each group would formulate its own vision since it was easier to reach a consensus with smaller numbers. The points in common of all four visions were then listed in the plenary - a process which also involved a good deal of discussion. Finally, in order to save time, the team also decided that each group would choose its own strategic question from its own version of the vision. A definitive version of the vision[7] was nonetheless produced by the NLTPS team some months later which bears no witness to the conflicts discussed above. To read the text without any knowledge of the social dynamics

[7] 'A country with a strong and dynamic productive system, well integrated into the world economy. A country endowed with durable human development, with a sense for the aesthetic and concern for the environment. Cape Verde, a welcoming country: beautiful, useful and credible' (my translation MCE 1997: 45).

involved in its production is misleading: the apparent authority of the printed document remains unchallenged.

It is significant that despite the predominantly external focus of the issues discussed in the seminar (aid, the world economy), local politics, whilst informing the debate, were rarely referred to explicitly. This highlights an important point in relation to my understanding of the dynamics of the seminar: comprehension of the literal sense of the spoken word was insufficient to fully grasp the significance of the discussions. In the words of Bourdieu: 'the truth of the interaction is never entirely contained in the interaction' (1977:81). Although seminar participants were engaged in a debate which reproduced the dominant development agenda, the close up lens of the middle ground reveals that their discussions were also influenced by the practical interests of local politics and power. In other words, despite the restrictive and prescriptive nature of the methodology, at least some of the participants had managed to ensure that their own agendas prevailed.

To what degree participants were disposed to take heed of each other's arguments throughout the seminar is open to question because discussions were also influenced by their mutual knowledge (and stereotypes) of their own life histories in this small island society. All of the seminar participants knew each other and consequently they could easily be prone either to dismiss the arguments of their 'rivals' or to listen selectively, in such a way as to confirm their own presuppositions regarding the 'irrelevance' or 'incorrectness' of the other's point of view. This is an important point[8] because it also leads us to question the supposed benefits of public participatory communication processes.

3.3.3. Participation and performance

The adoption of a participatory methodology is usually justified as a means of offering a flexible way of facilitating discussions. For example, the importance of facilitating dialogue, instead of imposing views from the outside, is also one of the principles of the approach known as participatory rural appraisal (PRA) which has enjoyed widespread popularity in the development field. The methods include: mapping and modelling; transect walks; matrix scoring; seasonal calendars; wealth ranking and so forth. PRA is described by Chambers as 'a family of approaches and methods to enable rural people to share, enhance, and analyze their knowledge of life and conditions, to plan and to act' (1994:953). Chambers claims that PRA is facilitating and participatory with the objective of empowering local people; however, as my examination of the methodology of the NLTPS seminar suggests, participatory methodologies may also be highly restrictive. The artificial elimination of issues for discussion through a rigid voting system, the construction of simplified scenarios, the di-

[8] My thanks to José Portela for drawing my attention to this issue.

rected inputs from the UNDP consultant and the comments from the technical team all served to guide the participants in a particular direction. Henkel and Stirrat reach a similar conclusion in their analysis of the use of maps in the PRA approach:

> The right of participants to 'draw their own maps' in the PRA circles gives them indeed some kind of ownership. But...it is also crucial to recognise that to a large extent PRA already presupposes the frame of what can and can not be done as it canonises the kinds of visualisations acceptable....What PRA does through its various supposedly neutral visual techniques is to encourage a particular way of seeing, understanding and representing the world which derives from the world of the PRA 'expert' (Henkel and Stirrat, 2001:182).

One of the consequences of the increasing popularity of participatory techniques is that processes of social change become transformed into simplified blueprints. Knowledge of the local socio-political context becomes less important than getting the techniques right. Anything that does not fit in with the methodology is then swept under the carpet and participation becomes a 'performance'. The failure of the methodology to maintain consensus throughout the NLTPS seminar, with the refusal of participants to abide by the results of the voting system, also reveals the potential consequences of attempting to 'impose' a participatory methodology at all costs: it resulted in the break-down of the seminar and the methodology burst at the seams. Like the postcolonial subjects in Mbembe's postcolony (2001), participants were prepared to 'perform' according to the 'rules of the game', but some of them were only willing to do so up to a certain point. The ability of individuals or social groups to gain control of their 'performances' and bargain in the conceptual market-place of development is likely to depend upon the local power relations in which they are embedded. The differentiated capacities of social actors to manipulate the political field are explored in more depth in Chapter Six.

3.4. Conclusion

One of the major activities that characterize the practice of development is the production of documents. Through a detailed analysis of the dynamics of the NLTPS seminar, I have attempted to elucidate the pertinence of analyzing them, not only as texts but also as social practice. That many of the participants' comments, discussed above, did not appear in the official NLTPS documentation, produced at the end of the project, reveals how documents misrepresent the social conditions of their production. They do not embody a single set of interests, but rather, conceal a range of conflicting interests. Whose voices have been silenced in the text? Which words have been omitted and why? What polemical issues have been ignored? In order to answer these questions we need to go beyond the printed word.

Although, initially, the methodology of the seminar had appeared to produce consensus, this was increasingly difficult to maintain as the discussions in the seminar became more detailed. Participants had found it relatively easy to reach a consensus in their choice of the Atlantic Dolphin scenario because it represented an ideal. The practice of development involves pursuing ideals which, due to their lack of a specific content, are often able to harmonize potentially conflicting positions. The construction of both the Atlantic Dolphin scenario and of the vision were a means of producing an 'imagined community' of an ideal Cape Verde in the year 2020. Once participants began to engage in more detailed discussions, which involved translating the ideal of development into specific practices, the maintenance of a consensus was no longer possible because other conflicting issues and interests came into play. Nonetheless, there is no documentary evidence of the turmoil that broke out when participants were unable to reach consensus over the formulation of the vision. Local political cleavages disrupted the seminar but they did not disrupt the written text. It would consequently be misleading to draw conclusions based solely on a textual analysis of the seminar documentation. This is also likely to be the case in the production of documents in other contexts, including smaller events such as in meetings or even in individually authored reports. Documents are always written with a particular audience in mind which influences the choice of content and style. For example, the author of a project proposal or activity report, written in order to secure funding from donors, is likely to 'dance according to the music'. The text may not necessarily reflect the views or indeed the practices of the development agency in question.

In the introduction to this chapter I argued that we cannot presume that there is a close alignment between centre/periphery relations and micro processes of cultural production. The effects of globalisation at the micro level - in the so called 'periphery' – cannot be taken for granted. By allowing ourselves to become immersed in a detailed case study of knowledge production, within the context of a regional project sponsored by a multi-lateral donor, we are in a good position to address this issue. To what degree do the dynamics of the seminar reflect global structural asymmetries? At one level, participants appeared to reproduce the dominant, neo-liberal development paradigm: they abided by the seminar 'rules', adopting the business language of SWOT analyses, as they responded to the question 'What should Cape Verde do? The seminar dynamics also exposes one of the central paradoxes of participatory methodologies by demonstrating how their characteristic emphasis on consensus-building sweeps divergent ideas and conflicting interests under the carpet so that the 'show' of participation may go on. Yet seminar participants did not simply hold up a mirror to the West. The seminar dynamics were also subject to the play of local politics and power. Moreover, the ultimate refusal of some participants to abide by the seminar 'rules' cannot be interpreted as a local united front against a donor-led intervention. It may be more helpful to turn to Mbembe (2001) and think in terms of the conceptual bargaining that took place in a field of local political cleavages in which the donor's agenda took second stage.

Chapter Four

'Idle' Peasants and 'Lazy' Officials: Mirror Images of Town and Country or The Politics of Development Categories

4.1. Introduction

> [W]e can all attribute gross stereotyped features to whole groups: but, for the members of those groups such stereotypes applied to themselves as individuals would almost invariably be regarded as gross distortions. In the public face, internal variety disappears or coalesces into a single statement. In its private mode, differentiation, variety and complexity proliferate (Cohen 1985:74).

This chapter examines processes of 'othering' in the language of everyday life in Cape Verde which construct differences between 'us' and 'them' based on the opposition of 'town'/'country'. The ethnography elucidates the ways in which mirror images of town and country produce group stereotypes which are used as foils for self-identification and legitimization. The concept of a 'shifting middle ground' helps to identify the transient and unstable nature of these stereotypes as they relate to the complexities of local realities.

I begin with a discussion of how stereotyped categories of 'idle peasants', prevalent in the heyday of theories of 'modernization', continue to circulate in urban Cape Verde. Thus peasants are commonly described as lazy, traditional and fatalistic. The majority of the ethnographic examples are taken from my 'urban fieldwork': casual conversations and semi-structured interviews in cafés, ministries and government departments, comments made in seminars and workshops and analyses taken from newspaper articles. Put together, they form a collective discourse of the urban elite on the rural population. (I am not suggesting that this is the only representation of rural society by the urban elite but rather that it is one of the most dominant ones). I then go on to demonstrate how countervailing discourses of categorization are produced in the countryside, based on an analysis of samples from semi-structured interviews and informal conversations with ten local leaders in rural Santiago, presidents of local associations and agricultural extensionists. These are informed by 'people-centred' approaches to development, which celebrate the rural population. The 'lazy' peasant thus becomes the 'authentic' and 'deserving' local and the urban elite 'idle' and 'corrupt'.

My analysis of how differences between 'us' and 'them' fall short of capturing the complexity of the real lives of people will come as no surprise to the anthropologist. For the study of the 'other' in terms of the observation of external manifestations of fixed traits has long been discredited in anthropology. And yet, the role of external categorization cannot be easily dismissed since, as Eriksen points out, to talk of identity in social anthropology is not to delve into the psychology of people's minds but rather to study processes of identification as an expression of social relations (Eriksen 1993:59-60). The underlying similarity between the mirror images of 'lazy' peasants and 'idle' civil servants is that they are portrayed as being excessively dependent upon the state.

The privatization of state construction projects provides the backdrop for a large part of the ethnography. It reflects a wider shift, in international development policy, from state-centred to market-driven approaches, to be discussed in more detail in the following chapter. The case material below suggests that the shift from one approach to another is never complete and is always open to reversals and contradictions. Assertions regarding the excessive dependence of workers upon the state, for example, may be seen as a reflection of the global shift towards neo-liberalism. Yet these assertions also reproduce the simplistic categorizations characteristic of outdated 'Modernization' theories. The shift away from the state in donor policy was also eventually reversed. Since the donor failed to guarantee the long term employment of project personnel at the end of the project cycle, the state was obliged to take them on as temporary employees.

The chapter introduces the concept and practice of community-based work fronts that led to the creation of local associations with a detailed case study that continues into the following chapter. The main focus of the case study, in this chapter, is on how an association president manipulated categorizations in order to maintain privileged access to resources, whilst projecting himself, to outsiders, as an 'authentic' representative of community interests. The ethnography also brings to light the existence of a 'shifting middle ground' of reversals and contradictions between 'top-down' and 'bottom-up' development, by examining how the funding exigencies of a participatory project granted legitimacy to undemocratic practices, enabling the president to conceal his own practical interests. The politics of development categories investigated throughout this chapter provide a window into the ways in which social actors strive to assert their 'authenticity' vis-à-vis each other, in the on-going struggle to secure their legitimate (or illegitimate) share of the 'development pie'.

4.2. The 'irrationality' of planting maize

During the early days of my fieldwork, I came across a newspaper article which drew upon Cape Verde's history of slavery to account for why small farmers continued to grow rainfed maize against all the odds. Moran argues that the introduction of maize by the Portuguese as a staple crop was inappropriate to the cyclical aridity of the islands (1982:81); however, it has since become the preferred staple for consumption even though yields are never sufficient to guarantee household food security for which the state has had to take responsibility (Langworthy and Finan 1997:9). The newspaper article turns to the history of slavery to account for this situation by arguing that family farmers have 'inherited' a fatalistic attitude:

> [B]e it in good or bad agricultural years, the slave was left with nothing (or next to nothing) from his work....This was his fate...it was the life that had been predestined for him.
>
> It is this lack of concern with the results of his labour[9] that our farmer has inherited from the former slaves. Without knowing it, he behaves just like them...Sowing in order not to reap is a Cape-Verdean destiny. This is our fate. If one insists upon a fixed principle without searching for alternatives, then this is surely a sign of fatalism (Monteiro 1996:15, my translation).

This viewpoint reflects the thinking of 'modernization' theorists such as Lewis who claimed, for example, that the Mexican subsistence farmers that he studied lacked considerations of production efficiency: 'so long as a man devotes himself to work, he feels secure and blameless, regardless of how little he produces' ([1960] cited in Rogers 1969:118). The farming practices of rural households are consequently construed as a 'cultural' problem.

In their study of household farming strategies in rural Cape Verde, Langworthy and Finan claim that farmers and researchers of rainfed agriculture have yet to find an alternative crop that can be successfully grown in such an arid climate and which can provide similar returns to those produced by the traditional mixed cropping of maize and beans. They argue that apart from the grain for human consumption, these crops also provide residue feed for animals which constitutes an important by-product for local farming systems. Given the high levels of unemployment in rural areas, the authors also point out that families will not necessarily consider it to be a waste of their time to plant these crops, even if the returns are expected to be low (1997:141).

Rather than attribute the act of 'sowing in order not to reap' to the fatalism of an inherited slave mentality, Langworthy and Finans' account suggests that it is, on the contrary, a measure of the farmers' dogged determination not to give up hope. The author of the newspaper article could have drawn upon historical examples of slave revolt in Cape Verde to support this contrary position. The article, which attributes a fatalistic mentality to Cape Verdean farmers, reflects an idea that is widespread amongst the urban elite; namely, that family farmers cultivate maize and beans out of a steadfast adherence to tradition. According to

[9] The term used in the original text is the creole word 'as-águas' which means the rainy period and is often used to refer to the agricultural labour which is carried out during this time.

Langworthy and Finan, this view is also shared by agricultural specialists whose insistence upon the allegedly symbolic importance of maize for the rural population obscures their understanding of the local motivations and incentives for cultivating these crops (1997:141). Whilst recognizing the significance of the spiritual, symbolic dimensions of local agricultural practices constitutes a lesson learnt by critics of the Green Revolution, in the case of Cape Verde, the focus on the symbolic dimension of maize growing has been construed as a 'cultural' problem, appearing to have overshadowed enquiries into the practical, material reasons for planting maize[10].

It is also noteworthy that both the Mexican farmers in Lewis' example, cited above, and the Cape Verdean farmers in the newspaper article are construed as hardworking: the Mexican farmers devote themselves to work and the image of the slave is evocative of hard, albeit forced, labour. This image of the industrious peasant contrasts with the assertions I came across in relation to the need to combat the idleness of workers on FAIMO - the state construction projects – referred to in previous chapters. FAIMO elucidates the existence of a systematic tendency to define problems of the poor as either 'natural' problems or problems inherent in the poor themselves, such as having the 'wrong' mentality. The following section provides some background information on FAIMO in order to set the scene for my analysis.

4.3. State construction projects: an overview

During the late colonial period the Portuguese government came under increased international pressure to be seen to be doing something to prevent famine in its colony. In order to improve its image, the state construction projects were consequently given a new name: 'Apoio às Populações Sinistradas pela Seca' which translates roughly as: 'support to the populations affected by the drought'. Often abbreviated to 'Apoio' (support) the term imputed the causes of famine to natural disaster alone, conveniently drawing attention away from the structural causes of poverty in the islands. The term also painted the colonial authorities in a good light: juxtaposing the word 'support' with that of 'disaster victims'. Thus we can see how the tendency to naturalize the problems of the poor dates back to the colonial period.

Shortly after independence (1975) 'Apoio' was abolished, following criticisms of widespread corruption inherent in the system. (Some of the individuals I interviewed spoke of food stolen from the warehouses and the inclusion in the register of people who had never worked or who had deceased in order to divert

---

[10] Relevant here is Lansing's study of how colonial administrators and development practitioners failed to recognize the practical role of temples in water management systems in Bali. Lansing points out that their symbolic role was integrated with their practical functions (Lansing 1991).

funds). 'Apoio' was nevertheless replaced by Emergency Programmes which were funded by the commercialization of international food aid. The donations of rice, corn, milk powder and vegetable oil were commercialized through the newly created state marketing agent EMPA (Public Food Marketing Enterprise) and the money deposited in a National Development Fund. Much of it was then used to finance these modified versions of 'Apoio'. There were often delays in paying workers' salaries out of the National Development Fund due to holdups in the arrival of the food aid which also took time to sell. So despite the formal abolition of the 'Apoio' workfronts, the system continued but with a new name: High Intensity Manual Labour[11], usually referred to as ‘AIMO’ or Emergency Workfronts. As this name suggests, the system was intended as a temporary measure and once again the social welfare objective was paramount: to guarantee access to foodstuffs through the provision of large scale employment in rural areas (Langworthy and Finan 1997:74).

The two ministries originally involved with running these emergency workfronts were the Ministry of Public Works (MOP) and the Ministry of Rural Development and Fishing (MDRP). Activities of the former consisted of the construction of infra-structure, mainly the building of roads and of the latter, soil and water conservation (SWC) work in order to combat desertification. The aim of the SWC work was to protect the scarce topsoil of the land through reforestation and the construction of rural structures designed to slow down sediment flow and to increase infiltration into the soil (Langworthy and Finan 1977:48). Most of the SWC work of the MDRP AIMOs was carried out on private land and on land that belonged to the state. It was very rare for rural structures to be built on land that was farmed by the AIMO workers themselves. A description of some of the different kinds of structures that were built is given in table 4.1 below.

Table 4.1: Rural engineering works (REW)

In the upper reaches of the valley slopes	In the gullies and ravines that feed into the valley floor	At places along the bottom of the valley
Contour rock wall terraces (arretos) Contour furrows (banquetas) and microcatchments (caldeiras) built around plants as water-harvesting devices.	Check dams (diques de correção torrencial) - to slow down surface flow and establish new agricultural land with the sediment accumulated behind the dam.	Catchment check dams (captações) to catch the subsurface flows through the alluvium.

(Source: Langworthy and Finan 1997:48)

Most of the rural engineering works (REW) that I visited consisted of contour rock wall terraces (arretos) and check dams (diques). Both were built in rocky

[11] Alta Intensidade de Mão-de-Obra

parts of the valley slopes. The different tasks involved in building the arretos, for example, consisted of the following: digging out the trenches, carrying rocks (usually on the head), chipping the rocks down to size with sledge hammers and building the rock walls in the trenches. The check dams were built in the gullies with much larger rocks which were usually dislodged from the earth with the help of a long metal rod and were then left to tumble down to the work site. The workcrews were made up of fifteen to forty workers whose wages were paid on a daily basis according to classified skill levels. There were various categories of stonemasons: those that only worked on contour rock wall terraces - second class - and those classified as first class who also worked on larger structures, including check dams. Very few stonemasons were women. The unskilled categories included: the servant (servente) whose task was to carry rocks and stones, the digger (cavaceiro) who were usually men and dug out the trenches and the waterwoman (aguadeira) whose job was to provide drinking water on demand to the workcrew. She was responsible for fetching water early in the morning before the workcrew arrived. This often involved walking long distances. The workcrew chief was responsible for the register and for overseeing the work.

Given the absence of alternative employment and the continued incapacity of local agricultural production to meet the subsistence needs of the poorer sections of the Cape Verdean population, the AIMO workfronts were eventually integrated into the government's first and subsequent National Development Plans. With the change of political regime in 1991, the new government altered their name to FAIMO (Ferreira Couto 2001:189, 197).

Although the intention of prioritising manual labour in order to generate maximum employment was part and parcel of the FAIMO system, this is not to say that machinery was never used. The MOP, in particular, introduced machinery in some of its workfronts because there were large extractions of earth to be made and manpower alone was not enough; nevertheless, as a MOP engineer whom I interviewed explained, the introduction of machinery created a degree of conflict between those who believed that it should be avoided wherever possible and those who were in favour of increasing mechanization, with a view to increasing production and efficiency. For despite the social welfare orientation explicit in most of the names given to these workfronts, criticisms of both AIMO and FAIMO have been levelled at their lack of productivity by the Cape Verdean elite. Whilst the differences between AIMO and FAIMO were not that great, the government's insistence upon a new name signalled its attempt to make the system more effective and productive.

4.4. 'Idle' FAIMO workers: the nation's burden

> According to some technicians who have a lot of experience in the field, peasants are not interested in projects which may be economically successful and consequently bring them more autonomy, if it requires them to stop receiving free aid. The beneficiaries' reactions to any successful initiative, is according to these technicians, one of authentic sabotage (MCE undated:37, my translation).

The above claim made in a draft version of a study on FAIMO[12] is typical of the assertions that circulated amongst the urban elite in relation to FAIMO workers. There is no reference in the above quotation to the nature of the high risk environment of rural Cape Verdean peasants. Everything has been reduced to a somewhat condemning account of peasant mentality - once again reminiscent of the 'modernization theories' discussed above. The definition of 'economically successful projects' also remains unclear in the text. The emphasis is placed on the peasants' apparent 'sabotage' without questioning whether such projects are considered 'economically successful' in their eyes. It would be unfair not to point out that this text was withdrawn from a later version of the study which concludes that the high rates of population growth and of unemployment indicate that the FAIMO system cannot at present be abolished (MCE undated:14-15); however, that the text should be written at all provides an indication of how common these 'mentality assertions' are.

Table 4.2 situates these 'mentality assertions' within a wide range of assertions that I came across in my 'urban' fieldwork in relation to FAIMO. Some of these statements were very common in the seminars and workshops that I attended, whilst others which go into more detail, have come from interviews that I conducted. None of the assertions come from FAIMO workers themselves, who shall be the subject of subsequent sections of this chapter. The point of bringing these statements together, in a compact and oppositional way, is to illustrate, on the one hand, the complexity of FAIMO and on the other, how this complexity could be simplified by drawing upon some assertions whilst ignoring others.

The table is divided into two separate columns. The statements in column A were frequently employed to lay the blame on FAIMO for what was perceived to be Cape Verde's lack of development. The statements in column B were often drawn upon in arguments intended to demonstrate the opposite: the valuable contributions that FAIMO had made towards the development of Cape Verde. It is no coincidence that the majority of the longer phrases are to be found in column B; this is because statements in favour of FAIMO addressed the complex

[12] Commissioned for the UNDP 'Fight Against Poverty Programme' during 1996-7.

causes of the inefficiencies of the system whereas assertions that denigrated FAIMO were generally more simplistic.

Table 4.2: FAIMO - Common assertions and arguments

Column A: Critical of FAIMO	Column B: In Favour of FAIMO
Statements that 1) identify FAIMO as the cause of Cape Verde's lack of development and 2) highlight the deficiencies of FAIMO and its workforce	**Statements that 1) identify the virtues of FAIMO and 2) give an explanation to account for the deficiencies of the system and its workforce**
FAIMO has created a welfare mentality: workers see FAIMO as their right because they know they can't die of hunger and it is the state's responsibility to provide for them. FAIMO creates dependency.	We, the government need to change our mentality to appreciate the potentials that FAIMO offers - we need well conceived projects. FAIMO has the potential for being the main agent for social and economic development
FAIMO is a brutal violation of human dignity with pick axes purposefully used instead of machinery to employ more people.	The widespread introduction of machinery by the Ministry of Public Works (MOP) meant that not every FAIMO was high intensity, unqualified labour: machinery required qualified operators and technical assistance. This gave a positive image to FAIMO.
There is a lack of supervision on FAIMO workfronts.	Supervision in the early years was not always easy; in Santo Antão it was done on horse back due to lack of roads.
The quality of work in FAIMO is very poor.	Workers have to walk long distances, arrive tired, are badly nourished and the work is physically exhausting.
Women are happy to carry a few stones for a day's work.	Given their meagre wages, we have to allow time for parallel activities, so that workers can earn elsewhere. Women also have to look after their children and walk long distances for water and wood.
Stonemasons could get more work in the private sector but they are too lazy or afraid to risk it - they prefer the security of the state.	The private sector, which includes agriculture, does not provide the guarantee of a continuous wage, nor social security in cases of illness and accident. FAIMO offers all of this now.
People prefer to work in FAIMO rather than in agriculture: it is an easy option. FAIMO drains labour away from agriculture.	A place on FAIMO is also a guarantee of obtaining credit from local merchants which is important in times of drought when families can no longer depend on home grown produce and have to buy everything.
FAIMO is an outdated strategy for resolving the problem of unemployment. Some of the workforce is too old to be productive.	FAIMO is everybody: we all want employment. Here in the Ministry we employ three people to pick up a stapler – it's simply more sophisticated high intensity labour.

Column A: Critical of FAIMO	Column B: In Favour of FAIMO
FAIMO is inefficient and has low productivity rates: it is a drain on the National Development Fund.	FAIMO can cost less than it appears because management may fake receipts to divert funds from FAIMO. There is a lot of scope for corruption in FAIMO. An enormous amount of basic infra-structures were built with FAIMO at relatively low costs. FAIMO is the country's survival.
FAIMO is pure social work.	FAIMO is better than pure assistance: it is a dignified way of using foreign aid because there are no free hand-outs: it is a way of fighting for economic independence.
FAIMO constitutes a disincentive to the private sector because people don't need to look beyond the state for work.	FAIMO provided opportunities for on-site training: it was an authentic training school, although few people recognise this now. Most of the civil engineers in Cape Verde began by working for MOP; FAIMO trained stonemasons and carpenters who are now working in companies.

The variety of assertions in table 4.2 illustrates how arguments ranged from the adoption of a 'macro' perspective which viewed FAIMO as a structural problem - a reflection of Cape Verde's historical situation - to organizational matters that focused on the capacity of the government to run FAIMO, through to a ′micro' perspective which concentrated on the role of individuals: the motivations and 'mentality' of workers.

Not everybody who discussed FAIMO took a stand for or against the system; many people were aware of the complexity of the issues involved. However, the structural positioning of individuals also affected their analysis. Arguments were often drawn upon selectively in order to meet different objectives. A civil servant, for example, explained to me how politicians working in the periphery felt the pressure of unemployment and consequently defended FAIMO, whilst the same politicians transferred to work in central government would then condemn FAIMO for draining the government's budget. Arguments that defended or criticized the organizational aspects of FAIMO were also commonly used to make political capital in party politics.

I came across numerous occasions, particularly in casual conversations and in seminars[13], when the urban elite drew exclusively upon the individualistic approaches listed in table 4.2 to criticize FAIMO. The complexity of FAIMO was thus reduced to a matter of 'changing mentalities', without any regard for the structural and organizational factors also listed in table 4.2. Two of the most frequent assertions that I came across in my 'urban' fieldwork, for example,

[13] See previous chapter.

were that women were happy to carry a few stones for a day's work and that the stonemasons could easily find work in the private sector but were too lazy or afraid to relinquish the security of the state. Social constructions of FAIMO workers by the urban elite tended to draw exclusively upon these mentality assertions without any mention of how Cape Verde's on-going drought, poor resource base and complex land tenure system could justifiably account for the perceived lack of viable income generation alternatives by FAIMO workers. These mentality assertions also ignored other factors listed in table 4.2 which affected the performance of FAIMO workers. For example, they had to travel long distances to reach the workfronts, so that they began work already tired and hungry. Neither did they receive any direct benefits, beyond their meagre salaries, from the SWC work that they carried out. The issues of distance and lack of direct benefits are two of the major factors which informed a US AID funded programme to promote community based workfronts (CBWF) in rural Cape Verde which will be discussed below.

In the social constructions of 'idle' FAIMO workers and of 'fatalistic' peasants, discussed above, both working in FAIMO and planting maize have been disembedded from the complex nature of social practice. This produces classifications which, as Escobar claims in his study of the categories produced through development discourse, reduce the complexity of a person's life to a feature or trait (1995:110). Moreover, these categories are also contradictory. As already mentioned, 'dependent' FAIMO workers are construed as 'idle', whilst 'fatalistic' maize growers are construed as hardworking. The contradiction lies in the fact that these categories represent in reality the same individuals. According to Langworthy and Finan, nearly all rural households cultivate some rainfed land in order to produce beans and maize (1997:67). These rural categories may also serve as models for the urban elite to position itself in society. Jenkins argues that the categorization of 'others' serves as a useful foil for self identification (1994:199). Implicit in the social construction of 'idle', 'traditional' and 'fatalistic' peasants then, is that those who construct these categories - the urban elite - are themselves 'modern', 'rational' and 'cosmopolitan'. Peasants and FAIMO workers, on the other hand, are constructed as 'obstacles' to 'national development'. FAIMO workers, for example, are commonly represented as obstacles that make excessive claims upon the state and display a 'welfare mentality' (see table 4.2). The category of the rural generated by members of the urban elite consequently enables the latter to represent themselves as agents of 'modernization' or bearers of modernity, in opposition to farmers and FAIMO workers who are represented as repositories of tradition.

The central feature of my analysis has been to demonstrate how simplifying discourses combine with complex – and continuously changing – structural realities. The following section examines these processes from the perspective of ‘people-centred’ approaches to development, in which ‘lazy’ officials are depicted as the locals’ burden.

4.5. Hardworking 'locals' and the 'ungrateful' state

The category of the 'authentic local' can be divided into two analytically separate forms of categorization: internal and external definition (Jenkins 1994). In both cases in Cape Verde, the 'authentic local' was constructed in opposition to an 'inauthentic' urban category. External definitions of the 'authentic local' tended to come from a small section of the urban elite which was predominantly comprised of Cape Verdean and expatriate NGO personnel.

'People-centred' development approaches and populist ideology both share a similar position regarding the importance of learning from 'the people'. In Cape Verde, internal definitions of the 'authentic, hardworking local' came from rural-based project personnel, who as I shall demonstrate below, represented themselves in opposition to the 'exploitative' urban-based civil servants. Parallels with populist thought are evident here too:

> Both "Left" and "Right" variants of populist ideology extol the "virtues" of rural society and its inhabitants and attack the "vices" of urban life, especially the corrupt, acquisitive nature of its inhabitants. The egoistic individualism of urban society is contrasted with the rural combination of independence and recognized communal obligation (Stewart 1969:192).

Populist celebrations of the 'authentic local' were also a statement of individual obligations: rural inhabitants should guard themselves against the 'corrupting influences' of the town and should not succumb to 'individual' aspirations which would 'erode' the 'community spirit'. These views were held by an expatriate working in Cape Verde for a US AID funded programme to promote community based workfronts (CBWF) whose work I followed closely. In our first encounter, he told me that he was an advocate of the 'Robert Chambers' approach to development, mentioned 'the centre/periphery theory', referred to 'the culture of silence' and to how city people dominate rural populations. His words created the impression that there was an enormous division between rural and urban people, the former being somehow morally superior. The ethnographic material discussed below reveals the ways in which these kinds of populist ideas informed and affected different individuals engaged with the CBWF aid programme.

US AID promotion of CBWF dated back to 1986 when Stephen, the expatriate referred to above, came to work in Cape Verde as a community development and agricultural extension specialist within the ambit of the 'Watershed Development' project (WDP). This project was implemented by an American company in association with the MRDP. Stephen had come to replace another expatriate who had been involved in the precursor to the WDP project, the 'Watershed Management' project (WMP). This was credited with not only training the first extensionists in Cape Verde, but more importantly, with having recruited them locally.

In the words of António, the Cape Verdean agronomist in charge of the Rural Assistance Programme (RAP) of the WMP in the Ministry of Rural Development and Fishilng: 'Technicians from Praia arrived late for work and then left the watersheds early because they were hungry, so we decided to recruit local people'. This justification for recruiting 'locals' not only challenged the 'modernization' perspective but also produced the same reversal characteristic of 'people-centred' approaches to development. Rather than representing peasants as 'lazy', his justification represented urban-based state technicians as 'inefficient' and 'lazy'. On another occasion, António described Praia based technicians to me as 'air conditioning technicians' - a reference to their preference for office work. A celebration of the 'authentic local' was also evident in the accounts from project beneficiaries who had been involved with the US AID programmes since their inception in 1982. A brief history of the first two programmes is given below.

The Watershed Management Project (WMP) initiated a Rural Assistance Programme (RAP) in 1982 in partnership with the Centre for Agrarian Studies of the Ministry of Rural Development and Fishing (MRDP). Four local farmers were recruited from the Santiago watersheds of São Miguel, Santa Cruz, Flamengos and Saltos and trained to work as extensionists providing community based technical assistance (CBTA) to farmers on their irrigated lands. The main activity was to cultivate demonstration plots in order to encourage the growth of more profitable crops - vegetables instead of sugar cane and manioc. In 1986 the WMP came to an end but the RAP was extended to thirteen Santiago watersheds within the ambit of a new project: the Watershed Development Project. The original core group of extensionists interviewed over eighty people in watersheds and selected thirty three for pre-service training in Tarrafal, seventeen of whom eventually qualified as new extensionists. The programme then created a system of paired male-female extension teams. By 1992, the group had expanded to twenty two extensionists providing a decentralised, grass roots SWC extension service for CBWF. Technical assistance in irrigated farming diminished over the years, with the growing problems of water scarcity (Gardiner 1988).

Hugo was one of the four extensionists to be recruited by the WMP. He went on to become the coordinator of the seventeen extensionists who were trained in Tarrafal and became RAP personnel. His account of what happened when the National Extension Service (NES) was created in 1986 by the government, with the help of Italian aid, is paraphrased below:

> Hugo claimed that this was when their problems began. Apart from the problem of duplication - about which he told me I should talk to Miguel,

> who had an amusing story to tell - there was also the fact that the national extensionists had a higher level of training than they did. Yet for all their training, the national extensionists did not know the areas that they were sent to work in as well as the RAP personnel, nor did they have the same amount of practical experience. Nevertheless, RAP personnel had now been barred from qualifying as permanent civil servants, because their training took place in the field, instead of in São Jorges[14] so they did not have a diploma. He who works has nothing whilst he who doesn't work has everything and without risk.

There is a strong sense of injustice in Hugo's account in which 'lazy' and 'undeserving' civil servants are set up in opposition to himself and his colleagues whom he represents as more knowledgeable and hardworking. Hugo's complaint that RAP personnel have been barred from a permanent state position and his reference to the lack of risk enjoyed by the national extensionists, highlights the importance that he affords to the state, in contrast to the project, in terms of securing a livelihood. What Hugo takes issue with is that the official criteria used to legitimize claims made on the state do not take actual performance into account. The exact word which Hugo used when referring to the diploma was 'canudo'. In its literal sense 'canudo' means 'tube' but in this context it is a derogatory form of slang used to refer to the rolled up certificate of qualification. According to Hugo, practical experience and commitment - of which he represents the RAP personnel of having plenty - are far more important criteria than academic qualifications.

Miguel's account also calls into question the fairness of a system in which diplomas endowed the national extensionists with a fixed value that did not have to be constantly proved and which qualified the extensionists for permanent positions. He represents the 'biological individual' who occupied one of these positions not only as lazy, but also manipulative, dishonest and exploitative of the work of others. Miguel, a young man in his early thirties, became a key informant during my fieldwork. Although his initial involvement with the Rural Assistance Programme was as a farmer - Miguel received technical assistance from Hugo - he was later trained as an extensionist. Miguel's account of his experience of collaboration with the NES is paraphrased below:

> When the national extensionists arrived, they found the RAP personnel already active in the field. The one allocated to Miguel's area told him that he had no vocation for the job, but that it was an opportunity he had to seize. Miguel stated that he was only trained in theory and that he made lots of false promises to the community which made it difficult for him to be accepted. The extensionist suggested that they work together and Miguel agreed. However, the extensionist used to arrive, give him orders dis-

[14] This is where the Cape Verdean National Agricultural Research and Development Institute is located.

guised in nice language, and then leave. If he saw a farmer's field had been attacked by pests, instead of showing the farmer how to treat the crops, he would refer him to Miguel. People prefer the towns. Then there was the training session. He invited Miguel to a meeting in which he presented him to his bosses of the National Extension Service as his best farmer instead of as his colleague from the RAP. Miguel stopped following his orders after this.

The national extensionist's alleged lack of interest in his job - seeing it merely as 'an opportunity' - represents him as being dependent upon the state for his livelihood in the same way that FAIMO workers are represented by the urban elite. Just as FAIMO workers are construed as the state's 'burden' - draining resources away from more legitimate allocations - the state extensionists are represented here as the locals' 'burden'. Not only were they seen as disqualifying the RAP personnel from what they saw as their moral right to permanent employment positions, but as Miguel's account indicates, they were seen to take advantage of the guarantee provided by these socially defined positions. The differences in philosophy and methodology between RAP and NES, presented in the WDP report, are given in table 4.3.

Table 4.3: Differences in philosophy and methodology: NES and RAP

Level of Action	**NES**	**RAP**
Education level of recruited personnel	Basic high school diploma of higher education	Minimum fourth grade education and functionally literate
Zones of recruitment of personnel	Larger cities (i.e. Praia, Assomada, etc.)	Local watersheds
Training	Specialized courses of 2 years duration followed by a nine month rural extension course	Two to four weeks of pre-service training followed by continuous in-service training
Extension methodology		
- locale of delivery of service	From regional extension offices	Local
- transportation	Motorcycle or jeep	By foot or bicycle (except for three RAP supervisors)
- methods employed	Flip charts, slides, films, other audio-visual materials, demonstration plots	Direct farmer contact and dialogue combined with demonstration plots
- main domain of action	Dryland and irrigated agriculture	SWC + CBWF (6 month/yr.) Dryland and irrigated agriculture (6 month/yr.)

*Contrary to classical workfronts (FAIMO) these CBWFs only operated for six months of the year, from 1 February to 31 July. (Source, Gardiner 1988:8).

The donor considered the differences outlined in table 4.3 to be sufficiently radical to argue against the integration of RAP into the NES on the grounds that the latter would bury the former in a bureaucracy (1988:11). Moreover, the success of the RAP had served to challenge the dominant perception of the supposed laziness of FAIMO workers. The WDP report claimed that the key to success was to address the organizational problems characteristic of FAIMO. One of the major factors that distinguished CBWF from traditional FAIMO, identified in the report, was that the SWC work was carried out nearer to the homes of the workers. FAIMO workcrews often had to walk between three to six kilometres to reach their work sites whereas the SWC work was usually carried out within one kilometre of workers' homes. Another major factor, deemed to increase motivation, was the enhanced benefits to workers. Although their average salaries were slightly lower than those of FAIMO, the SWC work was built on land that they themselves cultivated. CBWF were also more participatory. Crew leaders were elected by local crew workers rather than appointed by the Ministry of Rural Development (MRDP) and work plan decisions were negotiated between the local population and project staff instead of being handed down in a 'top down' manner from MRDP technicians. The technical assistance and quality control supervision which was characteristically limited and variable in FAIMO workfronts, was carried out by RAP personnel several times a week. According to the WDP report, it was a combination of all of these factors that resulted in an increase in worker productivity and efficiency as well as in structural improvements to the soil and water conservation (SWC) work built (Gardiner, 1988: iii, 17). CBWF consequently provided an alternative image to that of the 'idle FAIMO worker' which, as we have already seen, was frequently evoked by the urban elite to account for low levels of productivity and quality of work.

The representations of 'idle' peasants and 'lazy' officials discussed in this chapter reveal an underlying similarity: both are depicted as dependent upon the state. The national extensionists are not obliged to work hard because they are protected by their socially defined positions and FAIMO workers take advantage of the system to earn an 'easy day's work'. These representations serve as foils for self-identification. Categories of the 'idle' peasant serve to dissociate the urban elite from a 'backward', 'traditional' 'other' – held responsible for Cape Verde's 'lack' of 'development'. The category of the 'lazy' official feeds internal definitions of the RAP personnel as 'authentic', 'hardworking' agents of development. However, as we shall see in the following section, when these internal definitions function as external categorizations they can also become straight jackets that impose utopian, populist ideals upon individuals.

4.6. The 'moral tyranny' of place

The rationale behind the donor policy of recruiting personnel from the localities of project implementation was to guarantee the quality of services provided within the Rural Assistance Programme. The aid worker, Stephen, who had a long history of working with RAP, believed that there was a direct correlation between the degree to which personnel were integrated into their local communities and the extent to which they were committed to producing good quality work. As far as he was concerned, the less urban contact they had the more 'authentic' they were. This reflected populist beliefs regarding the need to safeguard the moral integrity of peasant society, described by MacRae as a 'self-righteous moral tyranny' (1969:160).

The conversation, paraphrased below, between Stephen and the Cape Verdean agronomist António, provides an example of the way in which Stephen's evaluation of the performance of RAP personnel was coloured by his populist beliefs. The conversation took place, in a meeting convened to evaluate the progress of a number of associations which were functioning as private contractors for the state, within the ambit of the CBWF initiative. The association under discussion was given high marks for 'conscience and participation of members' in the evaluation because it had been created prior to the US AID funded projects[15]; however, Stephen had also seen some bad technical work produced by the association in a CBWF which two and a half months later had still not been rectified.

> Stephen states that the association has weak managerial capacity because the president is in the capital, Praia.
> António rejects this by claiming that the association's management is satisfactory.
> Stephen insists that members are producing bad work: the extensionists are not going there...
> António replies that they are evaluating the association's managerial capacity and not its management of physical work.
> Stephen retorts that it is all the same thing.
> António argues that it is not. Why then do they have a separate item on quality of work if the two points are the same? What about their management of finances? He adds that they don't appear to have much leadership...
> Stephen replies this is because their president is in Praia...
> António laughs whilst telling Stephen that he cannot just say 'because their president is in Praia'...

Stephen's populist beliefs regarding the 'authentic local' required the association president to remain fixed in the countryside. However, contacts in Praia seemed to have been an important means of promoting the association's activities. The president told me, for example, how various foreign donors had funded a range of projects including the building of water tanks and improved ovens

[15] The history of the association dated back to the 1960s when a group of people linked to the area used to come together on an annual committee to organize the patron saint festivities. They eventually decided to engage more consistently in on-going activities and the association was created with one hundred and seven founding members.

and that he was also negotiating with a Praia based doctor to go several times a week to set up a part-time health centre. The president was constantly travelling to and from the association headquarters - just over an hour's drive away from the capital, Praia. From Stephen's perspective, establishing urban contacts was tantamount to succumbing to the personal ambition of upward mobility. It was interpreted by Stephen as an indication of diminished commitment to the community. This kind of reasoning provides an example of how populist ideals may generate expectations that impose restrictive or unrealistic demands upon individuals who occupy positions of leadership in their local communities. The case of Emilia below illustrates how Stephen also expected community members who had been donor trained as agricultural extensionists to display their commitment in accordance with his expectations.

Emília left secondary school in order to have a baby and a year later applied for work with the mass organization for women where she was eventually paid for giving literacy classes. During this period Emília began to work in FAIMO, carrying stones as a 'servente'. She then managed to train as a stonemason and was later recruited and trained by the WDP (see table 4.3). When I met her not only was she providing technical assistance for CBWF, but she had also become president of the local branch of the mass organization for women, which had recently been transformed into a nation-wide NGO[16]. During the course of my fieldwork, Emília was also invited to represent women in a new national farmer's organization; however, rather like the president of Picos, Emília's 'wordly' connections were used by some individuals to challenge her 'authenticity'. On one occasion, for example, Emília went to Mauritania for a fortnight as a representative of Cape Verdean women farmers. She claimed to have obtained permission from her employers for the trip and to have arranged for a substitute to provide technical assistance for the CBWF that she was responsible for. During her absence, a colleague carried out an unprogrammed visit to the work-fronts in question and found faults with the rural engineering works. Emília's absence was noted, the 'bad' news spread quickly and the next time I saw Stephen he told me that he had heard that Emília had stopped providing technical assistance and wondered whether she had 'forgotten her roots'.

The multiple roles of Emília and of the association President fitted uneasily with Stephen's conception of the 'moral obligation' of the 'authentic local' to be fixed in the rural space. Stephen himself felt very uncomfortable when he was obliged to stay in office headquarters to write reports and told me he would much rather be out in the field. Stephen was not the only one to link identity with place. Miguel, who had started out as a beneficiary of technical assistance before going on to become a RAP extensionist, also condemned the desire of his fellow villagers to move into the towns:

---

[16] The context within which the transformation of the mass organizations into NGOs occurred is discussed in Chapter Six.

> I detest people from poor families who as soon as they get the opportunity leave for the town - I think they should stay and share their knowledge.

Miguel had become a successful businessman: apart from providing technical assistance on CBWF he also kept his own animals, farmed irrigated land, owned a small shop managed by his wife and employed a driver to provide a taxi service with his car in the village. He also took pride in helping his fellow villagers. Miguel's representation of himself as an 'authentic local' was similar to the populist ideal of the moral individual integrated into the local community. He had been forced to stop studying at the age of fourteen because his parents could not afford to send him to secondary school in Praia. His brothers had emigrated, leaving behind a father who was blind and paralyzed, so Miguel remained in the village and took up agriculture. Whilst he continued to identify with his fellow villagers - he told me on two separate occasions that he was from the 'poor race' - he also distinguished himself from them, by emphasizing his affinities with 'urban' categories:

> Lots of people say to me why stay in this hole? You should come to Praia or Assomada.but I feel secure here. I have my business and I have a vocation for agriculture - it's what makes me happy. There are not many people on my level who choose to stay in rural areas.

Miguel's claim that many of his urban-based friends were exhorting him to leave the village - referred to in the derogative term of a 'hole' - suggests that he destabilized the internal definition of a ‘cosmopolitan’ identity, which separated the rural from the urban. Similarly, the residence of the association president in Praia, destabilized Stephen's external categorization of the 'authentic local'.

All of the cases discussed above demonstrate how categorization produces stereotyped models which do not correspond to the 'real' lives of individuals. Emília and the association president were what Ferguson calls 'worldly' and 'well-connected', which did not correspond to Stephen's model of the 'authentic' watershed resident. Miguel, on the other hand, was a successful businessman, living in a village which did not correspond to either of the models that the urban elite constructed of themselves or of rural inhabitants. Nonetheless, these stereotyped models still informed practice; they served as ideal role models which individuals were expected to emulate in their daily lives. Stephen expected Emília and the association President to be ‘more faithful’ to their ‘rural roots’ and Miguel's urban-based friends advised him to leave the village.

Having examined the different ways in which social actors strive to assert their own ‘authenticity’ and to project their expectations upon others, the question arises of how to deal with the problematic concept of the ‘authentic local’. Ferguson takes up the challenge of how to theorize the local by arguing in favour of deconstructing 'authenticity':

> Are we ready to jettison received ideas of 'local communities' and 'authentic leadership'? ....Can we learn to conceive, theoretically and politically, of a 'grassroots' that would be not local, communal, and authentic, but worldly, well-connected, and opportunistic? (2004:394).

Ferguson's depiction of a 'worldly' grassroots certainly helps to deconstruct the ideal role models produced by populist thought; however, we should bear in mind that it does not characterize the majority of the population that makes up the grassroots. The new kinds of subject relations and subject roles that emerge as a result of development interventions create new disjunctures within the grassroots between 'development outsiders' and 'development insiders' - people whose social and political capital enable them to reap more benefits.

The development of Emília's professional trajectory – from the lowest rank of a FAIMO worker to a relatively high profile development agent - provides a good example of the emergence of these new subject roles. When Emília was selected for training by the donor, it was her secondary school education that gave her an advantage over the many other women who were not selected. They had far less chance of ever becoming 'worldly' or 'well-connected'. Rather than identify Emília as evidence of a worldlier 'grassroots', it may be more helpful to interpret her upward mobility as a sign of the new opportunities, relations and roles provided by the on-going expansion of the 'development encounter'.

The increased access to material and symbolic power, made possible by development interventions, is also always open to abuse. In the following section, I demonstrate how the structural positioning of an association president – fixed in the rural space – enabled him to exploit utopian, populist ideals about 'authentic' locals to his own advantage. By projecting himself, to donors and politicians, as an individual committed to working for the development of the community, the president was able to conceal his privileged access to resources at the expense of fellow villagers. This, in turn, serves to debunk the populist myth regarding the moral integrity of peasant society and raises a compelling point about the kinds of things that assertions revolving around artificial dualities conceal. The president's residence in the rural space was no guarantee of his moral integrity, in the same way that the residence of an association president in Praia, contested by Stephen above, was not necessarily indicative of personal ambition. The following section illustrates the way in which the president manipulated populist notions of 'authenticity' in order to conceal his illicit 'helpings' to the 'development pie'.

4.7. Power relations at the community level

The success of the community based workfronts (CBWF), led the donor, in 1995, to work with and promote the creation of more local associations, thus enabling rural communities to contract directly with the state to implement soil and water conservation work (SWC). Initially, it was not obligatory to become a member of an association in order to be recruited as a worker, although, according to donor policy, the selection procedures should give priority to the poorest in the community. Association presidents, vice-presidents and treasurers were voted for by members. Two community members were selected to receive donor training in accountancy and the person who obtained the highest grade became the association accountant. More details of the transition process from CBWF to association are given in a description of the Food for Peace project, discussed in the following chapter. This section examines the internal dynamics of 'Batuque[17]': an association which became a beneficiary of the Food for Peace project in 2003.

My initial impression of Alberto, the president of Batuque, was that of a confident, eloquent individual who prided himself on his skills as a dynamic community leader. Nevertheless, it soon became apparent that he intended to mediate as many of my contacts as possible, in the community. At the beginning of my fieldwork in 2005, Alberto organized meetings with local youth and selected members. As time went on, I was able to break free of his control, speak with whom I chose and to stay in different houses in the village. I soon discovered that local opinions did not correspond to the image that he projected of himself as a disinterested representative of community interests.

I first met Alberto next to a water tank that the association was building as part of its SWC contract with the state. Alberto stopped supervising the work of a small group of people to talk with me. He claimed that the association had been created in 1997 with two main objectives: to bring water to the community (because women had to walk two or three kilometres in search of water) and to occupy the local youth. He explained to me that this had always been a concern for him. The association had negotiated with the local water board and with the help of an 'American project' had obtained finance to channel water from a spring further up the valley down to a community water tank. The association had also negotiated with the local council to bring electricity to the village. The president gesticulated towards the community centre behind us, where he told me, there was a television and video for the young people of the community. I asked if there was any particular reason why the association was created in 1997 and not before. Alberto replied that prior to that year he had been president of the residents' committee but had become too frustrated because 'every request became held up in the bureaucracy of the local council and community problems

[17] The name of this association has been codified. "Batuque" signifies drum.

were not resolved'[18]. He consequently decided to come together with four other men from the community to discuss the idea of creating an association. Together, they drew up a project proposal, presented it in a meeting to other members of the community and the association was then created with twenty-two founding members. Today the association had forty-three members.

Alberto projected himself as a natural leader. His account corresponds to an exemplary model of 'endogenous', 'bottom-up' development: the motivation for creating the association appeared to have emerged spontaneously at the community level. Upon the arrival of state technicians, the president excused himself from me and I was able to talk to some of the workers. The only woman present, Maria, was a stonemason and did not speak, nor did she stop working, throughout the whole encounter. The three men present stopped working and introduced themselves. Bernardo was secretary of the general assembly and, it transpired, the president's son. Augusto was president of the general assembly and, I also discovered, the president's nephew. The third man, Paulo, kept himself at a distance, acknowledging that he was also related to the president. I expressed the desire to meet non-members and Bernardo replied that some people had not yet joined the association because they did not understand what it was for. When I enquired into the association's purpose he replied 'to develop our community'. Before taking my leave, the president invited me to attend the next general assembly meeting. Having noted that three out of four workers were related to the president, I suspected that he may not represent the interests of all of the members of the community. My suspicion increased during the meeting, in which the dissident voice of Rogério, one of the four founding members, appeared to embarrass most of those who attended, by confronting the president with a string of complaints.

The meeting, conducted in Creole, took place on a Sunday afternoon in a small classroom in the community centre. Although Augusto, the president of the general assembly, was supposed to chair the meeting, Alberto took full control. Five women and six men attended. There were several reasons that could account for the low turn-out. According to the president, since it was the rainy season, many members would be engaged in farming activities. I suspected that since the REW had been completed, motivation to attend would also have diminished since there were no decisions to be made regarding who to employ. On the left hand side two women sat right at the back and two more sat on the first row. Rogério sat in the middle. On the right hand side, two men sat separately near the back, followed by a younger man in the middle, the president next to the secretary, a woman called Gertrudes, sat nearer to the front. Augusto, the president of the general assembly, sat next to me at the front. In a low, timid voice, he read out the agenda for the meeting after which the president took over in a loud and assertive voice. He began by creating an impression of clarity and transparency by gaving an account of the status of the rural engineering works

[18] 'Tudu pididu fika burokrátiku na kâmara. N dizisti pamodi es ka rizolvi prubulema di kumunidadi'.

(REW) stipulated in the 2005 contract: four check dams and three thousand and one hundred metres of contour rock wall terraces. Work had started on 14 March and was scheduled to finish by 31 July. On 30 June the work was already completed at a cost lower than that of the budget, enabling them to build an additional small check dam. The water tank, he explained, was a bonus for the good work carried out with no deadline for completion. He paused for questions, there were none. The meeting continued, each item introduced timidly by Augusto before it was discussed confidently by the president. One of the items was a proposal to organize an exchange with another association and the president asked members if they were interested.

In response to his question, Rogério cleared his throat and began, with a long-winded introduction, by stating that this was not really the moment to talk about certain matters, in front of guests, but he was unhappy about a number of things. His demeanour suggested that he was under the influence of alcohol. He spoke in a loud, slow voice, repeating the same phrases over and over, slurring his words in such a way that it was difficult to decipher them all. One of Rogério's complaints was that he was unaware of the total value of the contract. He had not inspected the check dams because he was too old to climb up the mountain. Also, he did not know how the auditing of association finances was being carried out. There had been elections in the association last March and yet the new president of the fiscal council had still not (in August) 'taken office'. Although he had been voted surrogate he had not been granted access to any information...Rogério spoke for a long time, repeating his complaints. As his speech continued, the two women at the back began to laugh and a woman at the front raised her eyebrows. Their body language appeared to indicate that his complaints were not to be taken seriously.

When Rogério had had his say, Alberto appealed to others present to speak so that their visiting guest would not think that 'badius[19]' did not talk. The secretary, Gertrudes, smiled at me and announced that this year they had all worked very well, better than last year because they had all gained experience and had produced better quality work. All workers should be congratulated. Nobody else spoke. Augusto appealed once again to members of the rather diminished general assembly but the only person to respond was Rogério, who proceeded to repeat the points he had raised earlier.

In keeping with the agenda of the meeting, a number of other issues were discussed by the President before he agreed to respond to Rogério, stating that the value of the contract had been announced in a previous meeting and that it had been clear to everyone who had attended. He did not repeat it here. Regarding the auditing of accounts, he requested that his secretary respond since she was the former president of the fiscal council. Gertrudes replied that although it was no longer, officially, her job to audit the accounts of the REW, she had done

[19] Santiago born Cape Verdeans, (see Chapter Two).

so and had explained everything to the incumbent president, with whom she suggested Rogério meet up to clarify any doubts. The matter was thus 'resolved' and the body language of those present seemed to express relief at the 'silencing' of a drunken, old man.

During Batuque's planned exchange visit to another association, referred to above, I finally managed to speak with Júlia, the new president of the fiscal council. Up until then, the association president had made sure that he was present in most of my contacts with villagers. I had not managed to talk with Rogério because every time I had visited his house he was not in. During the exchange, I explained to Júlia that I only knew the rosy side of her association and that, as a researcher, it would be good to get to know the 'real' association. She immediately replied 'Many people don't like to talk, but I will talk'. We agreed to meet at her house in which, on subsequent visits, I also met more disgruntled association members.

Júlia claimed that when she was voted president of the fiscal council the REW were already underway. This was six months ago and although Gertrudes had handed over some of the documents, she had not yet seen any of the receipts. Júlia confirmed that the president had communicated to members the value of the contract, but, went on to add that he had not presented them with any documents. As president of the fiscal council, it was her duty to inspect them. Unlike Rogério, she had not complained, for fear of creating conflicts. Moreover, Júlia believed that Gertrudes was an innocent dupe of the president. Unaware that she was also supposed to inspect the documents, Gertrudes had followed his recommendations and spent most of her time checking on the quality of the REW. Júlia was concerned that the lack of transparency in the accounts would eventually be detected by the donor and lead to a withdrawal of funds. She was waiting for the vice-president of the association, Egídio, to call a private meeting with the president to request that he hand over the documents for inspection.

My first meeting with Júlia also exposed an alternative version of the association's history. Júlia worked as a child carer at the local nursery – a room in the association's community development centre. Before the centre had been built, she worked in poor quality rented accommodation in which the children sat on the floor. Coming out of the nursery one day, before Batuque had been created, she overheard a conversation between Alberto and an aid worker from the United Nations Development Programme (UNDP). The aid worker was explaining that UNDP was willing to finish building a water tank that the local council had left unfinished in the village, as long as residents were prepared to create an association. UNDP did not want the local council to be responsible for the tank. The aid worker added that if they did not create an association, they would never acquire a new nursery because the government was not prepared to channel money into the local council[20]. If they created an association, they might even obtain funding for a community centre. It had not been in the interests of Alberto to divulge the contents of this conversation. His alternative version of events boosted his image as a dynamic 'authentic' community leader of a 'bottom up' association. It represented him as a disinterested hard working individual whose main motivation was to serve the community. As shall become apparent below, villagers had a different perception of his motivations.

On my way back down from Júlia's house, I walked past a group of villagers who were having lunch together in the open air and one of the woman called out to me to join them. Her name was Raquel and she was providing lunch for the workers she had hired to weed her crops. Raquel worked for the ministry of agriculture and told me she was not an association member because she wanted to maintain her independence. Another woman present, Carla, exclaimed that she wasn't a member either but had been called upon to work on an association workfront to build a check dam. 'Association work is too hard', she told me. Raquel agreed, 'Carla is ill and she is too weak to work for the association'. 'I only worked for a day', retorted Carla. 'The workcrew chief[21] employed me and two other women to carry 20 litre buckets of sand. He said we had to do 53 rounds. We had understood that it was 53 rounds between us; so, when we had finished we sat down to rest. Then he turned up accusing us of being lazy so I left and never went back'.

Subsequent visits to Júlia's house introduced me to association members who had worked in previous years and also complained about the president's behaviour: driving them to work too hard by setting excessive daily production targets and refusing to pay any wages at all if they failed to meet them. They were aware of Carla's case, claiming that the number of rounds demanded per female worker was excessive, given that each round equalled 100 metres. Cristina, one of the women present, stated that association work was too hard; women were expected to dig 10 metres of trenches a day and that this was too much for any woman. Júlia added that women who have had children cannot carry a lot of weight.[22] Cristina left the association in 2004 because she could not meet the production target. The earth was very hard and she could not dig 10 metres per day, it was too much for her. She went on to explain, that if, on one day, they only dug 8 metres because there were lots of rocks then they would not earn anything. Their complaints had no effect. In 2003 women from a more experienced association had been hired to dig trenches and build the contour rock wall terraces because there were not enough women in the village to carry out the work. Cristina explained how these women refused to accept the 10 metre target, claiming that in their association they only dug 5 metres per day. They also rejected the president's 8 metre production target for contour rock wall ter-

[20] The local council was from the opposition party.
[21] The workcrew chief, "controlador" was the association president.
[22] "Mudjer parida ka ta pode carega txeu"

races and Alberto had to settle with 3.5 metres instead. However, the following year, he employed women from elsewhere and reinstated his targets. The lack of transparency in association accounts led Júlia to suspect that the president was making personal profit out of the workers, which was why he drove them so hard, dismissing those who failed to reach the targets.

This year, Marta had not been chosen to work and she did not know why. She claimed that the selection of workers had taken place secretly during the night, instead of in a general assembly meeting, as had happened the year before. This time, people were summoned individually from their houses and two or three members from the same households were given work. She had nine children and twelve people to feed. What was the point of paying her subscription fee? Marta's husband, Paulo, one of the four founding members of the association, was unaware of the existence of any criteria for choosing workers, adding that it was not right to choose two or three people from the same family.

The members whom I spoke with in Júlia's house suspected that Alberto was not only using employment on an association workfront to employ his own family and possibly, to line his own pockets, but also to 'buy' votes for the next elections. The president's opponent in the last elections, Egídio, had lost by one vote and had become vice-president of the association. It was consequently in the president's interests to employ people who knew very little about the history and internal workings of Batuque. Most of the names on the list of workers, pinned up on the wall in the community centre, were new members; both Júlia and Paulo referred to them as 'members because of work' (*membru pamodi trabadju*). Júlia commented that the woman who was voted in as secretary of the fiscal council was illiterate. People had voted for her without any understanding of what her role should be. 'They are not aware of what is going on; they just vote because they have been given work'[23].

Whilst the CBWF provided an alternative image to that of 'idle' FAIMO workers, evoked by the urban elite, this section demonstrates how the new opportunities for increasing productivity also generated power struggles at the community level. The president's dismissal of individuals whom he labelled as 'lazy' workers, disguised a struggle to preserve his position of power and maintain privileged access to resources. Alberto's undemocratic procedures for recruiting new workers also contravened donor policy. The efforts that he put into maintaining his image as a disinterested community leader were evident in the ways in which he attempted to control my interpretation of events. For example, on one occasion, Alberto tried to prevent me from talking to Rogério, by insisting that I leave with the treasurer of the association so that I would have company on the way home. The treasurer tired of waiting for me and we were able to talk. The following day, the president expressed regret that I had missed the opportunity of company on my return journey. On another occasion, the presi-

[23] 'Es stá fora di asuntu. Es vota pamodi trabadju. Es ka konxi rialidadi'.

dent claimed that the daily production targets of other associations were higher than those he had set, although I knew from experience that this was not the case.

When I returned the following year (in 2007), the selection procedures for association workers continued to be shrouded in secrecy. In response to my questions regarding how they had been selected, workers replied that they had carried on from the year before. Most of them were now recruited from outside of the village. Members also complained to me that they had not held a general assembly meeting for over six months and that only a select few knew what the president was up to. Júlia, president of the fiscal council, was preparing to resign from her post because she was still unable to access any documents for inspection. I questioned the president regarding the lack of meetings and he explained that he was so busy working on association construction projects that he simply had no time to call meetings; making a point of showing me the project proposals that he had submitted to potential donors. The aim of one of these proposals was to bring water to people's homes. Alberto's projection of himself as a 'hardworking' president for the good of the community thus succeeded in masking his undemocratic practices which, as we shall see below, were unintentionally reinforced by the exigencies of donor funding.

Although the involvement of local residents in decisions regarding the location and execution of REW constituted a fundamental aspect of community based work fronts, donor funding dynamics sometimes proved to be incompatible with participatory processes. In 2005, Alberto was called to account, in a general assembly meeting, for failing to involve association members in the selection of sites for the REW planned for the following season. The demand for policy to be implemented did not come from the donor, but rather, from the vice-president, Egídio:

> Alberto says that he has surveyed the potential REW for 2006 which have to be submitted to the Ministry of Agriculture, but beforehand, he wants to present them to the general assembly to see if everyone agrees. Egídio asks if the proposal has been approved by the board. (He must know the answer because he is vice-president of the board). Miguel replies that he prepared the proposal on his own and he is now presenting it to the general assembly for approval. If they all approve, it can be signed and sent to the Ministry. Egídio asserts that if the president has carried out the appraisal on his own and the board has not been consulted then the procedures have been incorrect: the assembly is the last to be consulted, after the board. *Alberto claims that ever since the beginning, in 2003, the guidelines given by the donor never gave any indication that the proposal should be discussed in the general assembly.* But that is fine; if that is what he wants then they can wait and draw up a new proposal. Egídio remarks that *if the donor doesn't care whether the board or the general assembly met or not, then it is alright,*

but, if it really cared about the wellbeing of the association then it should give members time to think. The president is not a body, the board is the body. The proposal belongs to the association, not to the president. The president is not the only person who has ideas: one of the characteristics of grassroots associations is that they all have ideas and share them together.

Alberto responds by stating that the project cycle begins on 1st October and finishes the end of September[24]. The proposal for the following year should always be submitted by 31st August. They are already a bit behind. 1st October is the beginning of the New Year for possible finance, which is why there is this deadline. But he understands Egídio's concerns. He was never given any guidelines and the first time he did everything on his own *and didn't show it to anyone because it had to be done quickly.*

The vice-president responds that he is just making a suggestion for the future. Firstly, the proposal should pass through the board and then the general assembly. This takes time, so it all needs to be prepared well in advance. He concludes that there is no point in changing things now, if it is going to create delays for their project. *If the donor doesn't require the proposal to be approved by the general assembly, they will go ahead so as not to lose time and lose the chance of finance.*

The president's claim that the donor never required him to involve association members in the identification of potential REW contradicts the whole participatory philosophy of the project (discussed in the following chapter). Nonetheless, it would be too hasty an interpretation to disregard the president's claim as untruthful. Although according to project policy, the REW should be decided upon collectively, this was not always project practice, due to the pressure to approve REW in accordance with funding deadlines[25]. In his ethnography of aid, Mosse (2005) draws attention to the ways in which policy operates autonomously from field practice. According to Mosse, the main purpose of policy is to secure legitimacy and political support for donor activities – and specific interests that overlap with and are compatible with these. However, the implementation of these activities is less influenced by policy than by organizational and institutional requirements. The participation of beneficiaries in all of the stages of the implementation of REW was one of the cornerstones of donor policy, serving to distinguish community based workfronts from traditional FAIMO. Yet in practice, funding requirements, rather than policy, determined the amount

[24] The tax year ends in September in the United States and this was consequently a very busy month for the donor.

[25] Whilst the policy of the project was to promote and deepen local participation, the exigencies of reaching set targets within a pre-determined time scale resulted in non-participatory practices in the field. During fieldwork carried out in 1996, I accompanied a state official, linked to the project, during his first contacts with local residents in order to motivate them to form an association. When the first meeting with potential project beneficiaries took place, two of the richer, local farmers had already been involved in identifying the proposed REW with project personnel.

and levels of participation. Filling the donor's quota of REW for the financial year did not always give association presidents the time to involve their members, for whom funding was also paramount. In spite of his objections, neither was Egídio prepared to risk losing funds.

When the vice-president of 'Batuque' challenged Alberto, he was contesting the president's practices, with his own experience and knowledge of grass roots organizations, which, unknowingly to him, also corresponded to donor policy. It is a moot question, whether, in his defence, the president of 'Batuque' was aware of donor policy or not. Whatever the case, it is clear that the discrepancies between policy and practice could easily be manipulated by association presidents to justify undemocratic decision-making processes. For the most part, association members were not accustomed to holding the president to account, because in the words of Egídio, they were '*membru pamodi trabadju'*. The stonemason, Maria, referred to at the beginning of this section, was a young strong woman with an enormous capacity for heavy manual labour which I observed on various occasions. She often exclaimed, with a smile on her face, 'let's get to work'.[26]

The president of 'Batuque' made use of his external image as an authentic community leader to conceal manipulative undemocratic selection procedures, tailored to pursue his own practical interests. He also knew how to manipulate categorizations that constituted lucrative development labels. The reader will recall that he claimed that meeting the needs of the local youth constituted one of the motivations for creating the association. The Minister of Culture had donated a computer to the community centre; the local youth complained to me that the only people who were able to use it were the president's sons and daughters[27]. They told me that the president was always talking about them –the local youth - as a means of procuring finance which they never benefited from. For example, the president of the local council had given money to Alberto to help towards buying kits for those who were receiving classes of 'capoeira' – a Brazilian martial art in dance form – from a young teacher who lived in Praia[28]. Not only did they never see the money, but Alberto often prevented them from using the centre for their classes by locking the door. Conflicts with the capoeira teacher and his students were frequent. The president claimed that, during the training, the young people dirtied the bathroom of the centre. Very few houses had toilets in the village and it was common knowledge that the president and his family made personal use of the bathroom in the community centre.

Despite these internal conflicts, the success of Alberto's external projection of himself to local power holders as a committed representative of the commu-

---

[26] 'Nu mesti trabadju'

[27] One of his sons had used the computer to produce cards to sell for Valentine's Day.

[28] Originally from the village, he now lived in the capital and came once a week to give classes. His students could not afford to pay for the classes but covered his travel expenses.

nity was evident in how his bargaining skills won over their support. For example, the president of the local council was 'godfather' to the association, the Minister of Culture had donated a television and the former president of the Republic of Cape Verde had attended one of the association's anniversary celebrations. When the community centre was built, the Prime Minister had also provided funding to buy furniture for the day nursery; however, the child carer, Júlia, told me that as the number of children increased, Alberto refused to allow her to use a bigger, unoccupied room in the centre. A photocopying machine, donated to the community centre, was also kept under lock and key. When I suggested to the president that the association could sell photocopies to local school children as a means of generating income for the association, he replied that this would be difficult because photocopies were already given free of charge to the children of association members. The president's claim was vigorously denied by parents and children alike. Not even Júlia was able to access the photocopier for her work in the day nursery and there had also been conflicts over the children's use of the bathroom. Under the cover of his external image as a community representative, the president appeared to be enjoying more than his legitimate share of the 'development pie'.

4.8. Becoming the 'other'

The case of Alberto, discussed above, exposes what may lie hidden behind populist notions regarding the 'authenticity' of rural society. The following sections take a closer look at what is concealed in Cape Verde by assertions revolving around an artificial separation between town and country. We have seen how the urban elite construed the dependence of the rural population upon the state-run FAIMO system as an obstacle to the development of the nation. I argued that this 'urban' perspective was above all a narrative about the 'modern', 'cosmopolitan' and 'independent' urban social person. The case material below elucidates the fragility and mobility of the relations of difference upon which these assertions were predicated. It illustrates how events broke down one of the major distinctions upon which the category of the FAIMO worker was based: dependence upon the state.

4.8.1. Deconstructing difference

> FAIMO is everybody - we all want employment. Here in the ministry we employ three people to pick up a stapler: its simply more sophisticated high intensity labour[29].

[29] This quotation also appears in table 4.2 of Chapter Four as a 'structural' approach towards discussing FAIMO.

When I put the above point, made by an engineer who worked for the Ministry of Infra-structures and Transport (MIT)[30], to the director of the Praia delegation of MIT, the director passionately disagreed, claiming that whoever had made this claim was simply 'talking politics'. There certainly was political capital to be made from defending or criticizing both current and former FAIMO policies. For example, the government's continued financing of AIMO throughout the period of the first Republic (1975 - 1991), was sometimes used to accuse the PAIGC[31] of 'paternalism'. Criticisms of the current government's drive to privatize FAIMO led to accusations that the new government was insensitive to issues of social justice. Although the director of the MIT delegation was adamant that it was possible to distinguish between 'political' and 'technical' approaches towards FAIMO, this distinction was not easy to maintain, since what could be seen as a technical evaluation from one perspective, could easily be interpreted as an attempt to make political capital, from another.

The director of the Praia delegation of MIT told me that he had never got on well with FAIMO, claiming that it was 'anti-scientific'. The problem, he explained, lay in what he called the unjust relationship with the state: one of paternalism. The director spoke of the success of his experiences of the 'reconversion' of FAIMO in the island of Fogo. He had 'sacked' youths from FAIMO, allowing them to keep their tools so that they could set up their own workshops.

'Reconversion' was a term that was commonly used to refer to the restructuring of FAIMO in accordance with the exigencies of 'economic progress'. I soon discovered in my interviews that it was a concept which some people took objection to, on the grounds that it could simply be a euphemism for eventually abolishing the system all together, by transferring FAIMO from the state to the private sector. As one state employee put it to me:

> No government can abolish FAIMO. How can you justify to the outside world that you are receiving food aid whilst people are dying of hunger?

For 'reconversion' implied not only increasing efficiency and productivity, but also reducing the size of the workforce. Some of the MIT FAIMO had been 'reconverted': their contracts were open to competition in the private sector, leaving MIT with the role of supervision[32]. In the eyes of the director the consequent reduction in the size of the workforce did not pose a major problem. His words are paraphrased below:

---

[30] Formerly called the Ministy of Public Works (MOP).

[31] In 1980 the PAIGC was dissolved and the Cape Verdean branch of the party became the PAICV - the African Party for the Independence of Cape Verde. See Chapters Two and Three.

[32] The MIT FAIMOs which had not been privatized had been transferred to the local councils as part of the government's commitment to the development of strong local government. Some of the government's critics argued that an underlying motive behind this transfer was political: the MIT delegations had become very powerful over the years and were still associated with the PAICV, whereas most of the local councils were MPD.

> On the positive side we have efficiency, productivity, timeliness and quality. The negative consequence is that the contractor employs fewer people. The productive aspect is more important because FAIMO was only there to resolve social problems and these can be addressed through investing in the economy.

One of the underlying principles of the concept of 'reconversion' was that the FAIMO workforce was not exclusively comprised of the neediest: over the years FAIMO had attracted people who had alternative options for making a living but preferred to depend on the state (Lima 1990:19). I have already discussed above how this kind of argument became commonplace. Less common were questions related to the capacity of the private sector to absorb the surplus workforce of a reduced FAIMO system[33]. As far as the director was concerned, 'reconversion' was above all about changing welfare mentalities; nevertheless, his opinion changed in the wake of the mandatory scaling down of his delegation.

During the course of my fieldwork, I interviewed the director on several occasions and was always struck by the number of employees on the premises seemingly doing nothing. One day I arrived to find the place conspicuously quiet and the director in an uncharacteristically sombre mood. He had finally received orders to scale down the delegation. Two thirds of the workforce - comprised of one hundred employees - had been made redundant. Some of these employees felt cheated because they had no right to indemnification[34] since they had never been officially on the payroll, but had been employed as day workers for many years. It had clearly been a distressful time for the director. He told me that he had had to deal with women crying bitterly in his office who, he acknowledged, had little prospects of employment elsewhere. These were not simply categories but people whom the director knew well and his sombre mood told me that the issue of 'reconversion' had acquired a much more personal dimension for him, as he gingerly acknowledged that there was some truth to the claim that ‘we are all FAIMO’.

The scaling down of the MIT delegation of Praia served to break down the distinction between the ‘dependency’ of FAIMO workers and the ‘independence’ of civil servants - one of the distinctions upon which the social construction of rural categories was based. Representations of the category of the 'authentic local' in the CBWF initiative were also undermined by events which were beyond the control of the RAP personnel. The reader will recall how the RAP personnel produced group stereotypes as foils for self-identification and legitimization, representing themselves as ‘insiders’, more familiar with their

[33] I put this question to the director of DGASP in Ribeira Grande in the island of Santo Antão. His reply was that the funds available in the investment programme for 1997 were insufficient for the current employment needs and that the private sector would not be able to absorb the surplus.

[34] They would be entitled to a social pension once they reached the age of sixty.

working environment and hence more committed than the state extensionists, whom they represented as incompetent 'outsiders'. But as their structural circumstances changed, this simple opposition between 'insider' and 'outsider' also became a straightjacket that ceased to serve their practical interests.

4.8.2. The constraints of external categorization

The distinction between state employees and 'authentic' locals or 'insiders' was broken down by events following the end of the Watershed Development Project which resulted in the state taking on the RAP personnel as temporary employees. One of the consequences of their new structural positioning was that the RAP personnel became prey to the same kind of external categorizations that they had formulated in relation to state extensionists. This, in turn, brings to the foreground the transient and unstable nature of group categorizations as they relate to the changing complexities of local realities.

The government institution co-responsible for the CBWF initiative of the Watershed Development Project (WDP) was the General Directorate for Soil Conservation, Forestry and Rural Engineering (DGCSFER) of the Ministry of Rural Development and Fishing (MRDP). Although the salaries of the RAP personnel were paid through the DGCSFER, the funds came from the WDP. So when the project came to an end in 1990, there was no guarantee that the state would employ the RAP personnel since they did not have the necessary academic training to qualify for a permanent state position. Nevertheless, the DGCSFER eventually re-assigned the RAP personnel as temporary employees to work with the district delegations of the MRDP. The agronomist, António, who had been in charge of the WDP in the DGCSFER, gave an account of the events which is paraphrased below:

> The problem did not occur just with this project; it has and will continue to occur with other projects. The projects have autonomy and money so they recruit, train and pay people and then when the projects finish, those who are in the director's favour are allowed to stay, others are dismissed and new people are recruited....
>
> António had managed to get the RAP personnel linked to the MRDP district delegations, until another project came along. They may not have worked as much as before, but he was constantly checking on them, asking for follow-up data, so that the delegations would not complain about their work.

The state is represented in this account as a temporary back-up or safety net upon which individuals can rely until the inception of another project. This occurred in 1995 with the start of the Watershed and Applied Research Development project (WARD). The aim of the WARD project was to build on earlier experiences of the CBWF initiative by encouraging residents to form associations, so that they could contract directly with the government to implement rural engineering works. The incentives for efficiency were deemed to be greater than in the former CBWF since any money saved belonged to the associations. It was up to the latter to set their daily production targets so that they would outpace salaries and make a profit. A more detailed discussion of the associations' work will be given in the following chapter.

As a result of the implementation of the WARD project, the RAP personnel who were still officially employed by the DGCSFER - now called the General Directorate for Agriculture, Siviculture and Animal Husbandry (DGASP) - became in practice both project and state personnel. They consequently found themselves caught between the conflicting agendas of the donor on the one hand and of their official employer - the state - on the other. This situation was reflected in the fact that the donor and DGASP used different names to refer to them. The latter, employing them on a temporary basis to provide technical assistance in soil and water conservation, used the term 'técnicos auxiliares das ribeiras' (TARs) - 'watershed auxiliary technicians'. The donor, on the other hand, also depended upon the TARs to promote the associations in the watersheds and consequently referred to them in most of its written documents as 'community organizers' (COs). However, his was not a term that was used verbally in Portuguese or Creole because the donor could not afford to accentuate these conflicting agendas with DGASP which had turned the TARs/COs into 'piggies in the middle'.

As far as the director of DGASP was concerned, it was not the responsibility of any of his employees to engage in promoting the creation of associations. The responsibility of the TARS was, as their names indicated, to provide technical assistance. But the expatriate Stephen was aware that the low levels of education of watershed residents made the TARS' contributions fundamental to the functioning of the associations, even though they were not officially members. Whilst the associations were producing good quality rural engineering works for DGASP, this was not, in itself, enough. For the ultimate aim of the project, to be discussed in more detail in the next chapter, was for the associations to discover alternative sources of income generation. This required a more active engagement with the associations on behalf of its members than that of simply turning up to work: members were also expected to participate in association meetings. Failure to do so was frowned upon by the donor and Stephen was therefore constantly reprimanding the TARS for not devoting sufficient time to community animation.

Stephen often referred to the association work fronts as 'FAIMO in a different outfit'[35] to accuse the TARs and association members of lacking the will

[35] It was a more catchy term in Creole due to its alliteration: 'FAIMO di otu farda'.

and indeed the vision to view the associations as a means of freeing themselves from dependence upon the state. In this respect, the association work fronts were nothing more than FAIMO in disguise.

Stephen's demands were nevertheless problematic, given that the TARs were no longer employed by the donor. There was one occasion when Stephen cancelled a scheduled meeting with the TARs at the last minute in order to avoid accentuating tensions with DGASP. News had circulated quickly of how the director of DGASP had come across the TAR Hugo by chance in the donor headquarters in Praia and had snapped at him, asking Hugo what he thought he was doing there.

The events following the end of the WDP had turned the 'locals' into agents of the state by default. Following the re-instatement of the CBWF initiative, the TARs found themselves in a position of having to 'serve two masters' - an expression that they themselves used. The TARs continued to define themselves as 'locals' and 'insiders', whilst suffering the effects of the external categorizations of others. For it was not only the director of DGASP whose external categorization of 'state employees' created restrictions for the TARs. The donor field director - Peter - had also expressed his disapproval of the TARs becoming members of an umbrella organization called OASIS which had recently been created to represent the associations, on the grounds that they were not association members (more details regarding OASIS will be given in the following chapter). Stephen had nevertheless insisted and Hugo was even voted president of the directory council of OASIS. This resulted in the awkward situation of having to meet with his employer whenever Hugo represented OASIS in meetings with DGASP. Although this problem was resolved whenever such meetings took place by replacing Hugo with the president of the general assembly of OASIS (who was not a TAR but an association president) the underlying ambiguity of Hugo's position remained. This ambiguity was shared by all of the TARs and Peter argued that it posed a threat to the interests of OASIS. He knew of a case from America where both presidents and managers formed part of the directory council of an organization. Although the organization had lots of projects, Peter claimed that it never made a profit because the managers manipulated the decisions to make sure that they got higher salaries as well as other benefits. Peter's fear was that if the TARs had a voice and a vote then they could easily manipulate OASIS to their own advantage. The solution, according to Peter, was for the TARs to leave DGASP and work on a private basis. For many of the TARs this constituted a risk which they were not ready to take.

Having initially recruited the RAP personnel as 'locals' and 'insiders', the donor was now construing them not only as 'outsiders' but as potentially manipulative 'state employees'. Moreover it was the failure of USAID to provide continuity to the CBWF initiative that had led DGASP to employ the TARs in the first place. These events had consequently turned the 'authentic locals' into the 'stigmatized other' which had served as their foil for self-definition. The difference through which the 'locals' had represented themselves had been taken away. The external constraints that were imposed upon the TARs' self-definition of 'authentic locals' or 'insiders' highlight the structuring constraints of practice upon processes of identification. The TARs were constrained by their new status: irrespective of how they perceived themselves, they had now become state employees. Their '*positioning*' (Hall 1990:226) of themselves as committed 'locals' was constrained by their '*structural position*'. This led to further constraints produced by the external categorizations of others: Peter's refusal to see them as 'insiders' and the director of DGASP's protestations that as his employees the TARs should not be engaged in community organization. The question that I have not addressed here is what lay behind the director's objections to their involvement with the associations? Was it simply a matter of maintaining professional boundaries or was something else at stake? I shall return to this question in the following chapter.

4.9. Conclusion

The processes of identification described above should not be confused with the study of reflexive constructions of self-identity. As I stated in the introduction to this chapter, they should be analysed as an expression of social relations, including political struggle. The insecure status of the TARs highlights the precariousness of the contexts in which individuals become 'development insiders'. Projects open up new possibilities of training and employment. However as the words of António above warn us, projects come and go, often leaving an institutional vacuum in their wake. Those who are left behind must compete with each other for their survival and it is in this context that the problematic concept of 'authenticity' becomes an increasingly valuable commodity; be it as an 'authentic' local, representative of a community or as an 'authentic' professional – with the necessary qualifications, experience and 'modern' characteristics. The processes of 'othering' investigated in this chapter have elucidated a vulnerable and changing 'middle ground' between reified images of 'town' and 'country' which not only challenges populist notions of authenticity but also raises questions about the nature of power relations at the 'grassroots'. As more development 'outsiders' become 'development insiders' the struggle to hold on to this precarious position intensifies and the ability to do so is partly dependent upon an individual's success in the 'conceptual market place' (Mbembe 2001) where, as Escobar points out, 'labels determine access to resources' (1995, 110). This is evident in the case of the president of 'Batuque' whose ability to win over the support of donors and local politicians, who were unaware that it was for his personal gain, testifies to the quality of Alberto's bargaining skills in the development market place. That the funding dynamics of a purportedly participatory, 'people-centred' project should also contribute towards concealing the president's undemocratic practices, warns us to take heed of what may be obscured by the dualisms of development jargon such as that of the shift from 'top-down' to 'bottom-up' development.

The transfer of CBWF from the state to local associations – the privatization of FAIMO – reflects the shift in both the global political economy and international development policy away from state-centred Keynesian approaches towards the adoption of market-driven neo-liberal approaches, aimed at reducing the role of the state in the economy. This chapter has also revealed how the shift away from the 'state' towards the 'market' and private initiative was neither stable nor complete; dependence upon the state for employment constituted a recurrent critical issue which shall also be addressed in the following chapter.

Chapter Five

Market and Community Values: Vying in the 'Shifting Middle Ground'*

5.1. Introduction

> What has been happening to poverty? What has been happening to unemployment? What has been happening to inequality?...If one or two of these central problems have been growing worse, especially if all three have, it would be strange to call the result 'development,' even if per capita income doubled (Seers 1972:124).

> [T]he conversation concerning how to divide our economic life between community and market must take place outside the market discourse. We ought not to let ourselves be persuaded that the coin has only one side (Gudeman 2001:163).

Nearly thirty years after Seer's legendary challenge of the assumptions underlying the dominant market discourse of economic growth, Gudeman's appeal, cited above, testifies to the persistent influence of the economic liberal view upon established conceptions of the nature of the economy. Thus the market realm and the community realm are often placed in opposition to each other, conceived in terms of a trade-off between efficiency and equity (Gudeman 2001:65). Equity is understood to belong to the complex realm of ethics and morality, whilst efficiency is construed as value-free: a matter of objective, rational 'economic' sense. Although this liberal view continues to inform market-driven development initiatives, issues of equity and social welfare have also gained prominence. The current shift towards the market in international development policy has been accompanied by a renewed commitment to poverty alleviation. Halving extreme poverty, for example, constitutes one of the UN Millennium Development Goals[36]. That conventional growth models of development had failed to eradicate poverty was one of the major ethical concerns of academics and development practitioners back in the 1970s. Seers argued that equality

---

*An earlier version of the first part of this chapter, entitled "The Role of Associations in Local Development: Reflections from the Case of Cape Verde on the Interface between Market and Community", was presented at the II International Conference on Sócio-Cultural Research and Development in Paredes de Coura, organised by AGIR on 28-30 October 2004. An earlier version of the second part of the chapter, entitled 'Whose Knowledge Counts? Following the Trails of Development Knowledge Production in the Cape Verdean Third Sector' was presented at the International Conference on Knowledge and Science in Africa in Frankfurt, organised by the African Studies Association (VAD) on July 24-27 2006.

[36] The Millennium Declaration was signed by 147 countries during the Millennium Summit that took place in September 2000.

should be considered as a development objective 'in its own right' (1972:124). He is often cited for having put ethics on the development agenda (e.g. in Slater 1993:105-6, Midgley 1995:130). This chapter explores the contradictions and tensions inherent in the drive to integrate market growth with poverty alleviation. The ethnography demonstrates how these kinds of interventions may create inequalities or exacerbate existing ones. This is partly because market driven interventions continue to endorse the putative divide between efficiency and equity, creating an artificial division between 'market' and 'social' problems.

The ethnography revolves around a US AID funded programme, referred to in the previous chapter, aimed at pursuing profitability in the name of social welfare. The programme encouraged local people to form associations, so that they could contract directly with the government to implement rural engineering works in community based work fronts (CBWF). The incentives for efficiency were deemed to be greater than in the former CBWF since any money saved belonged to the associations. It was up to the latter to set their daily production targets so that they would outpace salaries and make a profit, to be invested in new income generation activities. The shift towards the market in donor policy could not be clearer; yet, the issue of wealth creation proved to be a contentious one. The idea that local associations should generate a 'profit' created frictions with the state, since the purported role of associations was to address 'social', rather than 'market', concerns. The issue of how best to use the associations' funds, created tensions between the donor and community members whose demands for social welfare were at odds with the donor policy of targeting productivity.

The chapter is divided into two parts. The first part explores the tensions inherent in reconciling profitability with social welfare across a range of programme beneficiary associations. The second part offers more thick description as it takes a closer look at what happens at the micro-level. It expands upon the case study of the association 'Batuque', initiated in the previous chapter, in order to produce a comparative analysis with 'Funaná' - another beneficiary association.

The ethnography reveals the ways in which social actors, with diverse agendas and differential access to capital and information, negotiate the discursive and institutional paradoxes of delivering social welfare through market driven development, in order to promote their own interests and/or the interests of poorer community members. The variety of ways in which they do this brings to light a 'shifting middle ground' where donor policies are simultaneously reproduced, appropriated, questioned and rejected. This, in turn, elucidates the relevance of the concept of a 'shifting middle ground' to describe a transactional space between politically differentiated social actors. I show how people, with competing priorities, are vying in this 'shifting middle ground', negotiating the contradictions of market-growth and poverty alleviation and in different ways, influencing the shape and outcomes of these interventions. My analysis of their differential abilities to negotiate and impact upon these paradoxes and tensions draws upon Mbembe's (2001) ideas on conviviality and conceptual bargaining, (outlined in Chapter One) as well as upon Bourdieu's concepts of 'symbolic capital' or 'credit' and 'symbolic violence'.

Part I

5.2. Setting the scene: The WARD and Food for Peace projects

The global shift towards the market is reflected in USAID donor policies in Cape Verde which turned their focus from targeting employment to targeting productivity and profit. The USAID funded programme which became the main focus of my fieldwork, called 'Food for Peace' (FFP), was a five year programme commencing in 1997. This was a somewhat artificial inception since the part of the programme that I was studying - the promotion of community-based workfronts (CBWF) - was in many aspects a continuation of its antecedent: the Watershed and Applied Research Development Project (WARD). The major difference of philosophy underlying the CBWF of the WARD and FFP projects, compared to earlier initiatives (see previous chapter), is spelled out in a section of the FFP project proposal, under the heading 'Lessons Learned'. It too is informed by the idea of a line that separates the efficiency of the economy from the social concerns of the non-market world.

> **Targeting employment and income with local currency sales proceeds does not produce sustainable improvements in the economy; targeting productivity and profitability does.**
>
> The strategy behind previous programmes was to improve incomes so that individuals would be able to purchase food. While this is laudable and may contribute to lower levels of chronic or acute malnutrition, it creates a dependence, as the funding for the public works has invariably come from outside the economy with no emphasis on developing sustainable institutions. By targeting activities which increase productivity there is an improvement in the performance of the economy, and more assets are generated to meet the needs of the society. Profits and increased incomes are in turn rolled into investments which increase economic activity and self-reliance (ACDI 1996b:52, emphasis in original).

The text presents a simplified and rational model of change in which programme inputs are unproblematically transformed into programme outputs. The substitution of the needs of individuals for the needs of society and the economy provide an indication of the conflicts of interest that may be subsumed by this presentation of a smooth transition towards the market. Yet, in its attempt to integrate market growth with poverty alleviation, the project proposal also identifies woman and the poor as target groups. A summary of the projects' aims and major activities is given in table 5.1 below.

Table 5.1: Aims and activities of the WARD and FFP projects

Watershed and Applied Research Development Project - WARD (1995-96)	
Government Institutions	General Directorate for Agriculture, Siviculture and Animal Husbandry (DGASP) of the Ministry of Fisheries, Agriculture and Rural Extension (MPAAR former MDRP)
Aim: to transfer SWC FAIMOs from the state to the private sector by encouraging watershed residents to form associations, so that they could contract directly with the government to implement rural engineering works (REW) in CBWF. 1995: 1) DGASP contracted directly with five Santiago based associations. Technical assistance provided by many of the RAP personnel who had become 'watershed auxiliary technicians' (TARs). All of the associations made a profit. 2) Additional Workfronts Programme - more SWC activities to fight soil erosion and alleviate unemployment caused by the drought of 1994, by setting up additional CBWFs. The programme also served as an apprenticeship for the groups involved to become fully legalized associations. By end of 1995 13 local watershed groups had became legalized. 1995-6: Technical training for the associations as well as training in bookkeeping and management, including how to enter into SWC business contracts. 1996: 1) 16 associations signed REW contracts with DGASP. 2) Targeting of women to help them take on leadership roles on the work crews and in the associations. 3) Creation of an umbrella organization - OASIS - in June 1996. .	
Food For Peace - FFP (1997-2001)	
Government Institutions	DGASP of the Ministry of Agriculture, Food and Environment (MAA, former MPAAR)
1997-2001 - Aims: Expand to a total of 50 associations nation wide (approx. 8 new associations per year). 80-90% of the REW to be built by these associations. 1997: 1) Additional Workfronts and training for 12 new associations 2) More REW contracts signed between DGASP and the old associations. 3) Some of the profits generated by the old associations used to grant loans to their members for income generation activities. 4) Expansion of the activities of the umbrella organization - OASIS.	
Additional components of the projects, which did not form a part of my fieldwork, include: the introduction of agricultural technologies, a small business lending programme and a micro enterprise training and lending programme.	

(Sources: interviews and project documents: ACDI 1995, 1996a, 1996b)

As can be seen from table 5.1, the projects were not only engaged in promoting the creation of associations, but also in making sure that they became fully legalized. The benefits to local residents of legalizing their associations were explained to me by Benjamim - president of a local association. His words are paraphrased below:

> In 1995 a friend from the DGASP district delegation asked Benjamim if he wanted to be a work crew chief on an additional WARD workfront in Mato Raia and he agreed. Benjamim's workfront made a profit so the donor ex-

patriate Stephen said that they should set up an association. Their profit was then transferred to pay for the salaries of his friend's workfront nearby, which had failed to be as productive, just like the old FAIMOs. The idea of creating an association became even more appealing to him because then no-body could take their profit.

The transfer of funds from one FAIMO to another appeared to be a common practice. I was told by another informant of a similar case in the same year when an additional WARD workfront was also denied its profits, which were used by DGASP to cover the costs of a less productive workfront elsewhere. (This practice supports the point made to me, by the director of a government department, of how easily funds could be diverted from FAIMO workfronts, making the latter appear more costly and hence more inefficient than they actually were[37]). The profit that was generated by the workfronts of the legally constituted associations was deposited into the associations' own bank accounts and therefore could not be diverted by the state. Initially, up to thirty per cent of the profits were distributed to association members in order to foment a sense of ownership. The remaining funds were set aside to be used to provide credit to members for investing in income generation activities. In later years, the donor began to discourage the distribution of profits to members so that more money could be invested in activities that would guarantee the financial sustainability of the associations.

Evidence that members had developed some sense of ownership is manifest in the following statements, made by association workers, in response to my question regarding the difference between association work fronts and those run by the local council:

> - With the association, people give all they have got. With the local council, people work less;
> - With the association, people work harder because there is a contract. In council work fronts people don't make much of an effort because they belong to the state. So they don't want to give all they have got;
> - With the council, we just work as we go along. Nobody says anything. With the association, the work is done properly; they say it has to be;
> - Association work is for making money; work with the council is for chatting with your friend. (How do you account for this difference?) The association is ours whilst the council work front belongs to the state[38].

---

[37] See Table 4.2 in Chapter Four.

[38]-Asosiason ta da kabidal, kâmara trabadju mas poku.
-Asosiason trabadju mas duru pamodi empretada. Kâmara, algen ta bai, ka ta desenpenha pa trabadju. Pamodi é di stadu. Djá es ka ta kre da kabidal.
-Kâmara, sima nu faze, nu faze. Algen ka ta fla nada. Asosiason, ta fazedu dretu, ta fladu tem ki faze.
-Asosiason é pa da rendimentu. Kâmara pa djobi companheru. (Pamodi kel diferensa?) Pamodi asosiason é di nos propri, kâmara é di estado.

Together with this sense of ownership came the raised expectations that the associations meet the needs of everybody. Yet, the rationale behind the programmes was based on a classical 'market model' that envisaged the promotion of 'profit-making organizations run on a businesslike basis' (ACDI 1996b45). The associations were more like the Cape Verdean micro-enterprises studied by Grassi (2003): they contravened the dominant market model. Unable to operate as 'hard core' businesses, because they could not turn their backs on the social issues of their communities, I have chosen to call them 'soft core businesses'. The following section discusses how the donor had unwittingly exacerbated the tensions between the community and market realms, by encouraging the watershed groups to become legalized as associations instead of as cooperatives. This placed them in a cross-fire between conflicting interpretations of their role. Associations were, by law, non-profit-making organizations and their mandate was usually associated with the social concerns of development assistance. Cooperatives, on the other hand, could generate a surplus and were more commonly associated with market activity.

5.3. 'Profit': the unspoken word of 'soft-core' businesses

Despite the shift in donor policy towards the market, the terms 'profit' and 'cooperative' were words that programme staff were careful to avoid in their everyday encounters with beneficiaries and in any public statements that they made with regard to the associations. This was because the donor's attempt to avoid alienating potential members had unwittingly created an ambiguous legal situation for the associations:

> The new farmer-based entities in Cape Verde are called *associations* since the word *cooperative* has a bad connotation. The GOCV [government of Cape Verde] set up a system of centrally-planned "cooperatives" that were cooperation in name only. Instead of farmer-owned and controlled, these activities were staffed by government employees and used to carry out government policy. Serving the needs of rural stakeholders was not their forte (ACDI 1996b:49).

Evidence that the cooperatives had acquired a bad name is reflected in the account that I was given by the watershed technician, Hugo. He told me how residents from his watershed had been encouraged by 'technicians of community participation' each to pay an entrance fee of five hundred escudos in order to set up a cooperative. Hugo had assisted in finding a suitable location to serve as a shop and a warehouse. However, when the lorry of corn arrived, Hugo claimed that no-body knew anything about how the cooperative was supposed to function and it consequently failed to work. Hugo remarked that there had been lots of corruption, pointing out to me that residents never got their money back and concluding that 'it was the same old story - people coming from the outside'.

The consequences of avoiding the 'bad connotation' of the word 'cooperative' were to deny the watershed groups the legal right to generate a surplus. Since they could not be called 'cooperatives' neither could they be legalized as such. The groups were consequently constituted on the basis of the 1987 law of non-profit making associations (Boletim Oficial 31 December, 1987), even though the legislation for cooperatives was far more appropriate for them. The latter permitted the generation of what was referred to in legal terms as a 'surplus', up to fifty per cent of which could be distributed to members. Activities permitted by this law also included the provision of credit (Boletim Oficial 23 November 1990:30). There were nevertheless two activities permitted within the 1987 law of non-profit making associations which provided the loophole for the associations to be able to sign SWC contracts with DGASP. These were the protection of the environment and the promotion of community development (Boletim Oficial 31 December, 1987:6). So although the associations were barred in legal terms from generating a 'surplus' or a 'profit', in practice they were able to do so: the unspoken word 'profit' was in reality an open secret. The director of DGASP was nonetheless uncomfortable with this. He told me in an interview that since the associations were not businesses they could not distribute their profits to members. The issue of legislation had been raised by the donor, at the end of the WARD project. But the director explained that changing the legislation would only create conflicts with other organizations. An informant gave me an example of the kind of conflicts that the director may have been referring to. He told me that the director had recently received a letter from a private contracting firm accusing DGASP of preferential treatment towards the WARD/FFP affiliated associations, since their contracts were not put to tender. Avoiding the term 'profit' thus served to protect local people from outside competition.

This raises the issue as to whether the associations could become legalized as businesses. I put this question to a lawyer hired by the donor to look into the legal status of the associations. He explained to me that the associations would no longer qualify for exemptions which would raise the costs of SWC contracting to the extent that the associations would lose their comparative advantages over state FAIMOs[39] and would be unable to make a profit. In other words, it was not only the legal status of the associations that prevented them from becoming hard core businesses. Their financial viability also depended upon receiving a helping hand from the state.

Implications of the associations` legal situation became more complicated when they joined together to form an umbrella organization, called OASIS, which was subject to the same law as that of its member associations. The donor requested the lawyer to look into the possibility of changing the legal status of OASIS so that it could import materials at a lower cost and be able to compete

[39] The WARD project final report claims that 'Watershed associations performed SWC contracts at approximately 60% the cost of the competing state-owned construction firm' (1996a: v).

legally with other institutions including the state-owned construction firm – the National Institute for Rural Engineering and Forestry - INERF.

The most appropriate status for OASIS would be that of a cooperative, however, as the lawyer explained to me, there were a number of legal problems with this which originated in the initial legalization of the watershed groups as associations. Whilst it was legally possible for associations to become cooperatives, this was only possible for first degree associations - whose members were individuals. Since OASIS was a second degree association - an association of associations - it could not become a second degree cooperative unless all of the association members of OASIS were to become cooperatives. Besides the various difficulties that this would entail, there was still a legal problem because the membership of OASIS was mixed: comprised of individual members - the watershed technicians- and collective members - the associations.

The lawyer took pleasure in describing these legalities to me. He displayed such enthusiasm in his attempt to resolve the matter that I was left with the impression that the legal predicament of the associations and OASIS was more of a lawyer's puzzle than a serious problem, in practice. The lawyer went on to tell me that whilst a federation of cooperatives existed in the law, there was no such legislation for creating a federation of associations: 'but it is not prohibited either, so OASIS was legalized anyway. This is the conversation that I had with the Minister of Justice'. The lawyer had also spoken with the director of the General Directorate for External Commerce who had told him that he was prepared to grant a licence to OASIS for the occasional importing of materials, such as gabions and drip irrigation technology. So despite the ambiguous legal situation of OASIS and its member associations, both the General Director and the Minister seemed willing to turn a blind eye. Their attitude provides an example of the discrepancy between official norms as stipulated in the law and the irrelevance of these norms in practice (Bourdieu 1998:60).

The director of DGASP did not show the same willingness to ignore the official norms as his colleagues had done. He told me that he objected to the term 'association contractors' which was frequently employed to refer to the associations, not only in donor documentation but also in the every-day conversations of individuals involved with the projects. This term served to blur the legal distinctions between 'associations' and 'contractors'. The director of DGASP argued that the watershed groups should make a choice: either they were contractors or associations. The function of the latter, he claimed, was above all a social one in which the whole community should participate in order to contribute towards the development of the locality. Despite his protestations - many of which were voiced 'backstage' rather than 'onstage' (Scott 1985:284) - the director of DGASP was collaborating with the project. The following section explores the reasons for the director's ambivalent position, by examining the institutional history of DGASP.

5.4. Relations of interdependence and competition

Unlike his colleagues from the Ministry of Justice and from the General Directorate for External Commerce, the director of DGASP had a direct stake in the WARD and FFP projects. His insistence upon the incompatibility of profitability and social welfare, despite the working consensus that had been achieved, reveals a desire to exploit the tensions between the market and community realms to his own advantage. Although the director seemed to be appealing to the kind of 'people-centred' approaches to development, discussed in the introduction to this chapter, his constant muddying of the waters reflected a covert interest that he could not afford to express openly. The director's insistence upon the social goals of the associations and upon the legal impediments to profit-making could thus be interpreted as a form of 'symbolic violence' in which 'interests can only be satisfied on condition that they be disguised in and by strategies aiming to satisfy them' (Bourdieu 1977:191).

DGASP was the operations department of the Ministry of Agriculture, created in order to contract with the state-owned construction company - the National Institute for Rural Engineering and Forestry (INERF). Both of these institutions had been created as a result of a re-structuring of the Ministry of Agriculture in 1991, when the MPD government came into power. The motivation for the creation of INERF was to render FAIMO more productive - an example of the concept of 'reconversion' referred to in the previous chapter. Although workers of INERF FAIMOs received higher salaries, they were no longer paid simply for turning up, but only if and when they reached their daily production targets. The role of DGASP was to draw up the work plans of soil and water conservation (SWC) and to contract INERF to implement them. However, given that the latter was a semi-private business, its salaries were higher than those of DGASP and it had managed to attract the best technicians. DGASP consequently lacked the technical capacity to draw up the SWC plans which were usually produced by INERF employees. Although DGASP was officially responsible for plan approval, in practice INERF was not only carrying out the design and the construction of REW but was also engaged in the billing of the quantities of work produced (ACDI 1996a:4). There were consequently often disputes between DGASP and INERF technicians.

It is within this context that DGASP became a beneficiary of the WARD project, under the rubric of 'institution building' (ACDI 1996a:4). The donor provided DGASP with computers, electronic survey equipment, training and technical assistance (ACDI 1996a:4). The justification for this support was that in order for the associations to be able to compete with INERF as viable SWC contractors, DGASP had to develop the capacity to draw up its own technical designs and to supervise SWC work. In other words, in order to develop the private sector, the donor also had to strengthen the state. Although the long term goal of the FFP project was to reduce the associations' dependence upon SWC contracts with the state, in the short term, at least, the associations were still dependent upon contracts with DGASP. The privatization of FAIMO did not automatically produce the predicted increase in 'self-reliance', referred to above.

Failure of DGASP to honour its side of the contracts was a common complaint voiced in OASIS meetings. Two of the most frequent cases that I heard were related to money. The first was DGASP's failure to hand over twenty per cent of the value of the contract at the time when it was signed - usually needed for the purchase of materials, such as cement, in order to start work. The other complaint was that the watershed technicians never benefited from the five per cent of the value of the contract that DGASP received from the donor, out of which it was supposed to pay for the watershed technicians' transport expenses. There was a rumour circulating that the director of DGASP was using this money for some infra-structural improvements at the office headquarters. Whether this rumour was true or not is a moot point. However, that large amounts of money were at stake was brought home to me when I discussed the legal situation of association contracting with António, who was now employed by the donor within the ambit of the FFP project.

When I questioned him about the legality of association contracting, António dismissed the issue, asking me somewhat irritably where it was written that associations could not sign contracts. He then went on to explain that there were fixed budget ceilings for which putting the contracts to tender was obligatory. The way round the problem was to divide the contracts up into parts, so that they never exceeded these ceilings. António seemed to be implying that the director's uneasiness with the legalities of the situation masked another agenda. António went on to mention the five per cent of the budget that DGASP received from every contract, already referred to above. He then proceeded to give me an example: in a contract worth one hundred and twenty million escudos, six million[40] would go to DGASP. This amounted to a lot of money, he told me. DGASP's fear, according to António, was that if OASIS became too strong, instead of contracting through DGASP, the donor could contract OASIS directly and DGASP would lose a significant source of income[41].

The suggestion that DGASP was secretly hostile to OASIS, because both institutions were in competition for the same funds, seems quite a plausible explanation to account for the director's ambivalent position. His insistence upon the legal impediments to association contracting provided the director with the necessary vocabulary to express the inexpressible in disguise: a covert rivalry

[40] During the 1996-7 period of my fieldwork, 100 escudos was equivalent to just under one euro - one euro was approximately 105 escudos (Banco de Cabo Verde, Departamento de Estudos Económicos e Estatísticas, Boletim 10 Anos 1995-2005).

[41] By 2005 this is exactly what happened. OASIS had become the general contractor for the thirty seven associations in Santiago that were beneficiaries of the FFP programme. DGASP continued to be the owner of the works but it now contracted with OASIS which then sub-contracted with the associations. These paid three per cent of the value of their contracts to OASIS.

with OASIS. In Bourdieuian terms, it served as a 'practical disclaimer' to satisfy an economic interest in a purportedly 'disinterested manner', 'inspired by pure respect for the customs and conventions recognized by the group' (1977:194), in this case, inspired by respect for the law. This also sheds new light upon the director's reluctance to allow the watershed technicians to lend support to the associations (see previous chapter). Seen from this perspective, the degree to which the director of DGASP tolerated the involvement of the watershed technicians with the associations may be an indication of DGASP's dependence upon donor funding. DGASP was also indirectly dependent upon the associations, since the securing of donor funds was contingent upon their continuing to contract through DGASP.

The director's recourse to symbolic violence illustrates how tensions between productivity and social welfare can be exploited to meet covert practical interests. The 'middle ground' where 'market' and 'community' intersect is also a political space in which actors not only collaborate, but also compete with each other as they negotiate their 'working ambiguities' and strive to secure a share of the resources generated by the development encounter. From a structural perspective, this 'middle ground' between 'market' and 'non-market' is, as Mitchell (2007) has poignantly illustrated, a 'broad terrain' with a long history of battles over the power to control resources.

The relations of interdependence and competition between DGASP and the associations also raise questions regarding the nature of the relationship between the 'state' and 'civil society'. The director's insistence upon keeping the waters murky, instead of adhering to the working consensus that had emerged, reveals how obfuscation is equally important as creating a 'mutually comprehensible world' (Conklin and Graham 1995, 295) in the political space of the 'shifting middle ground'. These issues are addressed in more detail in Chapter Six.

5.5 The 'up-close' community and the role of symbolic capital

The donor's representation of the associations as profit-led businesses was based on the assumption that it was not their responsibility to respond to the social welfare demands of their communities. It reflected a transnational policy imperative to liberate people to be autonomous producer-consumers in a free market. Bourdieu (1977:177) describes this separation between 'social' and 'market' concerns as 'the unconscious acceptance of a *restricted definition of economic interest'* which is set up in opposition to 'symbolic interests (often described as "spiritual" or "cultural"), and 'reduced to the irrationality of feeling or passion'. Bourdieu's thesis regarding the interconvertibility of economic and symbolic capital is corroborated by the ethnography below.

A local primary school was in risk of losing its two cooks who had discovered that they could earn more on an association workfront and were consequently threatening to leave. For many children in the village, the school meal was the most important - if not only - meal of the day. The local watershed technician, Miguel, called a meeting with all of the association work crews to decide what could be done. Salaries on an association workfront amounted to 6500 escudos per month, whereas the cooks earned 2500 escudos. Miguel calculated that if each of the four workfronts produced an extra metre of contour rock wall terrace per day, then the profit generated could be used to pay the difference in salaries. It was agreed with the cooks that they would only receive the 4000 escudos subsidy when the association had contracts. Miguel claimed that it was still necessary at times to remind the work crews to build the extra metre because they sometimes forgot which risked creating an imbalance in the association's funds.

These gymnastics with association funds reveal the initiative and creativity with which Miguel mediated the internal disjunctures created by the new employment opportunities of the WARD and FFP projects. The need to accommodate the cooks' demands testifies to the interconvertibility of economic and symbolic capital. It also corroborates Gudeman's point that the economy is constituted through local relationships anchored in context specific values. In the words of Barth: 'people interact strategically and accommodate one another in many other frameworks than that of a monetised market' (1997:235). The associations were unable to operate as 'hard core businesses' since they could not free themselves from an implicit expectation that they meet the needs of the whole of the community.

According to the lawyer whom I interviewed on several occasions, associations were connoted with the poor and helpless. 'The state prefers associations,' he told me, 'because the benefits go to society. Associations can relieve unemployment, taking the weight off the state'. The kind of pressure that he was referring to is evident in the case of the state-owned construction company - the National Institute for Rural Engineering and Forestry (INERF). Although it was intended to be an institution with business-like characteristics, INERF had been unable to free itself from the pressure to relieve unemployment, irrespective of the availability of funds. In the wake of the drought of 1994, for example, the number of people employed by the Ministry of Agriculture FAIMOs soared from the 1993 figures of 11000 to 16800 in 1995 (MCE undated:38)[42]

Despite attempts to privatize FAIMO, the legacy of state sponsored development programmes persisted and people still relied upon them for their subsistence. The elite at various levels also depended upon FAIMO for their continued legitimacy: positioning themselves competitively in order to guarantee the continuation or re-opening of state sponsored FAIMO for their constituencies.

[42] These figures are taken from definitive version of the report.

FAIMO workfronts were usually shut down during the rainy periods, as an incentive to encourage people to work in agriculture, and were only re-opened when the rain failed to come. Officially, these emergency FAIMOs were supposed to open in the neediest areas. However, they often appeared to operate in areas where the local council, church or political opposition had managed to exercise the most pressure on central government[43]. The responsibility of dealing with the issue of unemployment in these circumstances also fell upon the associations' shoulders. One of the watershed technicians complained in an OASIS meeting that neither INERF nor the local councils were prepared to offer places on emergency workfronts to people who had worked on the association workfronts the previous year. Candidates had been told that since they were members of an association, the association could give them work. Many of the associations came under increasing pressure to employ more people as a result of the bad agricultural year. Miguel claimed that in his locality even the richer farmers of irrigated land had come asking for work. However, following the criteria used in state run FAIMOs, association workfronts were supposed to give priority to the most needy and only recruit one person per household: another indication of how the associations were expected to function as 'soft core businesses'. In the case of a tree planting FAIMO contract that one association had signed, for example, a member told me that they had decided to give priority to women who were heads of households because the contract was very short.

Another association had programmed double the amount of rural engineering works that DGASP agreed to finance. The watershed technician, João, and association president had consequently found it difficult to resist the pressure to employ increasing numbers of people on the workfronts. João explained to me that the association had also felt obliged to employ more people because the government's emergency FAIMOs had been shut down and many people were left without work. The association had consequently succumbed to the same pressures as those of INERF, discussed above, and ended up employing more people than it had budgeted for. The result was an overall reduction in both the number of months of work and the amount of profit generated. In terms of 'hard core' profitability, the association's decision made no economic sense; unless we are to broaden the definition of 'economic interest' to include Bourdieu's concept of 'symbolic capital' (1977). João justified the decision to employ more workers on the grounds that it was important to build up people's trust in the association. Given the notorious history of the cooperative movement, already referred to above, 'trust' is undoubtedly one of the 'rare goods' that can be included in Bourdieu's list of what constitutes 'symbolic capital':

> [T]he theory of strictly economic practice is simply a particular case of a general theory of the economics of practice. The only way to escape from

[43] During the 1996-7 period of my fieldwork, workers in Santo Antão went on hunger strike in response to the government's closing down of FAIMO workfronts. The workfronts were eventually reopened (Correio 15 1996:2).

> the ethnocentric naiveties of economism...is to carry out in full what economism does only partially; and to extend economic calculation to *all* the goods, material and symbolic, without distinction, that present themselves as *rare* and worthy of being sought after in a particular social formation.- which may be "fair words" or smiles, handshakes or shrugs, compliments or attention, challenges or insults, honour or honours, powers or pleasures, gossip or scientific information, distinction or distinctions etc. (1977:178).

Seen from this perspective, the decisions of the associations to employ more people and to subsidize the work of the cooks are both rational and economic. For even though the accumulation of symbolic capital - trust and the provision of cooked meals - could only be accumulated at the expense of the accumulation of economic capital (Bourdieu 1977:180), it was nevertheless a form of 'credit':

> Once one realizes that symbolic capital is always *credit*, in the widest sense of the word, i.e. a sort of advance which...give[s]...the best material and symbolic guarantees....it becomes possible to grasp the economic rationality of conduct which economism dismisses as absurd (Bourdieu 1977:181).

Conflicting views over the economic rationality or absurdity of investing in symbolic credit is exemplified in the disagreements that emerged over the use of association funds. The finances of each association were audited by Raquel, an expatriate employed by the donor. The watershed technician, Miguel, told me how Raquel had disapproved of the way in which his association had spent money on photographs: an expense which he had no problems in justifying. His words are paraphrased below:

> Miguel told her that you can convince donors with a photograph. The association had sent a photograph of the school, before it was repaired, to UNICEF [United Nations Children's Fund] which had agreed to finance the repairs. Raquel did not like this but the association was free to do as it pleased with its funds. Miguel also had a photograph of the president of the local council in his locality. The president had told them that if they worked the local council would help them. The photograph was proof that he had been there. Photographs are documents.

The photographs taken by the association provide an example of the interconvertibility of symbolic and economic capital (Bourdieu 1977:177). The photograph of the president's visit to the village was a 'valuable form of accumulation' (Bourdieu 1977:179) since it offered the best guarantee within the association's reach that the president's promise of financial assistance would be honoured.

One of the most contentious uses of association funds, which could not be classified under the restricted definition of 'economic interest' of the classical market model, was in the case of an association which lent fifty thousand escudos to an association member to travel to the United States to receive medical treatment. She had fallen off a motor bike and had damaged her spine. The case was brought up by the expatriate Stephen in a meeting with the watershed technicians. He began by asking what would happen if the woman did not return. Stephen said that whilst he could empathize with this kind of social assistance, it was important to realize that spending money in this way would not resolve the associations' problems. The way forward had to be through productive investments. Although this was a rare case, there were other associations that spent part of their funds on 'non-productive activities', such as Christmas parties for children and for the aged. One of the associations was actively encouraged to organize a Christmas party by a national NGO working in the area which specialized in the promotion of 'community development'. This provides an indication of the different kinds of expectations that were placed upon the associations by different development organizations.

Another association had lent four thousand escudos to every member for Easter. The president had assumed that members would be able to pay the money back out of their wages from the new contract for the construction of check dams and water tanks that the association was due to sign with DGASP. However, the market price of sand and cement went up unexpectedly and so the association had to submit a new budget to DGASP. By the time the paper work had been completed, the owners of the land no longer wanted the rural engineering works to be carried out because it was too close to the rainy season. Fifty people were consequently left without work and members were unable to pay back their loans. The president, Benjamim, told me that members would only be in a position to pay back the money in the following year, when new association workfronts would be opened. He added that no interest would be charged on the four thousand escudos loans due to the difficult situation members found themselves in.

The change in the market price of cement provides an example of the wider relations of interdependence that had an impact upon the associations. In terms of Gudeman's (2001) model of the economy, it illustrates how the 'Far-distant' market affected the 'Up-close' community' and challenges the neoliberal logic which assumes opportunities that will allow people to pay the loans back. The decision not to charge any interest on the loans is an indication of the association's inability to turn a blind eye to the welfare needs of its members. This issue was brought up by a Cape Verdean project consultant, in one of his reports:

> The question that remains is what will happen to the associations when the food aid[44] finishes or when they have to compete with private businesses

[44] The consultant was referring to the FFP project.

for whom social issues (which the associations despite everything are engaged with) don't count? (Vera-Cruz 1997:6 my translation).

Answers to this question from a 'market-driven' perspective would probably adopt a 'Darwinian' position that holds that weak competitors must simply be allowed to fail (Archer 1994:29). One of the major challenges of the FFP project was to promote 'economic progress', without displaying insensitivity to concerns of 'social justice'. This was an issue that had already been raised years earlier by a consultant for the Watershed Development Project (see chapter Four) who had argued that 'the implementation of contract work risks favoring the most ambitious and productive workers...while possibly discriminating against economically needy people who are physically unable to rigorously comply with the exigencies of the work' (Gardiner 1988:40). In other words the FFP programme found itself in a double bind of telling people that they needed to work harder for the good of the community, thereby making the work too hard for them to be able to carry it out. We have seen in the previous chapter how a number of women claimed that association work was too strenuous for them. The president of Batuque not only appeared to set excessive production targets, but also used employment on the association workfront to create relations of patronage in the local community. Whilst it was difficult for the associations to dissociate the welfare needs of their members from the adoption of a 'market-driven' approach, these same needs could also easily be manipulated to serve the covert interests (Bourdieu 1977) of demagogic leaders. Moreover, as we shall see below, the practice of concealing interests was not restricted to the village level. The need to negotiate the paradoxes of promoting social welfare through market driven development also led the donor to conceal intentions.

5.6. Profitability versus social welfare

The issue of how to reconcile the demands of social welfare delivery with the requirements of productive investment has constituted a central tension in development assistance and social spending (see Midgley 1995). The tension in the efforts of the FFP programme to pursue profitability in the name of social inclusion was reflected in the difficulties that arose in the provision of credit to association members.

The kinds of productive activities that association members were granted loans for included, the itinerant trade – 'rabidancia' – already referred to above (usually the buying and selling of imported merchandise or agricultural produce) and the acquisition of animals (goats, pigs, cows and chickens). The interest rates for these loans had been set at three percent per month, following the recommendations of the donor field director - Peter - who was a specialist in credit. Peter told me that he made no apology for these rates because interest rates from private money lenders in Cape Verde ranged from five hundred to three thousand percent. One of the association presidents, Benjamim, confirmed that three percent was an acceptable rate given the bad agricultural year. He went on to say that if the rains came, the interest rate could go up to as much as ten percent because people would no longer have to buy many of the products which they had presently been unable to grow for themselves. The fieldwork I carried out in 1996-7 was a particularly bad year for agriculture and many animals were dying for lack of pasture. One of the associations had given loans ranging from fifteen to fifty thousand escudos to ten members who had requested credit to save their animals from dying. The government and other organizations were also giving out special loans to help people buy food simply to keep their animals alive.

The issue of credit for income generation was discussed in an OASIS general assembly meeting, in which the field director was also present. As will become apparent below, he chose not to openly voice his intentions in the meeting, for reasons highlighted by Mosse's analysis of the role that ambiguity plays in 'project discourse':

> In project discourse...ambiguity facilitates and helps to maintain consensus, it helps contain varying interests. In project negotiation it is quite common to accept that the language of objectives and strategies mean quite different things to different actors. Indeed, the process of designing and negotiating a project often involves a progressive increase in ambiguity. Over-precise statements have to be replaced. To refuse that space is to kill a venture early on, or to cause serious problems later on (1998:5).

The watershed technician, Hugo, suggested, in the meeting, that the associations establish a means of exchanging experiences so that they could learn from each others' successes and failures. Hugo then spoke of the problems his association had encountered with credit granted to some of its female members for rearing chicken. The women had not yet been able to pay back the money because there were no chicks on the market for them to buy. Peter then asked Hugo if he knew what the real problem was. The problem, according to Peter, was that loans should not be granted for high risk activities.

Sitting on my right was the lawyer (whose involvement with the project has already been discussed above). He whispered something to me about lack of water in Cape Verde whilst the expatriate Stephen, on my left, muttered the word 'marijuana' with a little smile. The message behind both of these comments appeared to be that all of the activities that the associations were providing credit for could be described as high risk. The question that seemed to be on everybody's lips was what could be considered to be low risk in Cape Verde? This question, however, remained unspoken until weeks later when I confronted Peter with it in his office. 'To live in Cape Verde is a high risk activity', was the reply that I had been given from the director of DGASP to the same question. To my surprise Peter replied quite straightforwardly that he did not know. His reply is paraphrased below:

> Peter's concern was that the associations were going to give loans to individuals who would not pay them back. Peter wanted to see the associations in business, functioning as cooperatives, in business for their members, such as buying a truck and commercializing products. The more dynamic associations should put the experiences of the national cooperatives behind them and not be afraid. The money should be used for the business enterprises of the associations rather than granting small loans for individuals. At present many associations were hanging on to their profits because they did not know how best to use them.

I was able to confirm Peter's observation by talking with an agricultural extensionist who worked with a number of associations. She told me that the associations that were located in the more distant villages that had no electricity and little water did not know how to spend their funds because it was difficult for them to conceive of viable investment projects. She also complained that the donor had given very little support to help them identify alternatives.

Peter's response also reveals that the probability of defaulting on individual loans constituted the 'high risk' which he had alluded to in the OASIS meeting. Unlike the titling programmes promoted by De Soto, discussed in Chapter One, the associations could not take recourse to mechanisms of dispossession or eviction should a member fail to repay a loan. If Peter had made his views explicit, in the meeting, it would probably have created uproar, since the provision of credit to association members constituted one of the major incentives to encourage membership. 'Individual credit' and 'social support' were listed as some of the benefits of creating an association in hand-outs produced and distributed by the donor to encourage watershed residents to adhere to the programme. This apparent contradiction in donor policy reflects the dilemmas posed by the pursuit of productivity in the name of social inclusion. As Mbembe points out, in his discussion of the challenges faced by the economies of continental Africa, the issue of how to legitimize social exclusion has not yet been resolved:

> With or without international creditors, Africa must face up to the challenge of the competitiveness of its economies on the world level. This challenge cannot be victoriously met in the current world economy without an increase in productivity-that is, in the last analysis, without putting in place effective ways of constructing inequality and organizing social exclusion…As for the shift to democracy, this will depend on how the debate on whether social exclusion is legitimate is historically settled (and in favor of which social forces); otherwise, how will such exclusion eventually be legitimated and codified institutionally? (2001:57-8).

The transition from targeting employment to targeting productivity in the FFP programme was still at a relatively early stage and hence could not be seen openly to legitimize social exclusion. That Peter did not endorse personal loans was nevertheless reflected in the donor's failure to include income generation in its training programme. Association members were only receiving training for soil and water conservation techniques, book keeping and management. This omission was raised in a technician's report which advised the donor to pay more attention to income generation given that this was the ultimate reason for working with the associations (Vera-Cruz 1997:5). Income generation was the purported key to independence from the state. Yet, as the ethnography below illustrates, employment continued to be the major concern of most association members. In other words, the FFP programme had transferred the responsibility of meeting demands for employment from the state to the associations but it had not managed to reconcile the conflicting demands for social welfare and productivity. The case material in the second part of this chapter examines how these conflicts were negotiated at the local level.

Part II

5.7. Targeting the deprived or the deserving?

The FFP programme was due to terminate in 2001; however, the programme was renewed in 2002 for another four years. During this period, the donor adopted a 'graduation' policy: a euphemism to refer to the termination of donor funding for associations that had been programme beneficiaries for five years. This was the case of an association called 'Funaná'[45] which could no longer depend upon the programme to secure SWC contracts with the state. The philosophy behind this policy was to force the older associations that had gained experience in SWC contracting to stand on their own two feet and actively look for finance elsewhere. This released funds to provide the opportunity, for new associations, (such as Batuque), to enter the programme. By 2005, when I conducted more fieldwork in Cape Verde, fifty associations had 'graduated' from the FFP programme, twenty of which from the island of Santiago, including the association, Funaná.

The first time I met Alice, the president of Funaná, was on a mountainside in the interior of Santiago Island where she was sowing maize and beans. Alice told me that the association no longer had a contract and that consequently members had stopped going to meetings and no longer paid their monthly subscription fees. This year, some members had managed to find work on local

[45] The real name of the association has been codified. 'Funaná' is a genre of music with its corresponding form of dance, originating from the interior of Santiago Island, characterized by the use of the accordion.

council work fronts instead. I introduced myself as a researcher interested in the differences between association and state-run work fronts, thus opening the door, in subsequent visits, to speak with members of the community. For the most part, there was a lack of awareness of the donor's 'graduation' policy. Many of those whom I spoke with claimed that the association had closed down (*asociason dja finda*) or that it had come to a standstill (*asociason sta paradu*). Several women whom I asked why the association was no longer in the project, shook their heads, claiming that they did not know why. One woman stated that it was because the finance had run out, another that it was because the project had come to an end. Manuel, the work crew chief of the local council FAIMO, was the only association member I spoke to who replied that it was because Funaná had already been a project beneficiary for five years. The numerous occasions in which villagers stated that the association had closed, illustrates, how, in their eyes, if the association could not employ them, then it no longer existed.

In the discussions that I initiated over the difference between association and state-run FAIMO, hardly any members referred to the association fund. Many of them stated that the work was harder, payments were timelier and the quality of the structures built superior to that of local council FAIMOs. A walk through the village was sufficient to testify to their better quality, through a comparison of local council and association contour rock wall terraces. The latter had been built a year ago, in the final year of the contract and were in a better state than the former, which had only been completed a month ago. These were uneven, much higher in some places than in others and made with a mixture of very small and big stones. I asked a member whether some of the workers could have been the same people and she assured me that this was the case and went on to explain that the difference lay in the motivation of workers. In local council work fronts, all they had to do was turn up to earn a day's work. These work fronts did not have production targets nor were they inspected; it was just a matter of earning money.[46] In the case of association work fronts, it was the workers' responsibility to make a formal submission of the work completed[47], so everything had to be right. Similar points were made by other female association members whom I interviewed. One woman claimed that the major difference between state and association work fronts was that the latter had production targets – 5 metres per day[48]. People were unanimous in telling me that association workfronts were better; but, it was only due to my insistent questioning that the existence of an association fund was eventually identified by a few members as an added advantage over FAIMO. In these circumstances, the fund was merely referred to as a source of social assistance; I was told how money had been spent to improve the conditions of the local school kitchen.

[46] 'Es ka ten metrajen, ka ten fiskalizason. É só pa ganha dinheru'.

[47] 'Intrega obra'.

[48] Compare this to the 8 metre production target imposed by the president of Batuque (see previous chapter).

The intended transition of the FFP programme, from targeting employment to targeting productivity, was not reflected at the local level where conflicts over whom to employ constituted the major concern of association members. Many of their accounts of the history of Funaná testified to a progression from open to restricted access to employment. Given that the associations could not employ everybody, the criterion of employing the neediest in the community was gradually substituted by the exigency that workers become association members in order to qualify for a place. Membership thus became a form of 'symbolic capital' or 'credit' (Bourdieu 1977) that guaranteed employment, irrespective of income levels. As the examples below illustrate, the poorest were excluded from the opportunities of upward mobility that association membership provided.

Alice, the current president, claimed that the first two presidents of the association had restricted membership but that when she became president she told the local delegate of the Ministry of Agriculture that more people wanted to join and he advised her to open the door to everyone. This account differs to that of Clara, the association accountant, who explained that the association began by giving work to members and non-members. This changed in 2001 when the previous president, Luís, agreed to admit new members. From then on, you had to be a member to obtain a place on a work front. Felisberta claimed to have become a member in 2000 because she had worked the previous year and had been told that if she wanted to continue working she must become a member. She had to pay a total of 3100 escudos (subscription and monthly fee) to join and decided to pay in order to keep her place on the work front. António recalled that-non members were not given work and that he was told if he wanted a place, he had to become a member; but, he could not afford to pay the fees[49]. This contrasts sharply with the case of Alice whose salary permitted her to gain a place. When she first joined the association, she was already working as a cook at the local school, earning 5500 escudos per month. Alice managed to obtain permission from the school manager to arrive late so that she could also work on an association work front. When Alice was voted president of the association, a full-time position paid for out of the association's REW contract, she found a woman to replace her at the school until the contract had finished. Alice then began to earn 20000 escudos a month and invested the money in considerable improvements to her home. She sent food prepared in her home to the school manager on various occasions whilst I was with her, anxious to guarantee her readmission to the school kitchen. This occurred in September 2005, despite protests from the substitute cook who was ousted from her position. As a result of the FFP programme, the association had provided Alice with the opportunity to more than triple her income and had prevented people like António, who could not afford to become members, from earning any money at all. In this respect, the aim of

[49] Temudo (2008) gives similar accounts of community members in other localities on the island of Santiago complaining that they could not afford to become association members and were thus excluded from association work fronts.

the FFP programme – to pursue profitability in the name of social inclusion – appeared to have failed. Wealthier village residents were also able to use their status as association members to employ relatives or friends.

Domingos lived in a comfortable house and was one of the few village residents who had electricity in his home. He was a founding member of the association and having lived in Germany for a number of years, claimed that he had never needed work but that he was happy to become a member to help develop the community. Membership, had, nonetheless, bestowed him with the power to employ a relative on an association work front. Domingos recalled that as an association member with the right to work, he had given his place on a work front to his niece, Clara, who was not a member and in need of work. He went on to complain that a year later, when Clara became affiliated, she and others refused to permit him to give his place to his adopted daughter, on the grounds that she was not his real daughter. Then, the new president, Luis, abolished the practice of place swapping altogether and only members who had paid their fees qualified for work. The deprived were consequently further deprived.

Underlying conflicts over who to employ were divergent interpretations of equity or social justice. To give priority to the poorest, an argument originally formulated by the donor, emphasized want and need; based on the social welfare model of development assistance. The argument of giving priority to members was founded on the market-driven model and lay emphasis on merit. Since employment was scarce, members held that those who had paid their fees deserved to be given work. In the case of Batuque, discussed in the previous chapter, the reader may recall how the president's strategy of employing non-members was contested by a member who raised the rhetorical question of what was the point in paying her subscription fee? Implicit in her words was the notion that she had 'invested' in the association and should receive a fair return.

The transition, in Funaná, from open to restricted access to employment appeared to go against donor recommendations of employing the neediest members of the community; however, these recommendations had been made in the early years of the programme. In later years, the donor chose not to interfere with the associations' criteria for worker selection. It is noteworthy that reserving employment for members who had paid their fees also addressed the donor's long-term concerns of financial sustainability, by increasing the amount of money deposited in the associations' funds. But, the majority of Funaná members were too anxious about their short term employment needs to concern themselves with the association's fund.

This section has demonstrated how the restriction of employment to paying members, exacerbated existing inequalities at the local level. Nevertheless, it was not only the issue of fees, per se, that determined access to employment. We have seen in the case of Batuque, in the previous chapter, that non-members were given priority over members. What was more significantly at stake, in both cases, was the differential access of social actors, not only to material capital, but also, to the symbolic capital (Bourdieu 1977) which enabled individuals to manipulate their local contexts in order to produce the best possible outcomes for themselves. Thus Mbembe's (2001) celebration of the bargaining skills of the postcolonial subject must also be treated with caution: the less access the postcolonial subject has to symbolic capital, the less skilled he or she is likely to be. I spoke to residents from both villages who claimed to want nothing to do with their local association because it only served to line the pockets of a few individuals. Their dismissal of the associations as vehicles for the personal advancement of a selected few also raises the theoretical question, who, in this context, is the postcolonial subject? Rather than think in terms of an essentialist category, it may be more helpful to adopt the notion of subject roles, referred to in the previous chapter. The degree of access to symbolic capital is context specific and an individual's bargaining skills will consequently vary accordingly.

The sense of indignation from being excluded, implicit in the criticisms referred to above, made by some of the villagers, stands in stark contrast to the public celebrations of community participation that I witnessed, during an exchange that took place between the two associations. The members of Batuque reproduced donor discourses in their representation of themselves to Funaná as a role model of participatory development and used Funaná as a foil to construct the public version of their success. My analysis of the case material below deconstructs this strategic essentialism and reveals that the associations were not so different to each other after all.

5.8. The success story of Batuque

The idea of an exchange visit with Funaná had occurred during the Batuque general assembly meeting described in Chapter Four. The president had suggested that since they had intended to carry out an exchange with another association, then they should make the most of my presence and choose an association that I was in close contact with. I explained that there was only one other association…The members of both Funaná and Batuque took up the proposal with enthusiasm.

The exchange took place in the village for a whole day[50] and served as a means of sharing experiences related to their involvement in the FFP project. Each association spoke about its practices, knowledge and experience: about the options made concerning their soil and water conservation contracts, about the use of their funds and about the future of the associations. The exchange was also a social event marked by food, drumming and dance.

[50] 28 August 2005

The president of the host association, Funaná, requested my help to prepare the contents of the formal part of the exchange and we consequently held a preparatory meeting with members in one of the classrooms of the village school. Around twelve people attended. The president's lack of 'bargaining skills' in the 'conceptual market-place' became evident in the way in which she addressed her peers. Alice declared that they had to decide what they were going to say to their visitors on Sunday. Offering no suggestions of her own, she added, 'It is not just for me to talk, is it?' followed by a prolonged silence in which no-body spoke. I eventually passed on the suggestion from the president of Batuque that both associations give an account of when they were created and of what their objectives and plans for the future were. The ensuing discussions produced disagreements over the year in which Funaná had been created. The distinction between an additional work front and a legalized association was not clear to all of those present. Some members claimed that Funaná had been created in 1998 whilst others disagreed, recalling that they had started to work in 1997. The legal constitution of the association appeared to have been an irrelevant process that had not involved or affected them. Paramount in most people's minds was the year when they had started working.

The insignificance of the legalization process for Funaná members also transpired during the exchange, in stark contrast to the alleged experience of Batuque which the vice-president presented in detail. Alice had asked the president, Alberto, how Batuque had found its partners. Affirming that the motivation for setting up the association was not to create employment, Alberto gave the official account of Batuque's history already described in the previous chapter. Egídio, the vice-president, built upon his account, by stating that the association was born from people who were lost and had nothing. They had no well, no water, no school, no social centre...but now they were in the FFP project. Some had thought it was not worth it, but they had never given up hope.

Egídio then enquired into the history of Funaná and this resulted in a public discussion of the differences between the histories of the two associations. The passage below that describes an extract of the discussions that took place, illustrates how Funaná served as a foil for Batuque to construct the official version of its history. Funaná is portrayed as a 'puppet' of exogenous intervention: created out of the sole purpose of celebrating a soil and water conservation contract with the state. Batuque is conveyed as a role model of endogenous development:

> Egídio says that he would like to know about the organization of Funaná. 'How did you start off? There may be some lessons for us'.
> Clara, the accountant of Funaná, replies that the former president came round knocking on people's doors asking if they would like to create an association for which they had to pay 500 escudos. He came from another village, saying that he had finance from the programme. They had a meeting

on the 2nd March and from then on they met every month…
Egídio expresses surprise. 'So you signed a contract and started working without sorting out your statutes?' Clara nods her head. Egídio insists, 'Has Funaná appeared in the 'Official Bulletin'[51]?' No reply.
The president of Batuque intervenes. 'I think Egídio is not satisfied with your reply. He wants to know if your association was created out of your own initiative…'
He is interrupted by Manuel, another Funaná association member. 'I was told the president kept the money for himself, so I wasn't interested in joining'.
'The association came from outside, it wasn't spontaneous', remarks the president of Batuque.
'The basis of our association is different to yours' exclaims Egídio. 'We decided to come together and analyse our situation, you copied ideas from elsewhere. This difference between us may account for the bad state you're in[52]. If you had a more solid base, things would be clearer and you would know what to do. We began without a meeting. We thought about our situation first…then we called a meeting and analysed the statutes together to see if everybody agreed. At that time we had no work crew chief, no check dams. We existed for 5-6 years without any project. Our basis is different to yours…'
Clara says 'Lots of people didn't want to pay the 500 escudos because they were suspicious….'
'This is why we have come to a standstill,' exclaims Manuel, 'our association president has already told you that we have no project for the future…'
…Egídio describes in detail the history of Beta's legalization process, concluding with the remark 'you responded immediately to the invitation and began your activities without thinking or discussing things together'.
Clara replies in a low, dry voice 'Since we had already begun, we decided to make the most of it'.
Egídio smiles, 'they began subsidized, because they already had a contract.' He then addresses Funaná members directly. 'In one sense, this was good because you had money, but now you mustn't just wait for funding. You must come together, not just to earn money, but out of friendship…forget about the money…You need to help your community to move forward. Regain the trust of your members. Don't keep anybody that was involved with the first president's embezzlements…'

Perhaps the most striking aspect about the above exchange is how donor logics became entangled with community logics. Alberto and Egidio's words mirror the people-centred development jargon of 'bottom up', 'authentic', 'spontaneous' participation. By capitalizing on the limited experience of Funaná, their representation of the history of Batuque corresponds to the ideal,

[51] This is a reference to the legalization of the association.
[52] The term used in Creole was "situason mariadu".

textbook model of participatory development. According to this account, there was no outside interference or engineering of social relations. The history of Funaná serves as a foil. It represents 'bad practice' and ultimately failure; thus emphasizing and enhancing the qualities of Batuque as an authentic association. Egídio's testimonial reference to the involvement of members in the discussion and approval of the association's statutes also contributed towards the representation of Batque as an ideal role model of participation. The urging of Funaná members to come together 'out of friendship' instead of 'to earn money' mirrors Gudeman's arguments regarding the importance for the community of valuing mutuality for itself rather than for the creation of wealth (2001:140).

It is important to emphasize that Egídio was speaking out of his own personal experience. He was totally unaware that the initial motivation for creating Batuque was identical to that of Funaná: the promise of financial assistance. The few people in the know had never told him about the role played by the UNDP (see Chapter Four). Alberto preferred to keep this knowledge to himself because his alternative account enhanced his image as an 'authentic' active community leader. Júlia, who had overheard the conversations between Alberto and the UNDP aid worker, chose not to say anything because she did not want to damage the good name of the association. She may never have told me, if I had not communicated to her my desire to probe deeper. Since the vice-president of Batuque was unaware of the initial material motivations for creating the association, as far as he was concerned, his experience of 'bottom up' development had had no outsider, donor influence. The association had emerged naturally; it was demand-led instead of supply-led, like Funaná. Neither does the existence of the alternative history invalidate the meanings that Egídio attributed to events which had concrete effects. They gained a social life of their own that passed unchallenged during the exchange in which the representation of Batuque as an ideal model of successful development took root. Nonetheless, this is not to say that Egídio was an unknowing dupe. He was also a knowing accomplice in the representation of Batuque as an exemplary model of participatory development.

Egídio's portrayal of cooperation and goodwill between Batuque association members contrasts sharply with the internal power struggles, discussed in the previous chapter. The reader will recall that association members accused the president of secrecy and patronage in the selection of workers and of driving them too hard. Egídio had also criticized Alberto, in a general assembly meeting, for failing to involve association members in the identification of new REW and had convened a meeting to demand more transparency in association finances. The president had also refused to allow Júlia to transfer the nursery to a bigger, under used room in the community centre. Members had also complained to me that they had not held a general assembly meeting for over six months. None of this was knowledge for widespread distribution; in the exchange, Egídio exhorted Funaná members to follow their example and work together out of 'friendship'.

This strategic positioning of Egídio reveals another level of 'entangled logics' in which he both challenged the president for his undemocratic behaviour and, like Júlia, colluded with him in order to preserve the association's reputation. Júlia could not afford to challenge the president directly because he had complete control over the community centre where she worked on a daily basis in the nursery. In the words of Mbembe (2001:103), their relationship was best described as 'convivial': she had to 'share the same living space' with the president. During the exchange, Júlia publicly thanked the association for improving her working conditions and praised the president, indirectly, for his fund raising abilities.

The ways in which Batuque members produced the success story of their association also bears similarities to the account given by Mosse (2004, 2005) of how the success of a development project is actively produced by subordinate actors. Mosse argues that development projects 'need "interpretive communities"' able to maintain coherent representations that coincide with dominant policy models regardless of the actuality of events in the field (2004:640, 646). The associations also needed 'interpretive communities' to sustain consistent representations of their organizations as genuine role models of endogenous development. The underlying difference between Batuque and Funaná was in their differential capacities to manipulate the interpretation of events.

The contrast between the presidents of Batuque and Funaná could not have been greater. On the day of the exchange, as she sat at the high table in front of about sixty people, the president of Funaná adjusted the jar of artificial flowers on the table so that it covered her face from the public gaze. When the president of Batuqe asked Alice what projects the association had in mind for the future, she replied that it had none because members no longer came to meetings and the association had come to a standstill. Later on in the discussions, Alberto invited Funaná to enter into partnership. He argued that the two associations needed to study ways of taking advantage of the first dam to be built in Cape Verde since it was located in their geographical area and due to be completed very soon.[53] Alice did not react to his proposal and it was only Manuel, the work crew chief of the local council FAIMO, who later on in the day, thanked Batque for the offer to help Funaná out of the blind alley it had found itself in[54]. The secret of Batuque's success appeared to lie in the bargaining skills of its president. The members of Funaná looked upon him with admiration.

[53] Both associations were in the same geographical area of Santiago Island. The dam was completed in 2006.

[54] 'Nu mesti obi forma di saída. Nu sta nun beku sen saída'.

5.8.1. The life of a ('worldly') cat

Batuque's 'recipe' for successful development, spelled out during the exchange for the benefit of Funaná members, did not mirror the FFP project's emphasis on the importance of making productive investments but appeared to elucidate instead Bourdieu's point regarding the interconvertibility of symbolic and economic capital (Bourdieu 1977:177). During the exchange, when Júlia expressed gratitude for the improvement in her working conditions, she exhorted Funaná members to 'open their eyes' and follow their example. Júlia explained how the president had contacted the prime minister and now the children no longer had to sit on the floor; they had toys and materials to work with and there was no more rent to pay. She told Funaná members that they should not be ashamed to ask for financial assistance. 'You must just keep on asking. I ask everybody. We are a non-profit making association. We are poor and deprived and we must show our needs in order to move forward[55]'. Her portrayal of Batuque was far from the vision that the donor field director had in mind in 1996, of the emergence of business-like enterprises, described in the first part of this chapter. Nonetheless, the strategy that she advocated required the development of particular 'bargaining' skills which the president of Batuque appeared to have mastered very well.

Alberto attributed the 'success' of the association to what he called its 'cat's life' (*vida di gatu*). 'We have become cheeky' he replied to a direct question from a Funaná member of how the association found finance 'we live the life of a cat'[56]. The president had used the same phrase with me on another occasion in which he had proceeded to reproduce the cat's characteristic crying sound to demonstrate the significance of the phrase. 'Not a week goes by', exclaimed Alberto in the exchange, 'when we don't go knocking on someone's door'. Alberto did not conceive the financial sustainability of the association in terms of developing business-like characteristics[57], but, rather, in terms of developing the necessary skills in order to know how to manipulate and 'bargain' with social welfare needs in the development market-place. Members of Funaná were aware that Alice did not possess these skills. The superior 'bargaining' powers of Alberto were commented upon in private during the exchange, in comparison to those of the president of Funaná.

During lunch, Felisberta came to talk to me, stating that all members needed to pull together to get the association Funaná back on its feet. 'We can't expect Alice to do it on her own', she said, 'it is asking too much of her. She

[55] 'É só pidi, pidi, pidi. Nos é pobre, koitadu, nu mesti mostra nesesidadi pa bai pa frenti'.

[56] 'Dja nu sta diskaradu: vida di gatu'.

[57] The president of Batuque referred briefly to the association fund, claiming that not all of the money could be spent on these kinds of exchanges and members still had to meet to decide how they were going to use the funds.

needs people to accompany her, especially since she is a woman. People will start talking and think that she has a man'.

Felisberta's comment reveals an awareness that Alice needed to be more proactive in her approach; to leave the village, to develop more contacts. In the words of Ferguson, she needed to become 'worldly' and 'well-connected' (2004:394). However, Felisbertas's observation that rumours might spread that she had a man also suggests that the problem was not just Alice's lack of bargaining skills but more importantly the local structure of gender relations that had prevented her from developing and applying them. Alice was a mother of six children. The father of the first three children had 'died'[58] – a local term she used to refer to his absence. He had immigrated to Portugal while she was pregnant with their third child and never made contact again. The two eldest children no longer lived with her. The father of the youngest three children had also 'died' although he still lived near by, having abandoned Alice for another woman.

At the end of the formal part of the exchange, whilst the drumming and singing got into full swing, Sara, another Funaná member, came to ask me how I thought the day had gone. I gave an encouraging reply and she exclaimed that at least it had been a different kind of day. But if Sara had had things done her way, then they would have presented the association Funaná in a more positive light. 'But we don't know any better: we are just a group of poor people. There is no one living here like the people from Batuque. We had someone, but he went to America. We don't have anybody here that is capable.'

Sara had made a discreet attempt to improve the image of Funaná before the exchange. We were sitting in her house days beforehand when she declared, in Creole, that she would like to ask me a favour. She wanted to make a small speech on Sunday to welcome the visitors from Batuque; without my help, she could not do it. Sara explained that no-body else would think of doing this but it would be a nice gesture. She also asked me not to tell anybody. Would I help her to write it? She got up and went and fetched a piece of paper that had a speech written on it that she had given when the President of the local council had come to make a formal inauguration of the provision of electricity to the village. A local teacher had written the speech for her. This time, he was too busy planting maize and beans because it was the rainy season. The speech, written in Portuguese, concluded with the following words: "Long live the president, long live work, long live development" (*Viva o presidente, viva o trabalho, viva o desenvolvimento*). I asked her, in Creole, if she was sure she wanted the speech to be in Portuguese? Why not make it in Creole? Sara replied that she did not know how to read and write in Creole. In an attempt to give her voice, I suggested Sara speak in Creole and I would try to translate and write down her words in Portuguese. Sara frowned claiming that she could not do this on her own be-

[58] 'El dja mori'.

cause she did not have enough education. If she knew how to do it, she would not be asking for help. It became clear to me that I would have to produce the speech and that it was a matter of prestige to make it in Portuguese. Sara's desire to speak in Portuguese not only served to create a sense of formality but also to express an idiom of social difference by distinguishing her from the rest. I consequently suggested the following: 'Funaná is very happy to welcome the members of Batuque here today. We hope that you will enjoy your stay and that we will be able to exchange lots of ideas which will be helpful to the development of both of our communities'. Sara suggested that the beginning be altered to 'In the name of the association of Funaná I welcome you…' and that the end of the speech conclude with 'Long live Funaná! Long live Batuque!' She gave her welcoming speech in Portuguese and the rest of the discussions during the exchange took place in Creole.

Although Sara appeared to be setting herself apart from Funaná members, by expressing awareness of their limitations and by taking the initiative to make a speech in Portuguese, she had also included herself as someone in need of assistance. The comments made by Felisberta may also be interpreted as a plea for help from members of the much larger section of the 'grassroots' which, as I suggested in Chapter Four, had far less chance of becoming, in Ferguson's words 'worldly' or 'well-connected'.

The 'well-connected' president of Batuque brings to mind the figure of the 'indigenous cultural mediator' referred to by Conklin and Graham (1995), who, in the attempt to secure international support, is obliged to produce essentializing discourses that meet unrealistic, Western expectations of 'authenticity'. We saw in Chapter One how Conklin and Graham use the term a 'shifting middle ground' to refer to this transnational arena of unequal relations. If the mediator's actions fail to correspond to idealized Western expectations, then international support may diminish. That Júlia and Egídio were also aware of the stakes is evident in how they colluded with the president to produce an idealized image of their association during the exchange with Funaná. But this did not prevent them, on another front, from challenging and resisting their president. My use of the concept of a 'shifting middle ground' proposes that we also pay attention to these smaller negotiations of power that occur at such a fine level of resolution that smaller types of inequities and exploitation may easily pass unnoticed. Let us return to the case of Batuque which offers a compelling example of this.

5.9. Behind the success story of Batuque

One of the major differences between Funaná and Batuque, emphasized by Egídio, in particular, during the exchange, was the lack of awareness of Funaná members regarding the legal procedures that had been followed to constitute their association. The founding members of Batuque, appeared, on the contrary, to be informed and engaged since we are told that they had discussed and approved the statutes in public meetings before they were made legally binding. Yet, their participation in the discussion and approval of the statutes had not in itself been sufficient to safeguard their rights. Members had unwittingly contributed towards the consolidation of the president's hold over power by agreeing to the adoption of statutes the implications of which they had not fully understood. Although they had been advised by a lawyer; he was also a relative of the president. There were a number of irregularities in these statutes, compared to the standard statutes of other associations. For example, the statutes stipulated that the members of the board could be voted in for three year periods that were 're-newable'[59]. The president was also given the power to 'punish' members. As we shall see below, it was the seemingly insignificant statute that authorized the president of the board to call general assembly meetings which was the most effective in securing the president's monopoly of the association's resources. In accordance with standard association statutes, it was the responsibility of the president of the general assembly rather than the president of the board, to convene these meetings.

The impression transmitted during the exchange of high levels of informed participation contrasted with local accounts. In 2007, Batuque members remonstrated that they had not held a meeting for over six months. As already noted in Chapter Four, the president claimed that he was too busy working and consequently had no time to call meetings. Egídio and Júlia were also waiting for the president to convene a meeting in order to repeat their requests for more transparency in the finances of the association. When I suggested to Egídio that somebody else convene the meeting, he explained that, according to the statutes, this was not possible. They were thus unable to call the president to account. Commenting upon this and other irregularities in the association statutes, Egídio added that when they had elaborated the statutes they didn't know any better. 'You could say we were oppressed. We were coming out of a one party state. And the priest who helped us to draw up the statutes was the president's nephew'. Whenever I asked the president, Alberto, if I could have a copy of the statutes, he claimed not to have one at hand.

The statutes conferred the president with the power not only to decide whether or not to call a meeting but also who had the right to attend. A number of villagers complained that they had been excluded from meetings because they had not been 'summoned' by the president. Those who did not receive a letter from the president did not attend general assembly meetings. Their way of protesting was to abandon the association altogether. The president was thus able to take advantage of the statutes to exclude and silence disgruntled members; however, most members were not even aware of the statutes. Even if the irregularities were corrected this was no guarantee that villagers' perceptions of the president's role would change. The most common form of protest for Batuque mem-

[59] The president was re-elected each time there were elections.

bers had been to discreetly dissociate themselves from the association; but, this also left the president's hold upon power and resources intact. Very few chose to challenge the president directly. There was also a third way which I have already referred to above: the maintaining of 'convivial relations' (Mbembe 2001). During a more prolonged stay in the village in 2007, I discovered that it was not only Júlia who had adopted this strategy. The work crew chief, Pedro, who was also a member of the board, never challenged the president but told me in private that he was constantly urging members not to leave the association because this was tantamount to playing into the president's hands. Júlia admitted to me that if it wasn't for Pedro's persuasive insistence she would have already left the association as well. Other villagers told me, in private, that if the association had another president they would join or renew their membership; however, this sounded more like wishful thinking. None of them seemed to think that it was in their hands to confront the president or dismiss him from his position. According to the president of the associations' umbrella organization, OASIS, with whom I discussed the case of Batuque, it was common for association members to view their presidents as all-powerful. 'Any member can convene a meeting,' she told me. 'The assembly has more power than the president. The problem is that they are not aware of the power that they have'. In accordance with Bourdieu (1977), members were mired in 'doxa': taking their president's power for granted without questioning its legitimacy. As for the president, he based his legitimacy on the market-driven model of development: he was so busy pursuing profitability, supposedly for the benefit of the association, that there was no time to attend to such 'secondary' matters as convening meetings. The aim of the donor was to pursue profitability in the name of social inclusion. Participation in meetings was consequently deemed important, as revealed in the following extract from the programme proposal (ACDI 1996b:44-45):

> One of the main strategic objectives of USAID is to encourage the empowerment of people, especially the poor. A principle technique employed in doing this is to decentralize decision making. The watershed associations created under this project are paradigm democratic institutions which will be making decisions on the location and type of rural engineering works to be undertaken. They will also carry out actual construction of the REWs and afforestation activities and will guarantee that the works are maintained. This directly and forcefully addresses AID's (sic) strategic objective of promoting democracy.

We have already seen in Chapter Four how, member participation in decision making was sometimes overridden by donor funding requirements; meeting the donor's quota of rural engineering works (REW) for the financial year took precedence over these social objectives. The president of Batuque provides an example of how 'local cultural mediators' could manipulate the tensions between market and social driven objectives in order to legitimize their own undemocratic decision-making processes. My uncovering of the success story of the association also reveals what else goes on behind the efforts of local development actors to maintain a coherent, legitimising representation of their actions and events (Mosse 2004, 2005). Friends in public turn out to be foes, formal expressions of gratitude veil relations of domination, resistance and uneasy 'conviviality', displays of competence and goodwill in the elaboration of association statutes mask inexperience, lack of knowledge and manipulation.

5.10. Raising member awareness

The concern that the FFP project had put too much emphasis on REW was raised by a new expatriate field officer whom I interviewed in 2005. In an attempt to resolve the tensions inherent in the project between market and social driven objectives she articulated them in the language of capacity building and described the 'graduation' policy to me as her worst nightmare. She argued that it made no sense to cut off finance from the associations without first assessing and strengthening their internal capacities, claiming that the associations had lost a lot of time since the beginning of the project. Their exclusive focus on REW had diverted them from their main remit: community development. It was the role of the associations to represent the interests of their villages and she expressed concern that the associations were benefiting some members at the expense of others. The tanks built by the associations, for example, should bring some kind of benefit to all of their members rather than just to those who benefited directly with irrigation for their crops. The money belonged to all of them. What about neighbouring associations that also wanted to build tanks but did not have a contract? They needed to make sure their voices were heard so that they too could get access to water. The programme needed to invest more resources in capacity building for the associations. The team was already trying to redress the balance by introducing new training material so that members learn the basics of what an association stood for. 'Associations are the same all over the world', the project officer exclaimed to me during one of our conversations. This constituted a major change in emphasis compared to nine years ago, when the implementation of the programme was based on the market model. New training materials were now being prepared, which, according to Cape Verdean donor personnel, were long overdue. They claimed to have identified training needs years before with the previous expatriate teams but the internal constraints of donor budgeting had been unable to finance them. The training was also open to associations that were no longer beneficiaries of the FFP project.

The training provided was consequently extended from SWC techniques and accountancy to include ideas for the use of association funds. This was intended to help members look beyond their individual concerns of securing a place on a work front and to invest in the long term potential of their associations. That the majority of members viewed the associations primarily as a source of employment on a work front constituted a major concern for the new expatriate team because it conditioned the motivation for members to participate in the association. Without a SWC contract, the majority were not interested in investing their time. In many cases, the overriding concern of employment on a work front also overshadowed any public discussions of the finances of the associations. In order to increase the levels and quality of member participation, the donor consequently paid trainers from the women's council of OASIS, who had in the early years provided some from training for associations, to provide additional training to raise the awareness of members of their rights and obligations. An experienced trainer, Isabel, involved in the FFP project since 1995, told me that initially the training had been carried out in teams. Now, there were so many associations in need of training that the team decided to split up in order to be able to reach more associations. My description of some of these sessions illustrates the creative ways in which Isabel negotiated the tensions between the market and community realms. As se shall see below, the contents and contexts of the sessions were not entirely within the donor's control. Although the approach adopted by her colleague, Maria, served as a channel for the transmission of door policies, Isabel's approach to awareness raising invoked the ideas of both donors and community while undermining powerful interests on both sides.

5.10.1. Money matters

The trainers from the women's council of OASIS were equipped with handbooks, prepared by the donor, written in Portuguese which described in detail the functions of the different bodies of an association. Separate sections described the rights and duties of the general assembly, the board and the fiscal board. On the occasion described below, Isabel invited me to accompany her to drop in on her colleague, Maria, who had asked her for some support.

The training took place in one of the classrooms of the local primary school. When we arrived, it had already begun. Maria was standing in front of eighteen men and women, members of the local association, who were spread out throughout the classroom, sitting on wooden benches in front of low desks. She was reading from the handbook in a loud, slow voice in Portuguese. The body language of her audience transmitted boredom and indifference. The whole scene appeared to correspond to Freire's (1970) critical description of teaching practices, expressed in his metaphor of 'banking'. The teacher transmits knowledge to the students by making 'deposits' which the student receives without any critical reflection. Maria had now begun to talk in Creole about paying membership fees. As soon as Isabel came into the room, the dynamics of the training session began to change:

> Isabel and I sit down and Maria carries on talking. I see the training handbook is on the desk in front of me. She says that the fees are for paying for

photocopies or for transport for the president to go to a meeting. "Is he/she going to pay for it out of his/her own pocket"? Maria asks rhetorically, "of course not". "The association money is for this kind of thing. If members don't pay for a period of 6 or even 3 months then they are out. Do you understand?"
"Yes", they all reply, like the chant of schoolchildren.
"Let us take a break for our visitors to introduce themselves".
Isabel shakes her head and screws up her nose. "Carry on" she says.
Maria insists. "But I don't know this lady".
Isabel ignores her, telling her to ask if they have all paid their fees and then proceeds to do so herself. Everyone laughs and many people shake their heads.
"Oh I see," exclaims Isabel, "so you all say you understand, but you haven't paid your membership fees, why not?" More laughter fills the room and a woman replies with another rhetorical question:
"How can we pay, if we haven't got any work?"'
'How much is it'?
'One hundred escudos per month[60]'.
'And you can't pay that? What happens if the president comes to visit your children's school for the day? You go and buy nice clothes for your children to look impressive[61] and you spend a lot of money. Isn't that so? But it is just for one day. And you can't find 100 escudos to give once a month for the association? Those who don't pay have to leave. It is better to have 20 people who comply than 100 who do not. Then when there is work, the association will give it to its members'.

Although her insistence upon the importance of paying membership fees addressed donor concerns of increasing the amount of money deposited into the associations' funds, Isabel's words did not reflect the outlook of the current expatriate team. She reduced the significance of association membership to a means of guaranteeing employment on a work front and actively promoted the exclusion of those who failed to pay their fees, based on the conviction that everybody could afford to pay. In this respect, Isabel's approach appeared to corroborate the point made by Mbembe (2001) of the need to come to terms with institutionalized ways of excluding people under a market-driven model. Yet, in another training session that I attended, Isabel stated exactly the opposite; claiming that the association was for the benefit of the whole community and not just for individuals. On this occasion, she coincided with donor policy by stating that members need not work on association work fronts because priority should be given to the neediest. The ambiguity of her approach reflects the on-going tensions in the objectives of the FFP project, discussed above, between the market and community realms.

---

[60] During the 2005 period of my fieldwork, 1 euro was equivalent to approximately 110 escudos (BCV).
[61] The term used in Creole was 'bazofu'.

When Maria took over from Isabel, she began to read from the handbook again in Portuguese. Maria concluded her sentences with the usual question, asked in Creole, 'do you understand?'[62] The trainees all chanted 'yes' in unison and blank expressions returned to their faces. From this moment onwards, the training session alternated between monotonous moments of 'banking' in Portuguese and more lively discussions in Creole between trainer and trainees, generated by inputs from Isabel.

Portuguese was spoken in more official contexts of everyday village life and was usually associated with individuals in positions of authority, such as the school teacher and the priest. Its use by Maria, in this context, served to evoke the presence of outsider authority and thus added to the foreignness of the training contents. Isabel knew how to translate the theory from the handbook into relevant everyday practices. The power of her message was strengthened by her use of Creole. She interrupted Maria to compare the general assembly of the association to the catholic mass; there were moments when only the priest spoke and other moments when everyone could speak. In a country predominantly catholic, it was not difficult for members to understand the parallel between the priest and the president of the general assembly. Aware of the importance of raising people's awareness of the need to make their leaders financially accountable, Isabel described the board as an 'errand boy': it could only do what had been approved of by the general assembly. If the owner of a house wants to have a party and someone does the preparations for him, that person will have to report back to the owner exactly what food he bought and how much he spent. In the same way, the board had to inform the general assembly how many contour rock wall terraces, reservoirs, check dams and cisterns had been built at what cost. Isabel compared the fiscal board to the police that stood in pairs on the roads of Santiago Island, waiting to fine the overloaded collective taxis that passed them by. It was the duty of the fiscal board to make sure that the names that appeared on the salary sheets of their CBWF corresponded to actual workers. The board should also present the monthly balance sheets at association meetings so that all members were in the know.

Although there was no guarantee that raising people's awareness of their rights and obligations as members would secure the democratic functioning of their associations, it was evident that Isabel's approach was far more effective than that of Maria's in getting the message across. Her use of everyday examples brought the contents of the training sessions closer to home and the pages of the association handbook to life. In the hands of literate members, caught up in local power struggles over access to development knowledge, the handbook served as a potential tool of empowerment. At the end of one of Isabel's training sessions, an association member commented to her that whilst he appreciated her translation of its contents into Creole, it was difficult to absorb everything

[62] 'Nhos intendi?'

that she had said. He expressed satisfaction at being able to take a copy of the handbook home to study more carefully. Júlia, the president of the fiscal board of Batuque, had also referred to the handbook, in conversations with me, as a useful tool for legitimating her demands for more transparency in association finances. But, for the majority of members, involvement in association life was confined to attempting to meet employment needs. Maria's 'banking' method was unlikely to change this. Her training sessions may even have served to distance illiterate, unmotivated members even further from association life, confirming their perceptions of the irrelevance of membership once there were no more REW contracts.

Notwithstanding Isabel's capacity to translate the contents of the handbook regarding members' rights and obligations into local experiences, the question still remains whether telling people 'how things should be', according to the dictates of an 'ideal' association, was in itself sufficient to empower them. To recall the expression of the president of OASIS, people were not aware of the power that they had. Some of the reasons for this are explored below.

5.10.2 Confronting 'cock's foot'

One of the causes of the low levels of member participation during association meetings was that many people had internalized the idea that to voice criticisms in public was negative and destructive. This was evident in the unease manifested by members, during the Batuque general assembly meeting, described in Chapter Four, when Rogério criticized the lack of transparency in association finances. The lack of public discussion in the general assemblies, regarding the finances of the associations, constituted one of the talking points in another training session that I attended given by Isabel. She provoked trainees by asking them if they knew how much money they had in the bank. In response to their shaking heads, she added, 'They may be robbing you then, you don't know'. Isabel told members that they should demand to be informed. One of the male trainees present replied that the fiscal board of his association had never worked. The current president of the fiscal board was brother to the president of the association and that was already against the association's statutes. He went on to explain that he himself had been president of the fiscal board but it had been impossible to carry out his work because there were so many barriers that he eventually gave up. Members did not know how association money was being spent. A female trainee remarked that if they did ask to be shown the accounts then they were accused of being 'cheeky'[63].

The attempt to introduce clarity in public forums could easily be dismissed as ill-mannered or disrespectful because the people, who made public demands for transparency and accountability, sometimes spoke in ungraceful,

---

[63] 'Diskaradu'.

accusatory tones. Those who protested were usually the ones who had nothing to lose: a farmer, for example, who, in the case of Funaná, was not looking for work and had joined with the expectation of receiving financial assistance from the association. After tiring of paying fees and receiving nothing in return he told me that he would no longer go to meetings because if he went he would have to be out spoken and people didn't like it. Isabel's training challenged the idea of being 'cheeky' by drawing on the concept of democracy, exemplifying how, according to the statutes of the association, all members were equal and free to speak. Yet, members who were more concerned with securing a place on an association work front, or who simply did not want to antagonize their neighbours, tended to keep quiet and talk outside of the meetings. This practice was also frowned upon. Isabel stated, during the training, that criticisms should be made in the general assembly, because this was more pleasant than talking outside meetings. A woman, sitting close to me, muttered 'cock's foot[64]'. I had already heard this phrase, on various occasions in informal conversations, to refer to the practice of making criticisms in private, behind peoples' backs. Attempts to understand the origins of this phrase have left me to suppose that the structure of a cock's foot - bent digits capped with claws - symbolizes the intrigue involved in behind the scenes politicizing.

Whilst it may have been unpleasant to know that members were talking about them behind their backs, the practice of 'cock's foot' also served the interests of association leaders. Following the exchange visit between Batuque and Funaná, it became apparent to me how, criticisms made in private, rather than in the public realm, could provide association leaders with an excuse for not changing their behaviour.

During the exchange, Alice had asked the president of Batuque how much they paid the president, accountant and treasurer. He had replied that before entering the programme they did not have a fixed salary because otherwise they would have spent all of their funds. When Batuque entered the FFP project, they began to receive salaries during the period of the rural engineering contracts. In the months when they had no contract, they did not receive anything. If they needed to leave the village to deal with the affairs of the association, then their transport costs would be paid for out of the fund and they would receive a small 'gratification' sum. During the period in which Funaná had been a beneficiary of the programme, the president, treasurer and accountant had all received a fixed salary all year round. The accountant, Clara, justified this in the exchange by stating that this had been the practice of their predecessors when they took office. Days later, in a private conversation I had with Alice, she brought up the issue of their continuous salaries, stating that if they had any contracts in the future, they would adopt the same practice as Batuque. Alice then commented that she had known at the time that there were members who were against their continuous salaries, but they had never said a word in the meetings. Her comment

---

[64] 'Pé di galu'.

appeared to imply that if members did not make their objections public then she could justify ignoring them. The local practice of 'cock's foot' had served her material interests. The president of Batuque actively avoided meetings in which he knew he could be called to account. Although he was aware that there were some people who criticized him behind his back, their criticisms did not interfere with his plans.

We have already seen in Chapter Four how the vice-president, Egídio, was prepared to challenge the president directly. Unlike Júlia, who had to share the community centre with the president on a daily basis, Egídio was a retired school teacher and consequently had nothing to lose by facing up to the president. In the words of Bourdieu (1977:169), he had 'the material and symbolic means of rejecting the definition of the real' that was imposed upon 'the dominated'. Júlia, reluctant to publicly accuse the president of denying her access to the necessary documents for inspecting association finances, had shared her concerns in private with the vice-president, Egídio. In local terms, this corresponded to the practice of 'cock's foot'. Egídio had then accompanied her to a meeting with the president and treasurer of Batuque to clarify matters. After the meeting, Júlia and Egídio came away annoyed and frustrated because they had both been accused of 'spreading confusion'[65]. Although Egídio had not internalized the view that public criticism was bad, the president had still been able to invoke this idea in order to side step any criticisms. This episode suggests that raising awareness, (or, to use Freire's (1970) term, 'conscientization') does not automatically empower the dominated. Egídio and Júlia were only too aware of the president's strategies; they had not yet managed to counteract them. Moreover, in the case of Júlia, another reason to account for her fear of confronting the president which is likely to be representative of many of the villagers was based on his supposed use of supernatural powers. Júlia, one of the most educated residents of the village, eventually confided in me that she could not rule out the possibility that he may take recourse to magical powers to harm her. The president's wife had become seriously mentally ill and, according to Júlia, since it was public knowledge that he was having relations with other women, some villagers believed that he had wished the illness upon her[66].

Despite the limited effects that raising awareness may have had upon the redressing of local power relations, the focus in the awareness training upon members' rights and obligations served to increase the bargaining powers of local people vis-à-vis the donor, leading some individuals to develop points of view that contravened donor policy. Isabel had also developed her own critical points of view; just as she was prepared to defy local practices, such as that of cock's foot, Isabel was also prepared to confront the donor policies that she disagreed with. One of these was the 'graduation' policy.

---

[65] To be "konfuzentu".

[66] For a detailed discussion of the role of the supernatural in modern day African see 'The modernity of Witchcraft Politics and the Occult in Postcolonial Africa' (1997) by Peter Geschiere.

5.10.3. Challenging donor policy

Unknown to Isabel, the 'graduation' policy was also challenged from within by a new expatriate field officer, working for the donor who, as we have seen above, argued that more resources needed to be invested in capacity building for the associations; only then would they be able to survive the withdrawal of external funding. Isabel challenged the 'graduation' policy for the opposite reason. As far as she was concerned, associations that had managed to strengthen their internal capacities should be given priority funding. She made her opinion known publicly on several occasions, in training sessions and meetings, arguing that it made no sense to withdraw finance from the best associations. Isabel interpreted the donor's 'graduation' policy, not as a means of working towards sustainability, but, rather, as a form of undeserved punishment. She claimed that there were only a small number of associations that functioned in accordance with their statutes. In the majority of cases, three or four people ran the association and the rest of the members were barely involved. It was for this reason that she held that it was unfair to withdraw finance from the few associations that functioned properly. There is, nonetheless, a degree of irony in the fact that on one of the occasions in which she made this statement, it was in a meeting with Batuque members, to praise the working of their association. Isabel, like many other outsiders, had been taken in by the official image of Batuque.

Another occasion, in which Isabel expressed her opposition to the 'graduation' policy, was in a training session in which one of the trainees, interrupted her to claim that if the associations decided to distribute thirty per cent of their profits to members, then there was nothing that the government could do about it. The reader may recall that donor policy had initially sanctioned this practice, in order to motivate members, but that donor concerns over guaranteeing the financial sustainability of the associations had led field staff not to recommend the practice any further[67]. Isabel replied that the donor did not want the associations to distribute the profits but the trainee insisted that the associations were autonomous and that it was up to the general assembly to decide. His response demonstrates how he had taken on board her earlier point that the general assembly was the most important organ of the association, equivalent to the head of a human body. To become aware of their right to exercise their rights increased the bargaining powers of association members, vis-à-vis the donor.

The trainee's defiance of donor recommendations was left in the air and Isabel made no attempt to account for the donor's point of view that distributing money to members did not produce profits nor guarantee the financial sustainability of the associations. The rhetorical question, 'what will happen when the

[67]The practice was also problematic for legal reasons, since, according to Cape Verdean legislation, only cooperatives could distribute a percentage of their profits to members.

white men leave?' posed to me by Peter, the donor field director in 1996, to justify his insistence upon the associations investing most of their funds in income generation activities, did not merit discussion by Isabel as she carried out her training in 2005. In Isabel's eyes, sustainability was not so much about finance, which nearly ten years later continued to be secured by the donor; it was more about what I would call 'social sustainability': motivating members to take an active role in their association. The more active they became, the more they deserved to continue to receive financial assistance. After all, who wanted 'the white men to leave'?

5.11. Success in the development market-place

In the first part of this chapter, discussions of the role of symbolic capital in association life could be seen as verging on the adoption of a 'harmonious' model of the community; the detailed case study of Batuque and Funaná demonstrates how this is not the case. If the associations were unable to operate as 'hard core' businesses because they could not dissociate themselves from the employment needs of community members, this in turn created new conflicts over access to employment as particular individuals gained the power to decide who to employ. Although the recommended criterion for hiring workers was to give priority to the neediest members of the community, neither Batuque nor Funaná appeared to have followed this recommendation. The president of Batuque exploited people's employment needs for his own personal gain. In the case of Funaná, membership became an obligatory criterion to qualify for a place; a criterion that excluded the poorest since it required the paying of fees. This criterion was actively promoted by Isabel in one of her training sessions to encourage members to pay fees and it was played down in another session, in which she stated that priority should be given to those most in need. The inconsistencies in her approach mirrored the balancing act inherent in the aim of the Food for Peace Project: to pursue profitability whilst promoting social inclusion.

Local interpretations of success also differed to the official market-led goals of the project. In the eyes of Alberto, it was about becoming a skilled 'beggar': not being ashamed to live the life of a cat. As far as Isabel was concerned, success was measured by the quality of the internal dynamics of association life which should be rewarded with the continuation, rather than the withdrawal, of external assistance. Success in the development market-place was about maintaining relations with paymasters and winning the approval of existing (or potential) benefactors; hence the importance of projecting a favourable image of the association. The underlying difference between the associations of Funaná and Batuque lay in their differential abilities to maintain, in the words of Mosse (2004:640) 'coherent representations regardless of events'. The official version of Batuque's history – a textbook model of 'endogenous development' - was intended to guarantee the exact opposite: the continuation of exogenous assistance. The actuality of events that contradicted the official history became a well guarded secret. Although their motivations for keeping quiet certainly differed, their silence reveals how both Júlia and Alberto understood the fundamental paradox of development aid: to obtain external assistance communities must appear to be independent sites of 'authentic' 'endogenous' development. Julia's silence reveals something more compelling. She was aware that securing external assistance for the potential benefit of the community also entailed concealing from the public eye the inequality and oppression which she and her peers were subjected to. The promise of development aid can thus be seen to produce disempowering effects at the micro level.

The best part of the meetings, negotiations of common ground and power struggles that I have described between different development interlocutors in the Cape Verdean ethnography were located in the 'core', or in the 'core' of the 'periphery': in the capital Praia, in district capitals, in NGO offices and association workplaces in the village centres. But what proportion of the 'grassroots' had access to these 'nerve centres'? Relevant here is Hoogvelt's discussion of a 'new social-core periphery hierarchy' to refer to the emergence of a privileged elite as a result of the intensification of capitalist integration which, she claims, excludes around sixty per cent of the populations of developing countries from reaping any of its benefits (cited in Kothari, Minogue and Dejong, 2002:32). Whilst we could adopt this concept of a 'new social-core periphery hierarchy', to refer to the forms of social exclusion created by the 'development encounter', this may lead us to make an overly static interpretation and runs the risk of contributing towards the creation of more rigid stakeholder categories.

The case material of the last two chapters has provided a number of examples of the new kinds of social relations and subject roles that emerge as a product of development interventions. Low ranking FAIMO workers receive donor training and become development insiders: community leaders, agricultural extensionists and association accountants. New employment opportunities, created at different levels, sustain livelihoods and in some cases, raise standards of living, often for limited periods of time. Success in the development market place is a precarious accomplishment and the possibility of exclusion is always close at hand. The new kinds of relations and roles that are made possible by development programmes and projects are inherently unstable; association presidents can be voted out of office[68], agricultural extensionists may find themselves without an employer at the end of a project cycle, association workers discover no new contract has been signed and there may be no funds available to pay the association accountant.

Igoe proposes that we study these new kinds of relations and subject roles by adopting the idea of interpenetrated networks that integrate vertically and laterally, shifting sometimes in unpredictable ways and which include and exclude

[68] In February 2007, the association of Funaná was preparing to vote for a new president.

people accordingly[69]. There may also be differing degrees of inclusion and exclusion. Consider the case of Alice, who became a new 'development insider' when she was elected president of Funaná. Local perceptions of gender roles and her lack of 'bargaining skills' had excluded Alice from the vertical networks necessary to create new funding opportunities for the association. In stark contrast to Alberto, the president of Batuque, she was part of the 'grassroots' that is mired in doxa; not knowing how to mediate between her local community and the national and international realm of government and donors. The silence of Alice compared to the eloquence of Alberto, during the exchange, testifies to this. On the other hand, at a finer level of resolution, we cannot conceive of Alice as being completely excluded from the 'development encounter'. The president of Funaná gained material benefit from her position in horizontal networks: manipulating her silence and indeed the silence of association members to her own advantage.

The case of Alberto suggests that individual characteristics, such as worldliness (Ferguson 2004) or being skilled at bargaining (Mbembe 2001) constitute significant indicators of an individual's potential for inclusion. The case of Alice reveals the importance of investigating silence: shyness and lack of 'bargaining skills' may constitute an unreliable indication of an individual's potential exclusion from the benefits of development aid. The issue of how to study the inclusions and exclusions generated by the 'development encounter' is addressed in the following chapter.

[69] Personal communication, 28 May 2007.

Chapter Six

Bargaining in the Development Market-Place*

6.1. Introduction

> Precisely because the postcolonial mode of domination is a regime that involves not just control but conviviality, even connivance - as shown by the constant compromises, the small tokens of fealty, the inherent cautiousness – the analyst must watch for the myriad ways ordinary people guide, deceive, and toy with power instead of confronting it directly (Mbembe 2001:128).

> The adherence expressed in the doxic relation to the social world is the absolute form of recognition of legitimacy through misrecognition of arbitrariness, since it is unaware of the very question of legitimacy, which arises from competition for legitimacy, and hence from conflict between groups claiming to possess it (Bourdieu 1977:168).

One of the commonest critiques of Bourdieu's theory of practice is that there is little scope for agency: it denies the dominated classes the capacity for interpreting and acting upon the world in a non-deterministic manner. This is because they are mired in 'doxa'; taking the social world for granted without questioning the dominant worldview. Any awareness that they may have of the existence of alternative views is shaped within the confines of what Bourdieu calls the 'field of opinion' which determines the degree of any questioning that takes place. Scholars have challenged Bourdieu's theory of misrecognition by demonstrating how subordinate classes are conscious of the nature of domination (for example, Abercombie et al 1980 and Mann 1973 cited in Garnham 1993). Scott's 'Weapons of the Weak' (1985) elucidates the nuances of peasant resistance which bear similarities to Mbembe's description above of how ordinary people 'play' with power in the postcolony.

Central to Mbembe's description of the postcolony is the relationship of conviviality between the 'dominant' and the 'dominated'. Outright opposition or resistance is not a viable option. Popular humour, on the other hand, deflates power and obliges it to face up to its own vulgarity. Mbembe examines numerous examples from the African postcolony of how state power is ridiculed and consequently disempowered. Playing and having fun allows ordinary people to

* An earlier version of this Chapter, entitled 'Up for Grabs, Civil Society in a Field of Conflicting Representations: a Case Study from Cape Verde' appears in 'African NGOs, Donors and the State: Between a Rock and a Hard Place' (ed. 2005) J. Igoe and T. Kelsall, Carolina Academic Press.

go through the motions of conformity to official rituals and rules, such as 'wearing uniforms and carrying the party card, making public gestures of support and hanging portraits of the autocrat in one's home' (2001:108) whilst, at the same time, stripping officialdom of its majesty and strength. However, for the government, laughter or simply indifference is tantamount to blasphemy and sacrilege, as Mbembe illustrates in his description of the beating of a man in Kenya by the police for failing to honour the flag (2001:109). The postcolonial subject has consequently learnt to adapt his or her behaviour in accordance with the different public spaces that make up the postcolony; in the words of Mbembe, he or she has learnt to 'bargain in this conceptual marketplace' (2001:104). Thus, postcolonial relations between the state and society are imbued with pretence and theatrical performance as social actors negotiate and manage their multiple identities (Mbembe 2001:104).

The question that remains is whether these insights into the agency and creativity of the dominated classes require us to jettison the concepts of misrecognition and doxa altogether. I would argue that this is not the case, since to do so would contribute towards the building of another rigid dichotomy: total awareness versus total unawareness. It may be more fruitful to think in terms of a 'shifting middle ground' between these two polar ends. Such an approach will not provide an all-encompassing theory to account for the relationship between structure and agency; however, it may help to generate a more nuanced analysis of the nature of relations of power and inequality within the 'development encounter'. Foreign aid creates opportunities of upward mobility – 'development outsiders' learn how to play the game and become 'development insiders'. But we should not be too hasty to celebrate their capacity for manipulating power. The game can be played at different levels; some players may take the proceedings at face value, unaware that there are other issues at stake. In this chapter, I look at how the official agendas in a Forum between government and non-governmental-organizations (NGOs) concealed a web of shifting alliances and struggles for legitimacy which cut across the state/society divide. Whilst on the one hand, these shifting alliances may be interpreted in the light of Mbembe's thesis of the nature of the postcolony, on the other hand, the differing degrees of awareness of these 'postcolonized subjects' may also be understood in terms of Bourdieu's notion of doxa. The two are not necessarily incompatible if we relate the practice of social actors to the concept of a 'shifting middle ground'; social actors may be more or less mired in doxa depending upon the context. The 'development encounter' is made up of several public spaces, to paraphrase the words of Mbembe, each with its own logic which can become entangled with each other in particular contexts. The ability of social actors to navigate the field of this 'shifting middle ground' depends upon their bargaining capacities in the 'conceptual marketplace'.

The concept of a 'shifting middle ground' not only describes a transactional space between politically differentiated social actors; it also opens up an analytical space which destabilizes our use of conventional categories. The web of shifting alliances, examined in this chapter, calls into question the validity of conventional models that oppose state and civil society. A number of authors have highlighted the limitations of this opposition by drawing attention to: the disunity of the concrete practices of the political institutions that make up the state (Abrams 1988); the 'elusiveness of the state-society boundary' (Mitchell 1991:78) and the way in which local-level encounters with the state blur the boundaries between state and society (Gupta 1995). The opposition between an abstract idea of a state/civil society divide and the concrete practices that cut across this divide is similar to the opposition Bourdieu makes between maps and paths. Bourdieu describes the abstract map as a 'homogeneous, continuous space of geometry' and contrasts it with the 'discontinuous, patchy space' of the 'paths' of practice (1977:105). This distinction between a map and a path is a very effective means of depicting the way in which the study of practice can challenge theoretical concepts: the 'beaten tracks' rendering the 'theoretically possible...routes' (Bourdieu 1977:37-8) obsolete in practice. The ethnographic material discussed below reveals how the boundaries established by the conventional 'maps' that distinguish the state from civil society were crossed by the 'paths' of practice. Nevertheless, it is not sufficient for the social analyst to reject the concept of a single cohesive 'state' because this is how the 'state' often appears in practice (Mitchell 1991:91). According to Abrams and Mitchell, the task of the social analyst is consequently to examine the practices that construct the *idea* of the state without postulating the material reality of a free-standing entity called the 'state' (Abrams 1988:75, Mitchell 1991:91). In the following section I shall analyse the way in which the boundary between 'state' and 'civil society' has been constructed in the development thinking of postcolonial Cape Verde.

6.2. Cape Verde: from 'state' to 'civil society'

Discourses regarding the role of the state in international development policies can be separated into two broad phases. The first phase is characterised by a deliberate attempt to strengthen and expand the state's capacities. The second phase is characterised by a dramatic reversal of this policy - to reduce the role of the state in favour of markets and private initiative. However, it would be misleading to conclude that this new agenda is an indication of the demise of the concept of the state. On the contrary, this lack of popularity has the paradoxical effect of strengthening the 'idea' of the state. For as Abrams argues in relation to Marxism, to oppose the state is to participate in its ideological construction (1988:70). Relevant here is the populist distinction between 'the people' and 'the state' that informs 'people-centred' approaches to development. The distrust of the state which characterizes these approaches reproduces the distinction between 'state' and 'society' by postulating a corrupt and power-grabbing state in opposition to 'authentic' locals[70]. The failure of state-led 'modernization' development approaches to eliminate poverty has resulted in strengthening the popularity and legitimacy of 'civil society'. The history of Cape Verde since its independence in 1975 provides a good example of these changing approaches towards 'state' and 'civil society' in development thinking.

After the fall of the dictatorship in Portugal on 25 April 1974, Cape Verde's right to independence was recognised by the new Portuguese government in an agreement signed in Lisbon on 19 December 1974 (Foy 1988:34). A government of transition was set up in Cape Verde to prepare for a general election consisting of three representatives of the PAIGC and three representatives of the Portuguese Armed Forces Movement (AFM) (Davidson 1989:124). Although the Lisbon agreement did not exclude the possibility of other parties participating in the election, by signing the agreement with the PAIGC the Portuguese government had in effect recognised the PAIGC as the sole representative of the Cape Verdean people (Foy 1988:34, Vicente Lopes 1996:405). The most prominent anti-independence parties were the Democratic Union of Cape Verde (UDC) and the Union of the People of the Cape Verde Islands (UPICV). According to Davidson, both parties were in collusion with the colonial regime and neither party had any significant support from the population (1989:112).

The results of the general election gave the PAIGC a landslide. The party won all of the seats and formed a new National Assembly which proclaimed the independence of Cape Verde on 5 July 1975 (Foy 1988:35, Davidson 1989:125). In the words of one of the PAIGC members: 'Once the elections were over we put our minds to the creation of the State' (cited in Vicente Lopes 1996:405, my translation). Pedro Pires, Cape Verde's first Prime Minister, recalls in an interview that it was in 1977 - when drought swept once again throughout the whole archipelago - that he felt the full weight upon his shoulders of the responsibility of having to govern an independent Cape Verde: the phantom of hunger was forever in his mind (cited in Vicente Lopes 1996:465). One of the fundamental objectives of Cape Verdean diplomacy was consequently to obtain foreign aid from as many countries as possible (Foy 1988:185). In a speech marking the tenth anniversary of the independence of Cape Verde in 1985, the President - Aristides Pereira - declared that the country's foreign policy was an integral part of the development programme of the state (1985:18 cited in Foy 1988:186). The political leaders also identified mass participation as one of the corner stones for the construction of the state in Cape Verde which served as a justification for the creation of a one-party state. The PAICV's conviction that it should be the main promoter of mass participation is evident in documents prepared for the Second Congress of the PAICV in June 1984:

[70] This binary opposition has already been deconstructed in Chapter Four through an analysis of how 'locals' became state employees.

> In defining the nature of the regime to be installed after independence - a democratic regime based on the action of the masses in the management of its social, economic and cultural life as in the government of the Nation - the Party's programme has defined mass participation as the key-element in the construction of the State....The task of acting as principal dynamizer and organizer of mass participation belongs to the Party... (cited in Davidson 1989:205-6).

Not everybody was in agreement with this position. Criticisms of the decision to install a one-party state were levelled at the PAICV's consequent suppression of an autonomous 'civil society'. Cardoso, for example, claims in his book entitled 'An Assault on Hope' (1993) that the promotion of mass organizations overrode existing forms of participation of civil society such as the publication of journals, newsletters and the proliferation of sport and radio clubs which had emerged during the late colonial period (1993:182). He also points out that the only institutions recognised by the state as NGOs up until 1988 were the mass organizations.

Towards the end of the 1980s the pressure was increasing upon the PAICV to listen to the voices calling for a multiparty constitution, particularly within a world trend of increasing political pluralism. One of the signs that the party was beginning to open up was the coming into force of the 1987 law of Associations which permitted the creation of civil organizations, followed by the decision thereafter to transform some of the mass organizations of the party into independent civil organizations (Dow 1995:12).

Following the defeat of the PAICV in the first multi-party elections of 1991 and the re-election of the Movement for Democracy (MPD) in 1995[71], the concept of 'civil society' became the new political currency of the day. The number of NGOs and associations in Cape Verde increased dramatically. Their activities ranged from theatre, dance, music and sport to funeral savings schemes, assistance for the disabled, protection of the environment and community development. Since there was no separate law for NGOs in Cape Verde, the latter were legally indistinguishable from this wide range of associations and debates began to intensify over how to define what constituted an NGO. Similar concerns have been voiced in both the academic and development worlds. Ways of distinguishing between different organizations include: the kind of work they engage in, their management structures, whom they represent and are accountable to, sources of income and ideologies. Whilst the term, 'non-governmental organization' bestows an identity upon these organizations by default, formal independence from the government has remained the official hallmark of a broad range of non-profit making organizations for which the umbrella term 'NGO' is widely used today. The table below (adapted from Dow 1995:13-14), distinguishes between 'open' versus 'restricted' membership and 'national' ver-

[71] As already noted in Chapter Three, the PAICV was later re-elected (in 1999).

sus 'local' because these criteria reflect the ways in which the classification of NGOs was contested in Cape Verde.

Table 6.1 Non-governmental organizations in Cape Verde

	National Organisations	Local Organisations
Organisations based on the concept of 'open' association	Delegations consolidated in nearly every municipality with a national network of members. For e.g. Caritas; the Red Cross and the former mass organisations transformed into independent organisations in 1991, such as the Organisation of Cape Verdean Women (OMCV). Organisations formed on the initiative of a group of individuals from the urban elite in order to promote development at the national level. Some were expanding their network of delegations and whilst others had only recently been created and were seeking to increase their membership. For e.g. Morabi.	Organisations formed on the initiative of individuals from the urban elite and/or aid donors to promote development at the regional or local level. For e.g. many of the OASIS member associations. Organisations formed on the initiative of community leaders in rural and suburban areas to meet the interests of their own members which ranged from funeral saving schemes to cultural and sport activities, some of which also included local development initiatives.
Organisations based on the concept of a 'restricted' association	Established by a small group of professionals to provide institutional cover for implementing projects. These organisations were not interested in recruiting lots of members. For e.g. Citi-Habitat, SOLMI.	The concept of 'restricted association' did not formally apply to any of the local organisations.

The director of a national NGO, with restricted membership, explained to me that it was important to distinguish between NGOs and non-governmental organisations for development (NGOD). He pointed out that this distinction was not of his own making but was recognised by the international development community. Organizations created for the exclusive benefit of their members were, according to him, 'member organisations' and should be differentiated from organisations such as his which had a national mandate for the professional delivery of development services. Taking the example of a member organisation which promoted development initiatives, he explained to me that it was not an NGOD, according to the international interpretation of the concept, because it only operated at the local level. This distinction was nonetheless contested by some of the 'member organisations' in Cape Verde which also considered themselves to be NGODs. The president of the member organisation in question, whom I shall call Pedro, told me that he was not interested in transforming his 'local' association into a national NGO. He claimed that aid donors preferred to finance associations and to by-pass national NGOs because they believed that the use of intermediaries often resulted in the 'loss' of funds. Pedro went on to add that other donors were more extreme and wanted to finance 'the people' directly. 'But 'the people' do not exist', he concluded with a smile. Pedro was not alone in his perception of how qualifying for donor funding had become increasingly contingent upon establishing the institutional legitimacy to represent the 'people'. Despite his comments regarding donor reservations in relation to intermediaries, it was also clear that there was money to be found in gaining the legitimacy to represent the institutional representatives of the 'people'. An umbrella organization for associations and NGOs already existed, known as the 'Plataforma', to which Pedro's organization was also affiliated. However, its constitution had been affected by party politics which threatened to undermine its legitimacy.

A report commissioned in 1995 for the United Nations on NGOs in Cape Verde states that many NGOs were often identified with the MPD or the PAICV, whichever was the party of the majority of their members (Dow 1995:14). The former mass organisations of the PAICV, for example were still connoted with their political history although they no longer had any formal links with the party. The president of the umbrella organization was also the director of the former mass organisation for women and a number of NGOs refused to join the umbrella organization on the grounds that it was associated with the PAICV. Some of the development NGOs affiliated to the umbrella organization, such as the national NGO referred to above, also wished to limit the access of member organisations to those engaged in development initiatives. Others, more concerned with party politics, were eager to recruit as many organizations as possible to the umbrella organization, irrespective of the nature of their mandates, in order to challenge its alleged connections with the PAICV. The organisations which had refused to join the umbrella organization were known to have close ties with the MPD. The directors of one of these NGOs held influential positions in government and worked on a voluntary basis.

Given Cape Verde's history of a single party state, it is not surprising that the majority of experienced and qualified professionals were state employees. In many cases financial restrictions prevented the NGOs from employing professionals on a full-time basis, so a large proportion of the directors and fieldworkers of the urban based NGOs retained their positions in government and worked on a voluntary and/or part-time basis. These actors were consequently able to secure political capital which placed them in a privileged position to influence both 'civil society' and the 'state'. The following section examines the 'shifting middle ground' as a transactional space between politically differentiated social actors.

6.3. The entangled logics of development contexts

My understanding of the dynamics of the Forum between government and NGOs that took place in the capital of Cape Verde, Praia, in 1997 would have been highly inadequate if I had not participated in the internal preparatory meetings between NGOs, as well as in the preparatory meetings that took place between government and NGOs. The strategizing and conceptual bargaining that occurred in these alternative official spaces could be likened to dress rehearsals for the grand performance of the Forum. Whilst these processes continued within the ambit of the Forum, they were partially concealed by the official agendas of the Forum programme. These constituted the 'field of opinion' (Bourdieu 1997, 168) for the majority of rural associations that were unaware of the alternative stakes which remained undisputed within the Forum.

The extent to which the logics of different public spaces of the 'development encounter' became entangled was brought home to me five months earlier, in a meeting which had ostensibly nothing to do with the Forum. This meeting was organised by the Plataforma within the ambit of a regional programme of the Permanent Inter-State Committee of the Fight against Drought in the Sahel (CILSS). The objective of the programme, entitled Sahel 21, was to engage the civil societies of the nine member countries[72] of CILSS in a series of participatory meetings and Forums at the local, national and regional level, in order to voice their views and reach a consensus on the desired vision for the future of the Sahel. The umbrella organization had been invited by the government to participate in Sahel 21 by organising meetings in different localities of the Cape Verdean islands. The Vice-President of the umbrella organization, Adriano, together with Pedro, had been 'allocated' rural Santiago. Pedro was in a privileged position because his association was member of both the 'plataforma', as well as of the umbrella organization – OASIS[73]. - of the rural associations affiliated to the USAID programmes discussed in earlier chapters. He consequently suggested convening a meeting with the OASIS affiliated associations which took place in the capital of the district of Santa Cruz. People came from all over the island of Santiago, many of whom had only recently become association presidents as a result of USAID's expansion policy.

Before talking about Sahel 21, Adriano made an appeal to all of the rural associations present to become members of the 'plataforma'. He argued that they were all NGOs simply because they were not government, carefully listing all the benefits of membership and arguing that they would find strength in unity. Much discussion followed as the association representatives questioned whether it made sense to join another umbrella organisation when they were already members of OASIS. The managing director of OASIS insinuated to me afterwards that joining the 'plataforma' may make the associations appear 'ungrateful' in the eyes of their American donors. Most of the organisations present had never heard of the 'plataforma'. The few organisations which were members of both OASIS and the plataforma had been created before the inception of the USAID programme and were consequently more well-connected.

---

[72] The nine member countries of the Sahel are: Burkina Faso, Cape Verde, Gambia, Guinea Bissau, Mali, Mauritania, Niger, Senegal and Chad.

[73] Organisation of the associations of Santiago Island.

The confusion caused by the entangled logics of different development contexts can be seen in the case of the watershed auxiliary technician, Emília, who announced in the meeting that she too was a representative of the 'plataforma' and seemed visibly troubled by her apparent exclusion from the preparations for the meeting. It later emerged that she was referring to another 'plataforma', recently created within the ambit of the Sahel 21 programme to represent farmers, for which she had been appointed to represent women (see Chapter Four). A further example of the entangled logics of this mixing of agendas, which had also caused some confusion, became apparent days later when I noted that an association president told me that he was considering joining 'Sahel 21'.

Adriano and Pedro - skilled at managing the entangled logics of different development contexts - had managed to take advantage of this meeting, to serve the 'practical interests' (Bourdieu 1977) of the 'plataforma', which were unrelated to the donor objectives of Sahel 21. Most of the associations present at the meeting were unaware of these dynamics. Both Pedro and Adriano were keen to increase the membership of the 'plataforma' for political reasons already discussed above, especially since they were already preparing for the NGO-government Forum which was to take place later on in the year in which they knew that the representational legitimacy of the 'plataforma' would be put to the test. The 'Sahel 21' programme consequently provided the orthodox discourse for this 'practical interest' which constituted the doxic field of the undiscussed.

6.3.1. Speak or forever hold your peace

The official agenda of the meeting read out by Pedro, was divided into three points: what is Sahel 21; why this reflection now; what are our aspirations and how can we contribute towards the reflection of Sahel 21? Some of the answers given to these questions in Adriano's speech are paraphrased below:
In 1973 there was a terrible drought in the Sahel and lots of people and animals died. Since most of the member countries were independent they decided to create CILSS to fight against drought and desertification and CILSS was given support from Northern countries, especially Europe. Cape Verde became a member of CILSS in 1976…

> The time for reflection has come because the amounts of aid are reducing. Northern donors think that we are not using the money properly. There have been many changes in the last ten years. With the fall of the Berlin wall aid is now going elsewhere and no longer to Africa. This is because independence in the 1960s for African countries has already been achieved. Fifteen years later they said we did not deserve so much support - enough is enough. So Africans were clever and said, 'OK we'll convert to democracy'. Europe considered this to be Africa's second independence. Now thirty years have gone by - what reason can we give? The reason now is giving

> the voice to the people: women, children, the disabled, peasants, rural populations, micro entrepreneurs. The target group is now local communities and social groups.
>
> Studies by technicians are important but we have been told by our ministers that they are not enough because the donors are not happy with this top down approach. When donors come and see that we know nothing about Sahel 21 it looks bad…We can't approve projects until farmers are involved because this is what the North wants. The technicians have written their reports but what do you think? We are two months behind because we have to prepare for an interstate meeting in March. So you must speak in the name of your people. The voice of women has been heard in CILSS, such as in Burkino Faso, but CILSS is not just women. There are four areas in the world that receive more money: women; poverty; aids and drugs. These are the projects that get priority funding now; remember this when preparing your projects…Now we want to gather data to produce a document…the grass roots must speak now because those who give the money say the grass roots have not been consulted. The idea is to elaborate projects and have a clear idea of what we want. It used to be the fight against desertification and then it was training; now what is it? The associations have a clear vision of what they want and this is what the donors are looking for. If you don't talk now it will be a lost opportunity…We need to prepare this document by the 31 January for the national Forum and then there will be a sub-regional meeting in Gambia in March…

Adriano made no attempt to conceal the donor-led nature of aid; on the contrary, he was in a celebratory mood as he catalogued Africa's history of the successful manipulation of donor trends. The 'grass roots' had to be consulted because such was the wish of the donors. There was no talk of participatory democratic values or rights. Adriano's appeal was to the 'practical interests' (Bourdieu 1977) of securing donor funds. The donor's demands were almost construed as whimsical: these were the rules of the game as they stood today and this was the best way to win points. The urgency of Adriano's message – speak now or for ever hold your peace – is similar to the practice of participatory rural appraisal (PRA) which also invites local people to participate in the production of shared, 'fast', palpable knowledge (see Chambers 1994). Unlike PRA, however, Adriano's invitation to speak was unstructured: there were no charts, diagrams or maps for the people to draw. It was Adriano's responsibility to produce a document based on this open consultation with the 'grassroots'. The first person to respond to Adriano's appeal was a new association president, Miguel, who expressed his difficulty in digesting this 'fast' approach towards grassroots consultations:

> Sahel 21 hasn't happened by chance. There is a lack of water, rain and food. Will the creation of Sahel 21 resolve these problems? I represent my

people. I need help to motivate people about the Sahel in my watershed. Will Sahel lessen the difficulties now that you say that the people have to be consulted? As their spokesman, I need to know what will make things better or worse. How can we participate?

Neither Adriano nor Pedro attempted to provide a concrete answer to this specific request. After clarifying that it was CILSS and not the Sahel that had been created, Pedro embarked upon a more general discussion of what had been achieved within CILSS at a regional level before going on to discuss what was achievable in general terms in Cape Verde. His inability to respond to Miguel's direct request highlights the lack of correspondence between the objectives and the concrete realities of grassroots consultations. The transnational donor concern to listen to the 'voice' of the 'people'[74] strengthened the authority of local Cape Verdean NGOs to speak on their behalf without necessarily giving voice to those who continued to be silenced. Adriano and Pedro may have replaced the figure of the international consultant, but they still pursued the same objective: the production of 'fast' knowledge for consumption by transnational donors. They had clearly learnt the 'rules of the game' and had become successful 'development insiders'.

Although he was oblivious to the unspoken dynamics of the meeting, Miguel was the president of an association created within the ambit of a donor programme: he was also learning to take on the subject role of a 'development interlocutor' and as time went on, was likely to become more informed and experienced in responding to donor trends. Miguel and many of the other new association presidents that attended the meeting could be seen as apprentice development interlocutors that were neither totally aware nor totally unaware of what was at stake. The following section analyses the dynamics of the government-NGO Forum which provide a good example of differentiated playing levels.

6.4. Bargaining in a 'conceptual marketplace'

The headline of one of the local newspaper[75] articles that reported upon the government – NGO Forum read as follows: 'Government, NGOs and CSOs [civil society organizations] put their cards on the table'. Given the strategies and counter strategies which I shall describe below, I would argue that some participants kept a few cards up their sleeves.

The newspaper's allusion to game-playing brings to light the significance of Mbembe's characterization of the postcolony described above. The Forum was a theatrical performance based on the logic of 'conviviality'. The more ex-

---

[74] This trend was also reflected in Cape Verde in the 'National Long Term Perspective Study' analysed in Chapter Three.

[75] Novo Jornal Cabo Verde 11 (June 1997:11)

perienced NGO development interlocutors were prepared to go along with the 'rules of the game' in much the same way that Mbembe argues that popular humour allows ordinary people to conform to the demands of officialdom whilst at the same time draining it of its power. Behind the official agenda of the Forum, something unspoken was at stake and actors on both sides of the state/society divide tested each others positions, modified their stakes and negotiated their identities according to the context. Actors that occupied posts both in government and in NGOs managed their 'splintered identities' (Mbembe, 2001:4) by spinning a web of shifting alliances according to their practical interests: depending upon what was at stake they either aligned themselves with their NGO colleagues or strategized against them in collusion with the government.

Around one hundred and fifty people from every island of Cape Verde participated in the Forum, out of which about one hundred and fifteen were members of associations, co-operatives, small businesses and NGOs. Some of the OASIS affiliated associations who had attended the meeting described above were also present. Much of the debate during the Forum focused on definitions: was it necessary to separate this mixed bag of organizations? If not, should the term 'civil society' organizations (CSO) be adopted to include them all?

Other participants in the meeting included a few representatives of international donors, a handful of observers (including myself) and officials from the local government and from the various Ministries. Some of the latter were officially present in the Forum as members of their organizations and not as civil servants. However, this distinction was not always so easily made in practice, as will become evident below.

One of the opening speeches in the Forum was made by the president of the Municipal Council of Praia, who was also president of the Association of the Municipal Councils and member of one of the local Praia based associations which had refused to join the 'plataforma'. During his speech, the President put forward the suggestion that the associations create a strong and broad national federation, arguing that this was as 'an indispensable condition for a common and global intervention strategy between the government and civil society organizations.'[76] For those who were 'in the know', this proposal constituted a challenge to the legitimacy of the plataforma.

By establishing a single policy with a wide range of organizations the government was ultimately refusing to distinguish between them. Organizations such as drumming, carnival, theatre and musical groups were consequently given the same status as organizations engaged in the promotion of development initiatives. Many of the latter were already affiliated to the 'plataforma'. However, if no distinction were made between the different kinds of organizations present in the Forum, then the legitimacy of the representative role of the 'plata-

[76] The contents of his speech were distributed in a handout.

forma' would be undermined and the need to create a more representative body would be established.

The government's justification for its choice of the term CSO is given in one of the preparatory documents for the Forum entitled: 'Regulations for the Establishment of Partnerships between the Government and Civil Society Organizations':

> The government would limit the participation of civil society, if it were to formulate a policy for the establishment of partnerships with civil society which were exclusively applicable to the civil associations that call themselves NGOs. Moreover, the term NGO does not have a "legal status" in Cape Verde, and is used to denominate civil entities which on the whole have the statute of non-profit making associations (MCE undated:2, my translation).

Note that there is no mention in the text of the specific mandate of NGOs for the promotion of development initiatives. Many of the organizations which were engaged in development and called themselves 'NGOs' believed that this mandate provided a justification for distinguishing them from other civil organizations. The government's intention behind introducing the term 'civil society organization' (CSO) was questioned by an NGO member in one of the consultation meetings that took place prior to the Forum:

> What is an NGO? How different is it to a CSO? Are we talking about every private association simply because it is not government? Surely the government does not want to regulate all of this? There is somebody here from the funeral association from the interior of Santiago. I can also see a drumming group, musical groups, carnival groups....The government cannot hope to co-ordinate and give funds to them all. We need to restrict the associations for this law. What are the priority areas? Is the fight against poverty to be given the same priority as groups involved in culture, theatre, music? What criteria are you intending to use to choose some organizations rather than others? This could provoke a lot of social conflict.

The government official denied that the government was trying to put all the organizations into the same bag and justified the use of the term CSO by claiming that the government's concern was to avoid exclusion. He argued that CSOs could also implement development projects and cited the example of a sport club from Porto Novo (Santo Antão Island) which had submitted a project proposal for community development to the Ministry.

The president's suggestion that the associations create a national federation was not part of the official agenda of the Forum which had been set by the Ministry of Economic Coordination. The agenda consisted of three main proposals submitted to the Forum assembly for discussion: a new law to regulate the creation and functioning of NGOs and CSOs; an 'agreement framework'[77] to institutionalize relations between the government and NGOs/CSOs and the creation of a national fund for the support of grassroots initiatives. During the months that led up to the Forum, the government had produced three or four versions of these different proposals. Each proposal was modified after a series of consultation meetings with NGOs and CSOs many of which I was also able to attend.

6.4.1. The proposal for a new law

During the negotiations with the government over the proposal for a new law, the NGOs put up a united front against the government's *apparent* intentions to exercise control over them. I emphasize the word *apparent* because although the government's proposed clauses of the law offer plenty of evidence of the 'control' politics characteristic of single party states, this evidence is not corroborated by the receptiveness of the government officials to the NGOs′ counter proposals. Whilst it may be tempting to interpret the documentary evidence of 'control' politics as an indication of the endurance of the habitus of single party state politics, a closer reading of the dynamics calls for a more nuanced interpretation. My analysis of the events leads me to suggest that the political history of colonial and post-colonial Cape Verde had not provided a sufficiently fertile ground for cultivating the verbal distinction between 'control' and 'accountability'. As far as the NGOs were concerned, their autonomy was at stake and this led them to ignore their underlying rivalries and speak in one voice.

A total of four versions of the proposed law were produced by a government lawyer in collaboration with his colleagues from the Ministry of Economic Co-ordination. The NGOs' reactions to the first proposal revealed a very strong concern that the government wanted to control them. A textual analysis of the document appears to support this interpretation.

With regard to the legal constitution of NGOs, Article 4 stipulated, inter alia, that the organizations had to have at least five years experience in their proposed activity and that they had to submit a dossier requesting 'admission' to a special committee that was composed of five government representatives and one NGO representative. Article 3 identified the Secretary of State for Decentralization as being responsible for the 'tutelage' (tutela) of NGOs. Article 18 stipulated that the 'Ministry of Tutelage' could visit the installations and infrastructures of NGOs, in the presence of one NGO representative, giving at least one week's notice (Unpublished document 1997a:2 -5).

---

[77]The Portuguese terminology - 'quadro de concertação' - has proved to be difficult to translate. The idea behind the concept of 'concertação' is basically to agree, to concert, to collaborate.

The freedom to associate had already been guaranteed during the First Republic under the 1987 Law of Associations[78]. It was somewhat ironic that with the advent of democracy, the first version of the proposed new law should be more restrictive, appearing to take away rights that had already been granted during the late period of single party rule[79]. Moreover, given that the Secretary of State for Decentralization was considered to be the appropriate governmental figure to exercise 'control', the lawyer seemed to be working within the framework of the former one party state. Pedro pointed this out to the government lawyer in one of the consultation meetings which he attended:

> We must not think that the organizations are a form of decentralizing the state. The state decentralizes itself.

An analysis of the changes in the different versions of the proposed law suggests that Pedro's comment did not fall upon deaf ears. The term 'tutelage', for example, was replaced in the second version with the concept of 'partnership'. Whilst this indicated a relinquishing of control, the second version of the document went on to state that the government was the NGOs' 'primary partner and interlocutor' (Unpublished document, 1997b, Article 4:2). However, following more consultations with NGOs and CSOs, the word 'primary' was omitted in the third and fourth versions (Unpublished documents, 1997c, Article 4:3, 1997d, Article 5:3).

Whilst these alterations constituted a 'victory' for the NGOs, a closer reading of the dynamics of the consultation meetings suggests that there may have been a more nuanced issue on the government's agenda than that of control. There were a number of occasions when NGO members challenged the legitimacy of the government's attempt to control NGOs which was always denied by the government officials. Criticism of the government's restrictions upon the freedom to associate, for example, was commented upon in one of the consultation meetings as follows:

> One thing is partnership and another thing is to control right from the beginning the constitution of an organization...The process of constitution has to be free and cannot be conditioned. The government may decide to support one organization over another according to certain criteria, but this is a separate issue and the two should not be confused.

The lawyer's passionate denial of any intention to exercise control over the organizations prompted a defensive reply:

---

[78] Article two of the law reads as follows: 'citizens...may constitute associations freely and without dependence upon any authorization' (1987:6).

[79] In legal terms the proposal was also anti-constitutional. Article 51 of the new constitution of the second republic states: 'The constitution of associations is free and does not require any administrative authority' (1992:2).

> I am speaking in terms of an objective reading of the document. The intention could be something else. I am not challenging you, I am simply responding to what is written in the document.

How is the lawyer's reaction to be interpreted? I would argue that his frustration over accusations of control were due to his inability to communicate what he considered to be legitimate concerns for *accountability*. The word 'accountability' does not translate easily into Portuguese which makes the dividing line between control and accountability harder to recognize. Although I would translate the word 'accountability' by 'responsabilização' or 'prestar contas' the only word I ever heard throughout all of the discussions was 'control'. Consider the words from one of the participants[80] of the meeting quoted below. Is he expressing the desire to control or an underlying concern for the accountability of NGOs?

> If we are going to decentralize from the lowest level NGOs have to be organized within the ambit of the process of decentralization. Projects need to be co-ordinated from top to bottom and from bottom to top - hence the need for the agreement framework. I consequently don't see why you are against the presidents of the local councils presiding the municipal committees (of these frameworks), particularly if the national committee is presided by the Ministry of Economic Co-ordination.....
>
> It is the councils who have experience. NGOs should be given freedom of action but in a first phase, it is a matter of control, the councils should be more involved. This is my own personal opinion.

One of the director's of a national NGO reacted immediately to this trigger by stating loudly and clearly:

> No-body is going to boss about the NGOs. When we submit a project there are presentation norms and control mechanisms in the project.

The limitations of the kind of project 'control mechanisms' referred to by this NGO director and the problems these limitations raise regarding who NGOs are ultimately accountable to, have been discussed in the literature on Northern NGOs (see Hulme and Edwards 1997; Marcussen 1996). Given that this is a contentious issue in the North, where NGOs are already firmly established within a democratic system, it should come as no surprise that the government of a young democracy - emerging from a long history of state control - should also be concerned with the accountability of NGOs. My reading of the events suggests that the necessary vocabulary for expressing this concern had not yet been formulated within the 'universe of discourse' (Bourdieu 1977:168). There may be historical reasons for this - beyond the scope of exploring in this chapter

[80] I was unable to identify which institution this participant represented.

- related to the restrictions imposed by the colonial and post colonial authorities upon the delegation of power in Cape Verde.

An analysis of the dynamics behind the creation of a new law for NGOs reveals the limitations of construing the state as a monolithic entity with unity of purpose. It is evident that the government's intentions cannot be read from the work of the lawyer and his colleagues alone. Why, for example, did the government not assign more (competent?) lawyers to the task of producing a new law? Had this omission been deliberate? A lawyer, to whom I spoke, from the Ministry of Economic Co-ordination, told me that she could not understand why she or some of her colleagues had not been included in the process. Whilst I cannot offer any answers to these questions, I would argue that the questions testify to the multiple levels and agendas of the state (Gupta 1995) which provide further evidence of the analytical limitations of creating a fixed 'stakeholder' category. The way in which the stakes change according to context were exemplified by the national NGO which allied itself with other NGOs in the consultation meetings regarding government 'control' but, as shall become evident below, was also in cahoots with the government in its attempt to undermine the 'plataforma'.

6.4.2. The Agreement framework

The rationale for the creation of an 'Agreement Framework' was to set up a permanent mechanism for negotiation to set the basis for a working partnership between the government and CSOs. The third version of the proposal envisaged the setting up of both national and municipal committees, composed of representatives of central and local government, donors, NGOs and CSOs (Unpublished document, 1997f: 4).

NGO criticism of the 'Agreement Framework' was voiced both in the Forum and in the consultation meetings. Many associations and NGOs disagreed in principle with this proposal, on the grounds that the committees would make relations with the government more rigid and bureaucratic. Nevertheless, there were still intense discussions in the Forum regarding who would sit on these proposed committees because the 'undiscussed' issue at stake was to test the representative legitimacy of the 'plataforma'. Opponents tried out their bargaining skills upon each other in a theatrical performance which for those who were not 'in the know' was taken at face value.

The government had allocated two posts for representatives of the NGOs and two posts for representatives of CSOs. The 'plataforma' argued that it should appoint both of the NGO representatives. However, the two NGOs which had refused to join the 'plataforma', including the national NGO referred to above, argued that this would lead to their exclusion. Finally participants agreed to vote and the ‘plataforma’ won the right to appoint both posts with a large majority.

The NGO directors who had lost the vote were furious and consequently tried to challenge the results by turning the debate back to the contested issue of definitions. Having failed to undermine the legitimacy of the representative role of the ‘plataforma’, they were no longer interested in blurring the distinctions between the different kinds of organizations but rather in accentuating the differences. The NGO directors consequently protested on the grounds that as NGOs they could not be represented by the CSOs.

The moderator of the Forum responded to their complaint by stating that the Forum had already resolved the issue of definitions. It had already been established in a vote that NGOs constituted a subgroup of the CSOs. At this point, the president of the council of Praia - who had made the appeal for the creation of a new federation of CSOs - also attempted to question the legitimacy of the vote. He pointed out that since there was no legal difference between NGOs and CSOs the Forum should respect the fact that NGOs did not exist in juridical terms.

The president of the council of Praia had invoked the law in order to create the impression that he was aligning himself with the ‘up there state’ that existed above local conflicts. As Bourdieu points out, the law serves to legitimize official representations of the state as ‘the site of universality and of service to the general interest’ (1998:59). Yet the president’s argument contradicted the claims of the NGO directors that NGOs could not be represented by CSOs. This contradiction was nonetheless compatible with the practical interest that they shared: to undermine the legitimacy of the ‘plataforma’.

One of the voluntary workers of the national NGO who was employed in the local council of Praia also found herself in a contradictory position in the vote for the representatives of local government in the ‘Agreement framework’. In order to appear consistent in her opposition to the ‘plataforma’ she was one of the very few people who voted against the motion that the Association of the Local Councils appoint the local council representatives, even though she worked closely with the president. Despite all of these efforts, however, the opponents of the ‘plataforma’ failed to overturn the results of the vote. The outcome was a show of strength which was celebrated as a major victory by the NGO members of the ‘plataforma’ who were ‘in the know’.

With regard to the voting procedures, it is interesting to note that everybody present was allowed to vote. This meant that government officials were able to vote upon what should have been an internal NGO affair and vice versa. Neither was the policy of one vote per organization adopted, since there were also various organizations that had more than one member present in the Forum, all of whom were free to vote. Although this lack of rigour with regard to the voting procedures was commented upon later by some participants, it did not seem to be a major issue. After all, as already stated above, many NGOs were against the 'Agreement Framework' in principle anyway. The whole of the proceedings corresponded to Mbembe's description of the postcolony as a 'hollow pretense' or a 'regime of unreality' (2001:108). However, the bargaining over the concepts of 'NGO' and 'CSO' also provided the 'orthodox discourse' (Bourdieu 1977:168) that concealed the underlying political struggles between rival NGOs that cut across the state/civil society divide.

Most of the membership organizations, particularly those based in rural areas had not participated in many, if indeed any, of the consultation meetings and were consequently only partially aware of the strategies that were being employed on both sides. When I later asked the President of one of the OASIS affiliated organizations if he had voted, he replied somewhat dismissively that there was no point. The President claimed that the 'plataforma' was only concerned with administrative issues and that organizations in rural areas were simply left out. There had been no victory or defeat for this association. One section of 'civil society' had remained marginalised from the whole process[81]. Those that did participate in the Forum were easily identifiable since they spoke in Creole whilst urban NGO representatives spoke in Portuguese.

6.4.3. Mechanisms for the creation of a national fund for the support of grassroots initiatives

The proposal for setting up a fund identified the concepts of 'decentralization' and 'participation' as fundamental elements of the government's national programme and announced its commitment to the 'reinforcement of the participation and autonomy of civil society', with specific reference to a programme to support the development of NGOs (unpublished document, 1997e:3-4).

This proposal generated prolonged discussions during the Forum. Some of the CSOs saw no reason to reject government funding. The director of an association for entrepreneurs, for example, spoke in Creole, arguing that the fund could be used as a form of collateral for associations to take out loans. Some of the NGOs, on the other hand, were very critical of the idea, seeming to prefer the current system of signing contracts with the government for specific projects. Their major criticism was related to safeguarding the autonomy of NGOs.

Notwithstanding these criticisms, none of the participants actually voted against the fund and an ad hoc committee was set up instead, to study the matter

[81] Lest we become too mired in 'nostalgic' sympathy for rural authenticity I should add that on a return visit to Cape Verde in 2002 I discovered that this particular association president had immigrated to Portugal taking all of the association funds with him.

further. One explanation that was offered to me, to account for this unexpected turn of events, was that the NGOs had decided that voting against the fund would alienate some of the CSOs from the 'plataforma'. Another possibly complementary explanation was simply that when it came to the crunch, the NGOs could not resist the temptation of government funding.

The moderator of the Forum whom I had interviewed beforehand had been prepared for the strategies and counterstrategies that I have described above. He compared them to rival military operations to seize a contested territory. He went on to explain that both government and NGOs were in competition with each other to dominate the process of the insertion of NGOs into the 'development process'. Due to the preference for NGOs by foreign donors, the government had realized that strengthening NGOs was a means of bringing in more resources for Cape Verde. However, the government did not wish to be marginalised from the process. The NGOs, on the other hand, aware of their institutional weaknesses, knew that although their survival depended upon entering into the 'development process', this could not be done at the margins of, or in opposition to the state. In other words, the relationship between NGOs and government is best understood in terms of the logic of 'conviviality' rather than that of resistance.

6.5. Relations of Power and Inequality

In this chapter, I have tried to provide an insight into the nature of 'local' political struggles to establish the legitimacy to represent 'civil society'. My analysis of NGO-government relations has produced a more complex picture than that of pitting 'civil society' against the 'state'. The ethnography challenges such reified conceptions of stakeholder categories by demonstrating how actors continually modified and negotiated their stakes within and across the state/society divide. That many of the organisations present in the Forum were only partially aware of what was going on, also reveals how theorising the 'intimacies' and 'complicities' of these alliances requires recognition of the existence of unequal power relations within civil society. The existence of internal relations of inequality within the NGO/CSO sector challenges received ideas of a homogeneous, harmonious and emancipatory civil society. It also alerts us against homogenising the postcolonial subject: not everybody has the same capacity to bargain in the 'conceptual marketplace'.

There was such a proliferation of aid projects, funds and seminars that it was sometimes difficult to 'untangle' them from each other. I have already referred to the case above in which participants were unwittingly referring to two different organisations which bore the same abbreviated name: the plataforma, (the NGO umbrella organisation and an organisation for Cape Verdean farmers linked to the Ministry of Agriculture). A similar confusion arose during discussions in the Forum over two separate funds. The government had proposed creating a fund for NGO projects and, during discussions, this fund became confused in the minds of some of the seminar participants with another fund which already existed within the government's national fight against poverty programme. Holding on to one's precarious status as a 'development insider' required a constant honing of skills at managing the entangled logics of these different development contexts.

The dynamics of the local political struggles described in this chapter also raise a number of questions regarding our use of analytical categories. It is tempting to argue that the membership organisations represent the 'authentic' grassroots in opposition to the 'worldly' NGOs. Unlike the NGOs, the membership organisations had had limited contact with the workings of the development apparatus and were consequently less skilled in bending the rules of the game to meet their own needs. Is this what it takes to be seen as 'authentic'? I would argue that it is misleading to conclude that people who are 'mired in doxa' are the only 'authentic grassroots' because this smacks of romantic paternalism: if you lose your 'innocence' you become 'disqualified'. This approach not only denies the grassroots access to knowledge and power but also fails to recognize the mobility between development categories. We have seen in previous chapters how a 'development outsider' may gradually become a 'development insider' and how precarious this role may also turn out to be. Likewise, to be 'mired in doxa' does not have to be a complete or permanent condition: it may be more helpful to see it as contextually determined, occupying a shifting middle ground between total awareness and total unawareness.

So how then are we to theorize the grassroots? Critiques of romantic conceptions of 'community' may be helpful here. It has become commonplace to state that the 'community' is neither homogeneous nor harmonious; why not talk of a *heterogeneous grassroots*? It too is shot through with unequal power relations and conflicts of interest. If we conceive of the grassroots in this manner, then the insights gained into the agency and creativity of the postcolonial subject need not blind us to the smaller and smaller types of inequities and exploitation created by the proliferation of 'development encounters', or to the existence of varying degrees of doxa. We should remember that most of the people who make up the 'grassroots' will never experience the social role of 'development insider', no matter how precarious that role may be. It could also be argued that it is in the interests of those who have secured themselves a role as 'development insider' for them to remain 'authentic' outsiders. Their 'authenticity' is a well-sought-after commodity in the development industry; however, this is not to argue that as analysts we should take their 'authenticity' at face value.

Theorizing the grassroots requires making a distinction between 'grassroots' as a category of analysis and 'grassroots' as a normative discourse that appeals to notions of the 'authentic' and the 'local'; nonetheless, the latter should not be taken lightly. Normative discourses of the 'authentic grassroots' are very important for securing the legitimacy of the work of African NGOs vis-à-vis donors and the state. As Kelsall and Igoe point out, in the introduction to their volume (2005), NGO researchers cannot escape the slippery challenge of elucidating the ways in which normative discourses gloss over the complexities of 'local realities' while simultaneously revealing the ways in which they may ultimately come to shape those realities. Our analysis of universal categories such as 'civil society', 'grassroots' and the 'state' requires us to adopt the stance of the ancient deity Janus whose two faces enabled him to look both forwards and backwards at the same time.

Chapter Seven

Conclusion

I begin this chapter with a vignette from my days at secondary school, where I was fortunate enough to have English teachers whose enthusiasm and sense of adventure transformed the reading of Shakespeare from drudgery into a whirlwind of passion and discovery. I recall, from a reading of Macbeth, our teacher explaining the 'true' meaning of 'in one fell swoop'. He claimed that most people used the term inaccurately to mean 'all in one go', unaware that the adjective 'fell' signified evil. Whenever I hear people use this expression, I remember my teacher's observation with a sense of privileged nostalgia. Although I have been alerted to the original meaning of the phrase, there is no point riding against the tide: the 'true' meaning is also determined by common usage. It is with a similar sense of cautious flexibility that I propose theorizing the 'shifting middle ground'.

My intention is not to offer a precise, fixed, and unambiguous definition of the concept. Throughout the pages of this book I have used the term 'shifting middle ground' in a variety of ways to refer to both a space for struggles over power between social actors and to an analytical approach for overcoming rigid dichotomies. With regard to the latter, I am also aware of the seemingly contradictory applications that I have made of the concept, by simultaneously referring to the 'shifting middle ground' as a 'blind spot' and as a tool of analysis: a close-up lens with a zoom which allows us to capture the fluid, shifting nature of the intersections between polar ends and thus reduce the size of our 'blind spots'. Whilst I may appear to be chasing my tail, the intention behind this use of mixed metaphors is heuristic: to explore the relevance of the concept, from a number of different perspectives, for questioning the use of universal categories both in the practice of development and in the social sciences in general.

Although I have made a point of distinguishing between binary categories as tools of interpretation and analysis and binary categories as normative discourses subject to interpretation and analysis, this distinction needs to be handled with care: normative discourses and tools of analysis can also become mutually implicative. It may consequently be misleading for the social analyst to place him or herself 'above' normative discourses that essentialize events through the use of binary oppositions in order to expose a scientific 'truth'. This is one of the problems encountered in Chapter Four, where I examine processes of othering in everyday life. For example, the juxtaposition of normative discourses, regarding the fatalism of growing maize and scientific discourses which reveal the rational and economic reasons for such a practice, does not in itself invalidate the meanings that social actors attribute to events. And these meanings have concrete effects which are equally important to investigate. Whilst at one level, I am proposing that we question the reliability of our use of generalized conceptions, at another level, I am also arguing that we cannot totally ignore their 'social life': the reality of dualisms must also be taken seriously. The way in which Batuque association members used Funaná as a foil, to represent their association as an ideal model of successful development, mirroring the development jargon of 'bottom up' development, provides another example. Anthropological fieldwork gets 'behind' the 'mirror' in order to expose an alternative history that debunks the myth in development theory of 'demand-led', 'authentic', 'spontaneous' participation. Batuque was not so different to its foil, Funana, after all; the creation of both associations was 'supply-led'. Nevertheless, its public image was consolidated during the exchange, leaving Funaná members in awe of Batuque's apparent achievements.

The notion of 'authenticity' is becoming an increasingly valuable commodity in development politics. In a global context of diminishing aid, Cape Verde's limited natural resources and its consequently extremely high level of aid dependence, illustrate the increasing significance of the 'shifting middle ground' - as a socio-political space of power relations – for the struggle to survive in contexts where people are losing access to the natural resources on which they depend for their livelihoods. The contradictions and tensions inherent in the drive to integrate market growth with poverty alleviation accentuate the urgency of these struggles.

One of the significant features of the 'shifting middle ground' is that it shifts; hence the relevance of conducting ethnographic fieldwork to be able to capture the transitional detail which may become obscured by the effects of external observation. This is not to take the naïve position of advocating the status of 'authentic insider' for the ethnographer; rather, my point is that ethnographic research tends to accompany events as they unfold and thus places the ethnographer in a privileged position to attend to the nuances of social practice. I have attempted to convey these nuances in the extended case studies of Batuque and Funaná by 'slowing down' the analysis, providing a detailed description of situations as they developed at the micro level. This in turn has revealed the importance of paying attention to the significance of the non-spoken; it was in the realm of silence that smaller inequities were to be found. The crowding out of silence with 'coherent representations' produced by communities for donor consumption (Mosse 2004), brings to light the potentially disempowering effects of the promise of financial aid upon the capacity of individuals to challenge inequities at the local level. These representations, which are produced regardless of the actuality of events, serve to silence their silence vis-à-vis the external observations of donor evaluations.

Uncovering inequities and exploitation is not just a matter of seeing through the silence of the oppressed and exposing the illusion of inclusion that their silence may create in public forums. We saw, in the case of Alice, how uncovering inequities may be a matter of exposing the illusion of exclusion that can also be generated by the practice of remaining silent. This brings to light the other side of the coin of Ferguson's argument regarding the need to accommodate a bold and sophisticated grassroots. Timidity, lack of skills in public speaking and inexperience in transnational networks are not always reliable indicators of an individual's incapacity to reap the benefits of external assistance. In other words, the significance of silence is by no means transparent.

One of the premises of this book is that there are exciting parallels to be drawn between the nuanced insights gained in the anthropology of development and those that have been produced in the literature on postcolonialism. In Chapter One, I explored the parallels between Long's actor oriented perspective (2001) and Mignolo's 'border thinking' (2000). So far, most of the explicit references to the relevance of postcolonial literature for development studies have been to elucidate the unequal power relations between North and South. Kothari, for example, claims that, until recently, postcolonial theory has had little influence upon scholars and practitioners of development studies and she welcomes the 'postcolonial challenges to development' (2002:39-40) made by authors such as Escobar (1995), Crush (1995) and Sachs (1992). Without denying the importance of reflecting upon the imperial origins and persisting inequalities of the 'development encounter', I would argue that postcolonial studies still have a lot more to offer, to enrich the vocabulary of our analysis of the complexities of development, than to simply critique 'Western structures of knowledge and power' (Kothari, 2002:39). To trace the changeover from 'colonized subject to aid recipient and from colonial administrator to development practitioner' (Kothari, 2002:36) may help to see how development has been influenced by colonialism; however, it also paints an over simplified picture of colonial and postcolonial relations, by failing to take into account the precariousness of (post)colonial power.

Mohan adopts the kind of approach I am advocating in his article on participation and empowerment in which he claims that the 'recovering of political agency' constitutes a strand of postcolonial studies that 'elucidates the practices of development' (2001:154, 155). By bringing to light this strand of postcolonial studies that challenges 'the premise that colonialism was hegemonic, implying a unity of purpose and totalizing effects' (2001:155) Mohan explores its relevance for an anthropological analysis of participatory research and development. Postcolonial theory does not only reveal the imperial origins of development, it also challenges the establishment of direct correlations between centre/periphery relations – between the Western and non-Western worlds - and the subaltern's lived experience of cultural production and interaction. Colonial history cannot only be explained in terms of the domination/resistance dyad. Quoting Fine (1994), Mohan identifies the need to '"work the hyphen" between dualisms because it is within these intersubjective worlds that meaning, knowledge, and political action will emerge' (2001:164).

The links between postcolonial and development studies are alluded to in the title of this book which adopts Mbembe's concept of bargaining in the conceptual market-place for elucidating what goes on in the field of development. Mbembe's idea that the postcolonial subject has learnt to negotiate and bargain in the face of state power evokes the political agency referred to by Mohan above; however, any metaphor has limited usage. The Cape Verdean ethnography demonstrates how the effectiveness of an individual's bargaining powers are context specific and are also determined by the degree of access to material and symbolic capital. Uncovering inequities at the village level may also render the category of the post-colonial subject somewhat redundant since the focus is no longer on the vertical power games between subjects and the state but on the horizontal power relations between subjects or fellow villagers. The precariousness of success in the development market-place also calls into question the relevance of attempting to establish any kind of category at all. In this respect, it may be more helpful to talk in terms of the new subject relations and roles that emerge and dissolve as a result of the ebb and flow of development interventions.

Whatever kinds of categorization we may use, there is always the chance that we will simplify reality. By referring to a wide range of literature, this book has also attempted to demonstrate the multidisciplinary relevance of applying the analytical tool of a 'shifting middle ground' for scrutinizing our use of analytical categories. Throughout this book, the reader will no doubt have identified 'blind spots' in my analysis. It is therefore fitting to conclude the book with a postscript in which a Cape Verdean colleague is given the first say.

Postscript

Interview on the National Long Term Perspective Study*

Challinor: Now that you have read the chapter, please feel free to give me any comments.

Director of the technical team, responsible for the study (DT): Well, my response will be somewhat limited because, as I said, I didn't have time to go back and consult the project documents which ideally is what I should have done. So you will have to bear this limitation in mind...However, the overall impression that I have is...well...we are dealing with issues that accentuate subjectivity and many times I was left with the impression that in front of this subjectivity there is more subjectivity. When I tried to gain a distance, in order to analyse events, I was confronted with this subjectivity. This is my overall impression. Your analysis needs to be theoretically grounded. What is lacking is a theoretical background on this subject in order to be able to make objective affirmations. Otherwise all we have is one subjectivism against another. This was my main impression...I may be wrong, but that is how it came across to me. All I could suggest is that you search for a theoretical framework to support your points of view; one that addresses the area of prospective studies and all the techniques that are used. I presume that there are academics who write about this.

There is another point where I don't agree with you, regarding the technique that we used. We begin by trying to cover everything, to get a general overview. But I don't agree what you say about our use of hierarchies. It is normal that we should establish hierarchies. It was a conscious decision to abandon certain things on the way, it is part of the technique; otherwise we wouldn't get very far. This is part and parcel of prospective studies. You can't please everybody. This is normal. If there is subjectivity or objectivity in the choice of what is left behind, this is a different matter. But the fact is you have to leave things behind. Anybody who works on prospective studies knows this. Then, for example, when you talk about sustainable development and say that it means nothing to you, it doesn't mean anything to me either. This is obvious. Streams of money are spent on these concepts and everybody pretends to understand. We also have to go with the flow. If you can't beat them, you have to join them!

It is also very important to bear in mind that all of the sessions were recorded; from the very first workshop with youth to the very end, including the one in Tarrfal[82]. We have the tapes and spent a lot of time over them. We obvi-

* Edited translation of a recorded interview conducted in Portuguese in Praia in September 2005.

[82] This is the seminar which is described in detail in Chapter Three.

ously couldn't write everything out but we took the time to listen to all of the tapes from beginning to end before we wrote up the reports and summaries. We used up a lot of tape – of course it is of no interest for people to hear everything. It was all carefully tested in the first workshop with youth. We were aware of the difficulties and took them into account. We were a team of three and worked together. For example, I did not write the summary, but I listened to the tapes to see if it was necessary to add or take anything away. It is important to state that we took the trouble to record everything. This is why it is a shame that we don't have the documents in front of us. Three main reports were produced but there was a total of at least ten. The questionnaire on national aspirations was dealt with by an expert from the group with the critical eye of an external evaluator.

Apart from the three members of the team, the project had a multidisciplinary discussion group comprised of eight people who followed everything closely which we ourselves took the initiative to set up. There was supposed to be an orientation and supervision committee, comprised of fifteen or sixteen people who had already been appointed, but we never managed to get it to function. So we set up our own discussion group instead and this one really worked. We discussed a lot of our work in this multidisciplinary group.

Challinor: Were they the same people?

DT: Maybe one or two were the same. I can even give you their names…When I talk about the reports it would be good if you could read the third report of March 1997 called "Scenarios and Strategies". I don't know if you had access to it. It has an introduction which explains the meaning of the whole exercise, also from a methodological point of view, and if you read it, it would help you to see things differently. For example, even in this report you will see that we talk about a "common interest": there is no such thing as a "common interest"! So what is all this business about consensus? All of this is in there: the conceptual framework and the explanation is all there. In other words the team not only reflected upon its main objectives but also upon the contents of its work. Maybe people who were not involved would not understand, but anybody who was involved would understand because the conceptual framework is there. The last report is very important. You can't talk about the exercise or evaluate it without looking at this report.

Now of course it is obvious that in these kinds of exercises there are always problems. I'm going to give you an example that you yourself cite which constitutes a flagrant example of how politics influenced the exercise: that business of Cape Verde verde (green). We couldn't adopt something that half of the participants were against. What kind of strategy would that be? You could say why not keep it because it is pretty? But this is not possible. We couldn't please one hundred per cent of those present, but we should at least please a considerable majority. If there is a conflict that is clearly political, some like it because their taste is political and ideological and others don't like it for political and ideological reasons; then what are you to do? You have to forget it. It is obvious. You have no choice. Even in normal situations, in normal straightforward development situations. This business about democracy and development, for example, where some people spend their time being constructive and others do nothing but destroy, this is a reality we can not get away from. But if we can avoid conflict, we will, because the people will thank us. This is just to say that all of this is normal…

Challinor: Are you referring to my comment about how politics was swept under the carpet? Are you saying that this is inevitable?

DT: They were always under the carpet. There are things that you are probably not even aware of; far more serious things. For example, just for you to see how you can't get away from politics. Imagine you are a professional; you have to work whatever your individual positioning may be. You have your expertise and you have to be able to analyse these things and to adapt according to circumstances because if you are not competent in your field, you might as well retire.

But to come back to the NLTPS exercise, you are not aware of the most serious thing that happened. At the exact moment when the government was signing the contract for the project with UNDP and the Dutch government, at the beginning of the project, that is to say, in order to get finance, the government had already commissioned the same exercise elsewhere. Do you understand what I am saying? You didn't know? Oh well. So we had to work. This was how we worked. It would be good if you were to find the parallel study. The government in power at the time, I don't know why it embarked upon this study with UNDP and Holland, when in reality it was interested in something else. The government did it just to please, but it already knew exactly what it wanted, it was already decided upon. Do you understand? So the government managed to get finance but in the meantime it already had finance for the other parallel exercise.

Challinor: Was it the same; exactly the same thing?

DT: Yes. Only, naturally, in terms of the methodology it was far less participatory. This is the only difference.

Challinor: And were they carried out at the same time?

DT: At least they both started at the same time. It was also called "Strategies" and I don't know what else. The work was supervised by a Portuguese professor and it was written in three volumes. The most important is the first volume; the remaining two volumes fail to reach minimum standards. And it was this study which gave origin to the phrase "strategy for the dynamic insertion into the world economy". This was what the government wanted. It wanted to justify something that it had already decided upon[83], I don't know how.

Challinor: In other words, it was all decided before hand. Even if you had reached the conclusion in the study that the fight against poverty and social exclusion was more important they would not have....

DT: Exactly, they wouldn't have. They had already chosen their strategy. When we began, when we went to the field, we started in the island of Fogo. I went to talk to the president of the council of Fogo, in São Filipe. He said to me, 'You are doing the same thing as the professor who is here'. Our workshop was scheduled for the following day and he asked me if he could invite the professor from the other study. 'Of course', I said and he invited him. He came but did not stay until the end. So here we had two initiatives, exactly the same, being implemented at the same time.

Challinor: So it was supervised by him and then carried out by local people?

DT: No. He had his team, comprised of members from Madeira, from the Azores...and they also hired a few nationals to produce the second and third volumes which are an absolute disgrace...Do you understand? So they paid another national, I don't even know who it was, who worked for them and they presented their first volume which corresponds more or less in terms of the methodology to our exercise. But of course, we began in June 1994 and finished in March 1997. They did the whole thing in a year.

Challinor: So when you started which government was in power? It was the same government wasn't it?

DT: The same government! The same minister!

Challinor: I don't understand. Why did the government need to do another study if you were already there doing the work with locals?

DT: It's politics! It's politics! Now we are touching upon confidentialities. All that mattered was what a group of two, three, four or five people thought. This is what was important: what came out had to be theirs...If you start taking issue and being ingenuous...

Challinor: Now you have to let me say something. I can understand how you must have been quite angry with my chapter because you must have felt that compared to the other study, yours was much more participatory and here comes a foreigner...

---

[83] The government chose this as the central strategy in a document produced to divulge its main planning options.

DT (laughing): more important than that is that when the professor finished his study he submitted it to the general assembly. The prime minister sponsored the presentation of the study and the government organized everything for its divulgence. The prime minister actually went there to the general assembly!

Challinor: And what about your study?

DT: Our study had to remain hidden. It was a titanic struggle for it to appear. It was better for it not to appear; we were in a position where it was better not to appear. But all of this began in the field. Because basically there were three phases, although there were supposed to be four. But conflict already broke out in the first phase. They didn't have any arguments. So what argument did they use? The government's argument was that it did not have enough faith in the technical team, in the people who had been appointed. Already in the first phase, the government claimed that the team must be made up of people it trusted in.

Challinor: But what about the other team member who was purposely put there by the government?

DT: I knew what was going on and I wasn't against it. I wasn't put there by anybody; I didn't have to fulfil anyone's agenda. They could appoint whoever they wanted to. But I was aware. I knew that it was the minister who wanted him there….

Challinor: So you were trying to work knowing that the government wasn't interested in your study?

DT: It was a matter of personal pride to do what we could. Otherwise there would be no point. It would all be over. This is how it is. But it's not a case about this party or that party; I'm not interested in that. But this is how things are.

Challinor: So it gets in the way of the professional who is not on either side and simply wants to get on with his work?

DT: You have to take sides. You want to try to understand what the other person is saying but you are not allowed to. No, no, no, you can't. What he says is wrong; without analysing what he said and what may be right….

Challinor: I would also like to clarify that the purpose of my study was not to argue that your work was done badly but rather to highlight the limitations of any study that claims to be participatory; to look at the limits of participation…

DT: It's obvious that any exercise that claims to be participatory does not manage to account for everything in all its complexity. We can never achieve this. There are people who talk about adopting a participatory approach, for example, in the case of the Portuguese professor, but just use it as an alibi when in reality there is nothing participatory about what they do. It is an alibi to claim that they have carried out two or three workshops but if you look at the contents of their study, they do not reflect a participatory approach. In our case, of course, we weren't that naïve, but we were serious about promoting participation. You can always get something out of it, although, clearly, there is no scientific method which will guarantee you one hundred percent satisfaction at the end…

…Even after the NLTPS study we carried on using a participatory approach. For example, for the Main Planning Options[84] we adopted a participatory approach for three months; although, of course, we did establish some milestones. In other words, it was participatory, but with an end in view. There are two types of participatory approaches: those where we don't know where it is going to end up and those with established milestones. We say it is participatory, but we know that we want to arrive here. The Main Planning Options were participatory; but there comes a time, when, as an intellectual, you have to pick up your pen, and after all the participation and all the discussion, write the summary and say "this is it" and finish.

You know I have experience of this with the big international aid agencies like UNDP or the Economic Commission for Africa. These regional and international bureaucracies all write in the same style; the way UNDP writes in New York is the same in Addis Ababa. The framework is the same everywhere, that's how it is. So you arrive at the meeting ready to discuss. You bombard them, you argue this is good, this is bad, you show, you demonstrate and at the end they all clap. After two days of discussions, do you think that they are going to change the report that has already been submitted? They don't change a thing; except, maybe, a comma here or there. Since they have already received their per diem, they haven't got any more time to lose. So you go there full of good intentions and end up blowing your top. This is ludicrous! You take the trouble to carefully present your arguments, not a soul disagrees with you and two days later you leave the conference as if you hadn't said a word. The whole thing is like a show, a play to entertain the Greeks. Those who take advantage of the system gain legitimacy by agreeing to minute changes and nothing more. And life goes on. It's a shame, but that is how it is. So what are we to do? When you go to these meetings to discuss and analyse your country, you have to be more 'cool', otherwise you won't get very far. Often we discuss problems just to entertain people. We need to find a way of discussing and following up problems, evaluating and questioning that is actually useful because, otherwise, well, it's like this business of development where we use up a lot of saliva, a lot of paper and ink, but often we are all just playing with each other. We are taking steps back-

[84] "Grandes Opções do Plano"

wards and forwards and backwards again: playing with each other, it's a shame but that is the way it is. Now of course, if within all of this you manage to avoid too much disaster, then you are doing well. You have obtained a good grade.

When I was in the arena, all of this helped me to advance…

Challinor: The arena?
DT: Yes the arena, where the gladiators are. You go after the lights, you look for the lights wherever you can, if you find a light, you go after it: this, for me, is participation.

Challinor: So you would argue that your study was a truly participatory study, taking into account the limitations inherent in participatory processes?

DT: I'm not sure I would go so far. Remember, this was a regional study. The methodology was designed by UNDP and by the regional project "African Futures" which was carried out in various countries. So each country adapted it according to its circumstances, vision and capacities. Based on what I had seen, I concluded that it was a useful instrument and that it could be helpful for Cape Verde and I tried to be loyal to the methodology, but also creative, working in a way that suited me and the team. We played the game. I know it took place in Guinea Bissau, Mali, Gabon, and Ivory Coast. We could even compare the studies to see which one was best. I'm sure that Cape Verde would not be at the end of the list. I'm confident about this and nothing else interests me. My conscience is clear. But it is a shame that the study existed, just for the sake of appearances. Still, something good always comes out of these things. You always discover something that can be of use.

At the end of the first phase there was already a shock. The team was no good. They had no arguments to support this. Really, it was a clumsy way of saying "we didn't choose the team members so we're not interested". This is what they were really saying.

Challinor: So who chose the team members? Wasn't it the government in power?

DT: The team members were not chosen. There was a public announcement, people applied for the posts and there was a jury….But then there was a proposal for someone else to be the team coordinator instead of me…but then when I was appointed…it wasn't easy…there were many things, many things…enough! It's better to remain quiet.

Challinor: I can switch the tape off, if you prefer.

DT: Yes. I think it would be better…

Bibliography

Abrams, P. (1988). "Notes on the Difficulty of Studying the State" in Journal of Historical Sociology, 1. 1 (March), 58-89.

Agrawal, A. and Sivaramakrishnan, K. (1998). "Regional Modernities in Stories and Practices of Development" in Yale Center for International and Area Studies: Working Paper Series, D&E O1 (citations from extended unpublished version).

Agricultural Cooperative Development International, (1995). "Micro-Enterprise Training and Lending Program, Cape Verde, PL-480 Monetization Project Proposal", Praia.

Agricultural Cooperative Development International, (1996a). "Watershed and Applied Research Development Project (WARD) Final Report", Praia.

Agricultural Cooperative Development International, (1996b). "Development Activity Proposal: P.L. 480 Title II Monetization Activity, Cape Verde, Fiscal Years 1997-2001", Praia.

Anderson, B. (1983). Imagined Communities, London: Verso.

Andrade, S. E. (1996). As Ilhas de Cabo Verde da 'Descoberta' à Independência Nacional (1460-1975), Paris: L'Harmattan.

Anthias, F. (1998). "Evaluating 'Diaspora': Beyond Ethnicity" in Sociology, Vol. 32. Issue 3.

Appadurai, A. (1990). "Disjuncture and Diffference in the Global Cultural Economy" in M. Featherstone (ed.), Global Culture: Nationalism, Globalization and Modernity, London: Sage Publications.

Appadurai, A. (ed.) (2001). Globalization. Durham and London: Duke University Press.

Appadurai, A. (2002). "Grassroots Globalization and the Research Imagination" in J. Vincent (ed.), The Anthropology of Politics: a Reader in Ethnography, Theory and Critique, Oxford: Blackwell Publishers Ltd.

Apter, D. E. and Rosberg, C. G. (eds), (1994). Political Development and the New Realism in Sub-Saharan Africa, London: University Press of Virginia.

Apthorpe, R. and Gasper, D. (eds), (1996). Arguing Development Policy: Frames and Discourses, London: Frank Class and Company Limited.

Arce, A. and Long, N. (2000). Anthropology, Development and Modernities, London: Routldedge.

Archer, R. (1994). "Markets and Good Government" in A. Clayton (ed.), Governance, Democracy and Conditionality: What Role for NGOs? Oxford: INTRAC.

Asad, T. (ed.), (1973). Anthropology and the Colonial Encounter, London: Ithaca Press.

Asad, T. (1993). Genealogies of Religion: Discipline and Reasons of Power in Christianity and Islam, London: The John Hopkins University Press.

Bakhtin, M. (1981). The Dialogical Imagination, Austin: University of Texas Press.

Barrows, P. W. (1991). 'The Historical Roots of Cape Verdean Dependency, 1460 - 1990', unpublished Ph.D. diss. University of Minnesota.

Barth, F. (1997). "Economy, Agency and Ordinary Lives" in The Journal of the European Association of Social Anthropologists, 5. 3, 233-242.

Barth, R. (ed.) (1969). Ethnic Groups and Boundaries: the Social Organization of Culture Difference, Oslo: Scandinavian University Press.

Benedict, B. (ed.) (1967). Problems of Smaller Territories, London: University of London/Athlone Press.

Bertram, I. G. and Watters, R. F. (1985). "The MIRAB Economy in South Pacific Microstates" in Pacific Viewpoint, 26, 3, 497-519.

Bigman, L. (1993). History and Hunger in West Africa: Food Production and Entitlement in Guinea - Bissau and Cape Verde, London: Greenwood Press.

Boletim Oficial, (1987). 4 Suplemento, 31 de Dezembro, No.52. Lei no. 28/III/87. "Regula o exercício da liberdade de associação.."(pp 6-8). Praia: INCV.

Boletim Oficial, (1990). Suplemento, 23 November, No.46. Decreto-Lei no. 101-H/90. "Aprova as Bases Gerais das Cooperativas..." (pp23-33), Praia: INCV.

Bordo, S. (1990). "Feminism, Postmodernism and Gender Scepticism", in Feminism / Postmodernism. ed. Nicholson, L. Routledge, New York.

Boserup, E. (1970). Women's Role in Economic Development, New York: St. Martin's Press.

Bourdieu, P. (1977). Outline of a Theory of Practice, Cambridge University Press, Cambridge.

Bourdieu, P. (1985). "The Social Space and the Genesis of Groups" in Theory and Society, 14, 6, 723-744.

Bourdieu, P. (1990a). The Logic of Practice, Cambridge: Polity Press.

Bourdieu, P. (1990b). In Other Words: Essays Towards a Reflexive Sociology, Cambridge: Polity Press.

Bourdieu, P. (1998). Practical Reason: On the Theory of Action, Cambridge: Polity Press.

Brooks, G. E. (1972). Yankee Traders, Old Coasters and African Middlemen, Boston: Boston University Press.

Cardoso, H. (1993). O Partido Unico em Cabo Verde: Um Assalto à Esperança, Praia: Imprensa Nacional de Cabo Verde.

Cardoso Mendes, D. (1995). Desenvolvimento Regional, Praia: MCE.

Carreira, A. (1982 [1977]). The People of the Cape Verde Islands: Exploitation and Emigration, C. Fyfe (ed.), London: Hurst and Company Limited.

Carreira, A. (1983). Migrações nas Ilhas de Cabo Verde, Praia: Instituto Caboverdeano do Livro.

Carvalho, A. Monteiro, H. and Rodrigues, N., (1995). Desenvolvimento dos Recursos Humanos, Praia: MCE.

Cernea, M. (ed.) (1985). Putting People First: Sociological Variables in Rural Development, Oxford: Oxford University Press.

Chabal, P. (1983). Amilcar Cabral: Revolutionary Leadership and People's war, Cambridge: Cambridge University Press.

Challinor, E. (2007) "Cape Verde" in J. Middleton, J. Miller et al (ed.) New Encyclopedia of Africa, 2nd Edition, Farmington Hills, MI: Thomson Gale.

Challinor, E. (2005) "Up for Grabs, Civil Society in a Field of Conflicting Representations: A Case Study from Cape Verde" in J. Igoe, and T. Kelsall (ed) Between a Rock and a Hard Place: African NGOs, Donors and the State, Durham, North Carolina: Carolina Academic Press.

Challinor, E. (2005). A cooperação e o Associativismo em Cabo Verde: um Estudo de Caso Comparativo, Actas do I Congresso Lusófono do Terceiro Sector/III Congresso Brasileiro do Voluntariado no Porto, 17-19 Novembro 2005.

Chambers, R. (1983). Rural Development: Putting the Last First, London: Longmans.

Chambers, R. (1993). Challenging the Professions: Frontiers for Rural Development, London: Intermediate Technology Publications.

Chambers, R. Pacey, A., and Thrupp, L. A. (1989). Farmer First: Farmer Innovation and Agricultural Research, London: Intermediate Technology Publications.

Chrisman, L. (1997). "Journeying to Death: Gilroy's 'Black Atlantic'" in Race and Class, Vol. 39. Issue 2.

Christian, M. (2001). "African Centered Knowledge: a British Perspective" in The Western Journal of Black Studies, Vol. 25. Issue 1.

Clammer, J. (1984). "Approaches to Ethnographic Research" in R.F. Ellen (ed.), Ethnographic Research: A Guide to General Conduct, London: Academic Press.

Clark, J. (1991). Democratizing Development: The Role of Voluntary Organizations. London: Earthscan.

Clifford, J. and Marcus, G. E. (eds), (1986). Writing Culture: The Poetics and Politics of Ethnography, London: University of California Press.

Cohen, A. (1985). The Symbolic Construction of Community, London: Tavistock Productions Ltd.

Collins, J. L. (1997). "Development Theory and the Politics of Location: an Example from North Eastern Brazil" in V. Tucker (ed.), Cultural Perspectives on Development, London: Frank Class and Company Limited.

Commins, S. (1997). "World Vision International and Donors: Too Close for Comfort?" in D. Hulme and M. Edwards, (eds), NGOs, States and Donors: Too Close for Comfort? London: Macmillan Press Ltd.

Conklin, B. A. and Graham, L. R. (1995) "The Shifting Middle Ground: Amazonian Indians and Eco-Politics" in American Anthropologist 97 (4): 695-710.

Cooper, F. (1994). "Conflict and Connection: Rethinking Colonial African History" in The American Historical Review, Vol.99, No 5, 1516-1545.

Correia e Silva, A. L. (1995). Historias de um Sahel Insular, Praia: Spleen-Edições.

Correio 15, (1996). Reabertura das Frentes em Porto Novo, 16 April, p2.

Crewe, E. and Harrison, E. (1998). Whose Development? An ethnography of Aid, London: Zed Books.

Crocker, D. A. (1991). "Toward Development Ethics" in World Development, 19, 5, 457-483.

Crush, J. (ed.) (1995). Power of Development, London: Routledge.

Davidson, B. (1969). The Liberation of Guiné: Aspects of an African Revolution, Middlesex: Penguin Books.

Davidson, B. (1989). The Fortunate Isles: A Study in African Transformation, London: Century Hutchinson Limited.

De Soto, H. (2001). The Mystery of Capital: Why Capitalism Triumphs in the West and Fails Elsewhere, London: Black Swan.

De Vries, P. (1992). "A Research Journey: On Actors, Concepts and the Text" in N. Long and A. Long (eds), Battlefields of Knowledge: the Interlocking of Theory and Practice in Social Research and Development, London: Routledge.

Dow, S. (1995). Non-Governmental Organizations in Cape Verde: An Analysis and Suggestions for their Greater Involvement in the Development of Cape Verde, Praia: UNDP.

Duarte, F. and Mertz, M. (1996). Joint Evaluation of European Union Programme Food Aid Stage Two. Cape Verde: an Extended Study, Praia.

Du Bois, W.E.B. (1989). The Souls of Black Folk, New York: Bantam.

Dunleavy, P. and O'Leary, B. (1987). Theories of the State: the Politics of Liberal Democracy, London: The Macmillan Press Ltd.

Epstein, A. L. (1978). Ethos and Identity: Three Studies in Ethnicity, London: Tavistock publications.

Epstein, A. L. (1981). Urbanization and Kinship: the Domestic Domain on the Copperbelt of Zambia, 1950-1956, New York: Academic Press.

Eriksen, T. H. (1993). Ethnicity and Nationalism: Anthropological Perspectives, London: Pluto Press.

Escobar, A. (1984). "Discourse and Power in Development: Michel Foucault and the Relevance of his Work to the Third World" in Alternatives, X (Winter 1984-85), 377-400.

Escobar, A. (1991). "Anthropology and the Development Encounter: the Making and Marketing of Development Anthropology" in American Ethnologist, 18, 4, 658-682.

Escobar, A. (1995). Encountering Development: The Making and Unmaking of the Third World, Princeton: Princeton University Press.

Esteva, G. (1992). "Development", in W. Sachs (ed.), The Development Dictionary: A Guide to Knowledge as Power, London: Zed Books Ltd.

Farrington, J. and Bebbington, A., (1993). Reluctant Partners? Non-Governmental Organizations, the State and Sustainable Agricultural Development. London: Routledge.

Farrugia, C. (1987). "The Professional Development of Educational Personnel" in The Challenge of Scale: Educational Development in the Small States of the Common wealth, London: Commonwealth Secretariat Publications.

Featherstone, M. (1995). Undoing Culture: Globalization, Postmodernism and Identity, London: Sage Publications.

Ferguson, J. (1990). The Anti-politics Machine: 'Development', Depoliticisation and Bureaucratic Power in Lesotho. Cambridge: Cambridge University Press.

Ferguson, J. (1997a). "Anthropology and its Evil Twin: 'Development' in the Constitution of a Discipline" in F. Cooper and R. Packard (eds), International Development and the Social Sciences: Essays on the History and Politics of Knowledge, London: University of California Press.

Ferguson, J. (1997b). "The Country and the City on the Copperbelt" in A. Gupta and J. Ferguson (eds), Culture, Power, Place: Explorations in Critical Anthropology, Durham: Duke Universtiy Press.

Ferguson, J. (1998). "Transnational Topographies of Power: Beyond 'the State' and 'Civil Society' in the Study of African Politics", paper given at the ICCCR International Conference on Transnationalism at the University of Manchester, 16-18 May.

Ferguson, J. (2004). “Transnational Topographies of Power: Beyond ‘the state’ and ‘Civil Society’ in the Study of African Politics” in J, Vincent and D, Nugent (eds) The Anthropology of Politics, Oxford: Blackwell.

Foster, G. (1962). Traditional Cultures and the Impact of Technological Change, Evanston: Harper and Row.

Foucault, M. (1980). Power/Knowledge: Selected Interviews and Other Writings, 1972-1977, C. Gordon (ed.), New York: Pantheon.

Fowler, A. (1988). "Non-Governmental Organisations in Africa: Achieving Comparative Advantage in Relief and Micro-Development", Discussion Paper, 249, Sussex: Institute of Development Studies.

Fowler, A. (1990). "Doing it Better? Where and How NGOs have a Comparative Advantage in Facilitating Development", in AERDD Bulletin, 28, 11-20, Reading.

Foy, C. (1988). Cape Verde: Politics, Economics and Society, London: Pinter Publishers.

Frank, G. (1967). Capitalism and Underdevelopment in Latin America, New York: Monthly Review Press.

Freire, P. (1970). Pedagogy of the Oppressed, New York: Herder and Herder.

Furtado, C. A. (1993). A Transformação das Estruturas Agrárias numa Sociedade em Mudança - Santiago, Cabo Verde, Praia: Instituto Cabo Verdeano do Livro e do Disco.

Furtado, C. A. (1995). "Efeitos da Prática Política no Tecido Social Caboverdiano" in C, Araújo (ed.), De Mindelo para Cabo Verde: Convergência para a Solidariedade, Mindelo: Forum Convergência.

Gardiner, T. (1988). "Republic of Cape Verde Watershed Development Project: Evolution of the Rural Assistance Programme and Community Based Workfronts within the Watershed Development Project", Oregon: Sheladia Associates, INC.

Gardiner, T. (1997). "Cape Verde - PL 480 Food For Peace Program: Consultant's Report", February 10 to May 10, Praia: ACDI.

Gardner, K. (1997) "Mixed Messages: Contested 'Development' and the 'Plantation Rehabilitation Project' " in R.D. Grillo and R. L. Stirrat (eds), Discourses of Development: Anthropological Perspectives, Oxford: Berg.

Gardner, K. and Lewis, D. (1996). Anthropology, Development and the Post-Modern Challenge, London: Pluto Press.

Garnham, N. (1993). “Bourdieu, the Cultural Arbitrary and Television” in Calhoun, C. Lipuma, E. and Postone, M. (ed.) Bourdieu: Critical Perspectives, Cambridge: Polity Press in association with Blackwell Publishers.

Gasper, D. (1996). "Essentialism in and About Development Discourse" in R. Apthorpe and D. Gasper (eds), Arguing Development Policy: Frames and Discourses, London: Frank Class and Company Limited.

Giddens, A. (1990). The Consequences of Modernity, Stanford: Stanford University press.

Giddens, A. (1991). Modernity and Self-Identity: Self and Society in the Late Modern Age, Oxford: Polity Press.

Gill, P. (1988). "Conclusion: Helping is not Enough" in R. Poulton and M. Harris (eds), Putting People First: Voluntary Organisations and Third World Organisations, London: Macmillan Publishers.

Gilroy, P. (1993). The Black Atlantic: Modernity and Double Consciousness, London: Verso.

Gledhill, J. (1994). Power and its Disguises: Anthropological Perspectives on Politics, London: Pluto Press.

Goulet, D. (1995). Development Ethics: A Guide to Theory and Practice, London: Zed Books, Ltd.

Grassi, M. (2003). Rabidantes: Comércio Espontâneo Transnacional em Cabo Verde, Lisbon: Imprensa de Ciências Sociais and Spleen Edições.

Gregroy, C. (2002). "The Anthropology of the Economy: Community, Market, Culture" in The Australian Journal of Anthropology, Vol. 13. Issue 3.

Greenfield, S. M. (1976). "In Search of Social Identity: Strategies of Ethnic Identity Management Amongst Capeverdeans in Southeastern Massachusetts", in Luso-Brazilian Review, 13, 1 (June), 3-17.

Grillo, R. D. (1997). "Discourses of Development: the View from Anthropology" in R.D. Grillo and R. L. Stirrat (eds), Discourses of Development: Anthropological Perspectives, Oxford: Berg.

Grillo, R. D. (1999). "'An African Railwayman is a Railwayman'...Or the Subject of the Subject of the Subject" in J. R. Campbell and A. Rew (eds), Identity and Affect: Experiences of Identity in a Globalising World, London: Pluto Press.

Gudeman, S. (2001). The Antropology of Economy: Community, Market and Culture, Oxford: Blackwell Publishers.

Guijt, I. and Shah, M. K. (eds) (1998). The Myth of Community: Gender Issues in Participatory Development, London: ITDG Publishing.

Gupta, A. (1995). "Blurred Boundaries: the Discourse of Corruption, the Culture of Politics, and the Imagined State" in American Ethnologist, 22, 2, 375-402.

Gupta, A. and Ferguson, J. (1997). "Beyond 'Culture': Space, Identity, and the Politics of Difference" in A. Gupta and J. Ferguson (eds), Culture, Power, Place: Explorations in Critical Anthropology, Durham: Duke Universtiy Press.

Hailey, J. (2001). "Beyond the Formulaic: Process and Practice in South Asian NGOs" in Cooke, B. and Kothari, U. (ed.) Participation: the New Tyranny?, London: Zed Books.

Hall, S. (1984). "The State in Question" in G. McLennan, D. Held and S. Hall (eds), The Idea of the Modern State, Milton Keynes: Open University Press.

Hall, S. (1990). "Cultural Identity and Diaspora" in J. Rutherford (ed.), Identity, Community, Culture, Difference, London: Lawrence and Wishart.

Hall, S. (1991). "Old and New Identities" in A. King (ed.), Culture, London: Sage Publications.

Hall, S. (1993). "Cultural Identity in Question" in S. Hall, D. Held and T. McGrew (eds), Modernity and its Futures, Cambridge: Polity Press.

Hall, S. (1996). "Introduction: Who Needs Identity?" in S. Hall and P. Du Gay (eds), Questions of Cultural Identity, London: Sage Publications.

Hancock, G. (1989). Lords of Poverty, London: Macmillan Press.

Hanlon, J. (1991). Mozambique: Who Calls the Shots? London: James Currey.

Hannerz, U. (1992). Cultural Complexity: Studies in the Social Organization of Meaning, New York: Colombial University Press.

Harbeson, J. W. (1994). "Civil Society and the Study of African Politics: A Preliminary Assessment" in J.W. Harbeson, D. Rothchild and N. Chazan (eds), Civil Society and the State in Africa, London: Lynne Rienner Publications.

Haug, T. Anderson, S, E; Grude, K, V. (2004). Goal Directed Project Management: Effective Techniques and Strategies, London: Kogan Page.

Henkel, H. and Stirrat, R. (2001). “Participation as Spiritual Duty; Empowerment as Secular Subjection” in Cooke, B and Kothari, U. (eds) Participation: The New Tyranny? Zed Books, London, pp 168-184.

Hobart, M. (ed.), (1993). An Anthropological Critique of Development. London: Routledge.

Holy, L. (1984). "Theory, Methodology and the Research Process" in R.F. Ellen (ed.), Ethnographic Research: A Guide to General Conduct, London: Academic Press.

Hulme, D. and Edwards, M. (eds), (1997). NGOs, States and Donors: Too Close for Comfort? London: Macmillan Press Ltd.

Instituto de Emprego e Formação Profissional (2006) Inquérito ao Emprego 2005: Apresentação dos Principais Resultados: www.iefp.cv

Instituto Nacional de Estatística (2000, 2004) Census: www.ine.cv

Inkeles, A. and Smith, D. H. (1974). Becoming Modern: Individual Change in Six Developing Countries, London: Heinemann Educational Books Ltd.

Jameson, F. (1998). "Notes on Globalization as a Philosophical Issue" in F. Jameson and M. Miyoshi (eds), The Cultures of Globalization, Durham: Duke University Press.

Jenkins, R. (1992). Pierre Bourdieu, London: Routledge.

Jenkins, R. (1994). "Rethinking ethnicity: identity, categorization and power" in Ethnic and Racial Studies, 17, 2, 197-223.

Kabeer, N. (1994). Reversed Realities: Gender Hierarchies in Development Thought, London: Verso.

Keane, J. (1998). Civil Society: Old Images, New Visions, Cambridge: Polity Press.

Kelsall, T. and Igoe J. (eds) (2005) Between a Rock and a Hard Place: African NGOs, Donors and the State, Durham: Carolina Academic Press.

Korten, D. C. and Carner, G. (1984). "Planning Frameworks for People-Centered Development" in D.C. Korten and R. Klauss (eds), People-Centered Development: Contributions Toward Theory and Planning Frameworks, Connecticut: Kumarian Press.

Kothari, U. and Minogue, M. (eds). (2002). Development Theory and Practice: Critical Perspectives, Hampshire: Palgrave.

Laclau, E. (1977). Politics and Ideology in Marxist Theory: Capitalism, Fascism, Populism, London: NLB.

Langworthy, M. and Finan, T. J. (1997). Waiting for Rain: Agricultural and Ecological Imbalance in Cape Verde, Boulder: Lynne Rienner Publishers.

Lansing, S. (1991). Priests and Programmers: Tecnologies of Power in the Engineered Landscape of Bali, Princeton: Princeton University Press.

Latour, B. (1993). We Have Never Been Modern, Hemel Hempstead: Harvester Wheatsheaf.

Lechner, F., J. and Boli, J. (ed.) (2000). The Globalization Reader, Oxford: Blackwell Publishers.

Lefebvre, H. (1995). Introduction to Modernity: Twelve Preludes, September 1959-May1961, London: Verso.

Lesourd, M. (1995). Etat et Société aux îles du Cap-Vert, Paris: Karthala.

Lima, S. (1990). "Frentes de Trabalho - Uma Contribuição para a sua Reconversão", Santo Antão:MOP.

Lipton, M. (1984). "Urban Bias in World Development" in D.C. Korten and R. Klauss (eds), People-Centered Development: Contributions Toward Theory and Planning Frameworks, Connecticut: Kumarian Press.

Lobban, R. A. (1995). Cape Verde: Crioulo Colony to Independent Nation, Oxford: Westview Press.

Long, N. (1992). "Introduction" in N. Long and A. Long (eds), Battlefields of Knowledge: the Interlocking of Theory and Practice in Social Research and Development, London: Routledge.

Long, N. (2000). "Exploring local/global Transformations" em Arce, A., e Long, N. (2000) Anthropology, Development and Modernities, London: Routldedge.

Long, N. (2001). Development Sociology: Actor Perspectives, London: Routldedge.

Lopes, B. (1993). Chiquinho, Lousã: ALAC.

Macpherson, S. (1982). Social Policy in the Third World, Brighton: Wheatsheaf Books.

MacRae, D. (1969). "Populism as an Ideology" in G. Ionescu and E. Gellner (eds), Populism: its Meanings and Characteristics, Hertfordshire: Garden City Press Ltd.

Malinowski, B. (1922). "Ethnology and the Study of Society" in Economica, 2, 208-219.

Marcus, G. E. (1998). Ethnography though Thick and Thin, Princeton: Princeton University Press.

Marcussen, H. S. (1996). "NGOs, the State and Civil Society", in Review of African Political Economy, 69, 405-423.

Marsden, D. (1990). "The Meaning of Social Development" in D. Marsden and P. Oakley (eds), Evaluating Social Development Projects, Oxford: Oxfam.

Mayer, J. (1990). "Development Problems and Prospects in Portuguese-Speaking Africa" in International Labour Review, 129, 4, 459-478.

Mbembe, A. (2001). On the Postcolony, Berkeley: University of California Press.

McGrew, A. (1992). "A Global Society?" in S. Hall, D. Held and T. McGrew (eds), Modernity and its Futures, Cambridge: Polity Press.

Meillassoux, C. (1981). Maidens, Meal and Money: Capitalism and the Domestic Economy, Cambridge: Cambridge University Press.

Meintel, D. (1981). "Cape Verdean Americans" in J. Rollins (ed.), Hidden Minorities: the Persistence of Ethnicity in American Life, London: University Press of America.

Meintel, D. (1984a). Race, Culture and Portuguese Colonialism in Cabo Verde, Syracuse, New York: Maxwell School of Citizenship and Public Affairs, Syracuse University.

Meintel, D. (1984b). "Emigração em Cabo Verde: Solução ou Problema" in Revista Internacional de Estudos Africanos, 2, 93-120.

Midgley, J. (1995). Social Development: the Developmental Perspective in Social Welfare, London: Sage Publications.

Midgley, J. Hall, A., Hardiman, M., and Narine, D. (1986). Community Participation, Social Development and the State, New York: Methuen.

Mignolo, W. D. (2000). Local Histories/Global Designs: Coloniality, Subaltern Knowledges, and Border Thinking, Princeton: Princeton University Press.

Ministério da Coordenação Económica, (1995a). Projecto NLTPS - Estudo Nacional de Perspectivas a Longo Prazo: "Cabo Verde 2020". As Principais Aspirações Nacionais - Relatório, Praia.

Ministério da Coordenação Económica, (1995b). Projecto NLTPS - Estudo Nacional de Perspectivas a Longo Prazo: "Cabo Verde 2020". As Principais Aspirações Nacionais - Mesas Redondas nos Concelhos, Praia.

Ministério da Coordenação Económica, (undated, c.1996). "Regulamento para o Establecimento de Parcerias entre o Governo e as Organizações da Sociedade Civil", Praia.

Ministério da Coordenação Económica, (1997). The 1997-2000 Plan's Main Options. Cape Verde's Dynamic Insertion in the World Economic System - an Option for Self-Sustained Economic and Social Development, Praia.

Ministério da Coordenação Económica, (1997a). Modalidades de Intervenção Das Organizações Não Governamentais (ONGs) e Quadro de Concertação Governo/ONGs. (Proposta de Decreto Lei). Praia: first version of unpublished proposal document.

Ministério da Coordenação Económica, (1997b). Organizacões da Sociedade Civil. Praia: second version of unpublished proposal document.

Ministério da Coordenação Económica, (1997c). Organizacões Não Governamentais e Outras Organizações Comunitarias do Desenvolvimento. Praia: third version of unpublished proposal document.

Ministério da Coordenação Económica, (1997d). Organizacões Não Governamentais e Outras Organizações Comunitarias do Desenvolvimento. Subsídios para a regulamentação da Constuição e funcionamento das ONGs e outras OCD. Praia: fourth version of unpublished proposal document.

Ministério da Coordenação Económica, (1997e). Fundo Nacional de Apoio As Iniciativas de Base. (Proposta de um Mecanismo para a sua Criação). Praia: third version of unpublished proposal document.

Ministério da Coordenação Económica, (1997f). Quadro de Concertação Governo/ONGs. Praia: second version of unpublished proposal document.

Ministério da Coordenação Económica, (1997g). Quadro de Concertação Governo/ONGs/OSC. Praia: third version of unpublished proposal document.

Ministério da Coordenação Económica, (undated). "Perspectivas de Reconversão das FAIMO na Optica do Combate a Pobreza", Programa Nacional de Luta Contra a Pobreza provisional and definitive versions of report, Praia.

Mitchell, K. (1996). "In Whose interest? Transnational capital and the production of multiculturalism in Candada" in R. Wilson and W. Dissanayake (eds), Global/Local: Cultural Production and the Transnational Imaginary, Durham: Duke University Press.

Mitchell, T. (2007). “The Properties of Markets” in D. Makenzie, F. Muniesa and L. Siu (eds), “Do Economists Make Markets?” Princeton: Princeton University Press.

Mitchell, T. (1991). "The Limits of the State: Beyond Statist Approaches and their Critics" in American Political Science Review, 85, 1, 77-96.

Mohan, G. (2001).”Beyond Participation: Strategies for Deeper Empowerment” in Cooke, B and Kothari, U. (ed) Participation: The New Tyranny? Zed Books, London.

Mohanty, C. (1988). "Under Western Eyes: Feminist Scholarship and Colonial Discourses" in Feminist Review, 30, 61-88.

Monteiro, D. C. (1996). Subsídios para o Estudo da Demografia em Cabo Verde: Situação Passada, Presente e Perspectivas Futuras, Praia: MCE.

Monteiro, F. (1996). "O Fatalismo das-águas" in Novo Jornal de Cabo Verde, 4 September, p15, Praia.

Moore, D. B. and Schmitz, G. J. (eds), (1995). Debating Development Discourse: Institutional and Popular Perspectives, London: Macmillan Press Ltd.

Moore, M. (1993). "Good Government? Introduction", IDS Bulletin, 24, 1, 1-6.

Moran, E. (1982). "The Evolution of Cape Verde's Agriculture" in African Economic History, 11, 63-86.

Mosse, D. (2005). Cultivating Development: an Ethnography of Aid Development and Practice, London: Pluto Press.

Mosse, D. (2004). “Is Good Policy Unimplementable? Reflections on the Ethnography of Aid Policy and Practice” in Development and Change 35 (4): 639-671.

Mosse, D. (1998). "The Making and Marketing of Participatory Development: A Sceptical Note", paper given at the conference entitled "Participation: the New Tyranny?" at the Institute for Development Policy and Management, University of Manchester, 3 November.

Mudimbe, V. Y. (1988). The Invention of Africa, Bloomington: Indiana University Press.

Novo Jornal Cabo Verde, (11 June, 1997:11). "Forum de Concertação Nacional. Governo, ONG e OSC Deitam Cartas na Mesa", Praia.

Organisation for Economic Cooperation and Development (OECD), (1995). Development Co-operation: Efforts and Policies of the Members of the Development Assistance Committee, Paris.

OECD Development Assistance Committee (DAC) Database: www.oecd.org/dac/stats/idsonline

Paul, S. and Israel, A. (eds), (1991). Non-Governmental Organizations and the World Bank: Co-operation for Development, Washington, DC: World Bank.

Pereira Silva, J. (1995). Subsídios para uma Política de Ordenamento do Território e Infra-Estruturação, Praia: MCE.

Persram, N. (1994). "Politicizing the Feminine, Globalizing the Feminist", in Alternatives: Social Transformation and Human Governance, Vol. 19 Number 3.

Pigg, S. L. (1992). "Inventing Social Categories Through Place: Social Representations and Development in Nepal" in Comparative Studies in Society and History, 34, 3, 491-513.

Pigg, S. L. (1996). "The Credible and the Credulous: the Question of 'Villagers' Beliefs' in Nepal" in Cultural Anthropology, 11, 2, 160-201.

Pires, J. (1995). Cabo Verde: Subsídios para o Estudo do Sistema Produtivo Nacional com Especial Incidência no Sector Primário, Praia: MCE.

Porter, D. J. (1995). "Scenes From Childhood: The Homesickness of Development Discourses" in J. Crush (ed.), Power of Development, London: Routledge.

Porter, D. Allen, B., and Thompson, G. (1991). Development in Practice: Paved with Good Intentions, London: Routledge.

Poulton, R. (1988). "On Theories and Strategies" in R. Poulton and M. Harris (eds), Putting People First: Voluntary Organisations and Third World Organisations, London: Macmillan Publishers.

Rahnema, M. (1990). "Participatory Action Research: the 'Last Temptation of Saint' Development" in Alternatives, Social Transformation and Humane Governance, XV, 2, 207-8.

Rew, A. (1997). "The Donor's Discourse: Official Social Development Knowledge in the 1980s" in R.D. Grillo and R. L. Stirrat (eds), Discourses of Development: Anthropological Perspectives, Oxford: Berg.

Rist, G. (1997). The History of Development from Western Origins to Global Faith, London: Zed Books Ltd.

Robertson, A. F. (1984). People and the State: An Anthropology of Planned Development, Cambridge: Cambridge University Press.

Robertson, R. (1995). "Glocalization: Time-Space and Homogeneity-Heterogeneity" in M. Featherstone, S. Lash and R. Robertson (eds), Global Modernities, London: Sage Publications.

Robinson, M. (1994). "Governance, Democracy and Conditionality: NGOs and the New Policy Agenda" in A. Clayton (ed.), Governance, Democracy and Conditionality: What Role for NGOs? Oxford: INTRAC.

Rofel, L. (1997). "Rethinking Modernity: Space and Factory Discipline in China" in A. Gupta and J. Ferguson (eds), Culture, Power, Place: Explorations in Critical Anthropology, Durham: Duke Universtiy Press.

Rogers, E. M. (1969). "Motivations, Values, and Attitudes of Subistence Farmers: Toward a Subculture of Peasantry" in C.R. Wharton (ed.), Subsistence Agriculture and Economic Development, Chicago: Aldine Publishing Company.

Rostow, W. (1960). The Stages of Economic Growth: A Non-Communist Manifesto, London: Cambridge University Press.

Sachs, W. (ed.), (1992). The Development Dictionary: A Guide to Knowledge as Power, London: Zed Books Ltd.

Sachs, W. (1992). "One World" in W. Sachs (ed.), The Development Dictionary: A Guide to Knowledge as Power, London: Zed Books Ltd.

Sahlins, M. (1976). Culture and Practical Reason, London: University of Chicago Press.

Said, E. (1978). Orientalism, London and Henley: Routledge and Kegan Paul.

Salústio, D. (1996). A Mulher no Quadro do Desenvolvimento Humano Sustentável: Situação Actual e Perspectivas, Praia: MCE.

Sampson, S. (1996). "The Social Life of Projects: Importing Civil Society to Albania" in C. Hann and E. Dunn (eds), Civil Society: Challenging Western Models, London: Routledge.

Sanches, A., (1996). Cabo Verde: Subsídios para o Estudo da Dimensão Internacional do Desenvolvimento, Praia: MCE.

Sangren, S. (1995). "'Power' against Ideology: A Critique of Foucaultian Usage" in Cultural Anthropology, 10, 1, 3-40.

Scott, J. (1985). Weapons of the Weak: Everyday Forms of Peasant Resistance, New Haven, Conn.: Yale University Press.

Seers, D. (1972). "The Meaning of Development" in N. T. Uphoff and W. F. Ilchman (eds), The Political Economy of Development: Theoretical and Empirical Contributions, London: Universtiy of California Press.

Seidel, G. (1985). "Political Discourse Analysis" in T. van Dijk (ed.), Handbook of Discourse Analysis, 4, London: Academic Press, 43-60.

Selwyn, P. (ed.), (1975). Development Policy in Small Countries, London: Croom Helm.

Selwyn, P. (1980). "Smallness and Islandness" in World Development, 8, 12, 945-951.

Shreshta, N., (1995). "Becoming a Development Category" in J. Crush (ed.), Power of Development, London: Routledge.

Slater, D. (1993). "The Political Meanings of Development: in Search of New Horizons" in F. J. Schuurman (ed.), Beyond the Impasse: New Directions in Development Theory, London: Zed Books.

Smart, B. (1988). Michel Foucault, London: Routledge.

Smillie, I. (1995). The Alms Bazaar. Altruism Under Fire - Non-Profit Organizations and International Development, London: IT Publications.

Social Development Division, (1995). "Guidance Note on How to do Stakeholder Analysis of Aid Projects and Programmes" in Stakeholder Participation and Analysis, London: Department for International Development.

Stewart, A. (1969). "The Social Roots" in G. Ionescu and E. Gellner (eds), Populism: its Meanings and Characteristics, Hertfordshire: Garden City Press Ltd.

Stewart, S. (1997). "Happy Ever After in the Marketplace: Non-governmental Organisations and Uncivil Society", in Review of African Political Economy, 71, 11-34.

Stirrat, R. L. (1997). "Cultures of Consultancy", paper presented at a workshop on consultancy at the University of Warwick in June 1997.

Suleri, S. (1992). The Rhetoric of English India, Chicago: Chicago University Press.

Swartz, M.J. Turner, V.W. and Tuden, A. ([1966] 2002). "Political Anthropology" in J. Vincent (ed.), The Anthropology of Politics: a Reader in Ethnography, Theory and Critique, Oxford: Blackwell Publishers Ltd.

Teixeira, A. and Monteiro, J.M.P. (1996). Estudo Sobre o Desenvolvimento Institucional, Praia: MCE.

Temudo, M. (2008). A Terra está a Emagrecer. Santiago, Cabo Verde, Lisboa: Periploi.

The Economist (1998). Country Profile - Guinea-Bissau, São Tomé and Príncipe, Cape Verde, the Economist Intelligence Unit Limited.

Tucker, V. (ed.), (1997). Cultural Perspectives on Development, London: Frank Cass and Company Limited.

UNICEF, (1995). "Cuidados Primários do Ambiente: Cabo Verde, Proposta de Projecto", Praia, Cape Verde.

United Nations, (1994). Development Strategies for Small Island Developing Countries, New York: UN General Assembley.

Unnithan, M. and Srivastava, K. (1997). "Gender Politics, Development and Women's Agency in Rajasthan" in R.D. Grillo and R. L. Stirrat (eds), Discourses of Development: Anthropological Perspectives, Oxford: Berg.

Veiga, M. (1995). Cultura e Desenvolvimento em Cabo Verde, Praia: MCE.

Vera Cruz, J. H., (1997). "Relatório Trimestral para o Periodo 01/04/97 a 30/06/97: PL-480 Programa Alimentar para a Paz", Praia: ACDI.

Vicente Lopes, J. (1996). Cabo Verde: Os Bastidores da Independência, Instituto Camões, Lisbon and Centro Cultural Português, Praia and Mindelo.

Wade, P. (2002). Race, Nature and Culture: an Anthropological Perspective, London: Pluto Press.

Wallerstein, I. (1974). The Modern World System, New York: Academic Press.

Wallerstein, I. (1984). The Politics of the World Economy, Cambridge: Cambridge University Press.

Wilk, R. R. (1996). Economies and Cultures: Foundations of Economic Anthropology, Oxford: Westview Press.

Williams, R. (1976). The Country and the City, London: the Hogarth Press.

Wolf, E. (1982). Europe and the People Without History, Berkeley: University of California Press.

Wood, G. (1985). "The Politics of Development Policy Labelling" in Development and Change, 16, 3, 347-73.

World Bank, (1994). Poverty in Cape Verde: A Summary Assessment and a Strategy for its Alleviation, Washington, D.C.

Worsley, P. (1964). The Third World, London: Weidenfeld and Nicholson.

Worsley, P. (1969). "The Concept of Populism" in G. Ionescu and E. Gellner (eds), Populism: its Meanings and Characteristics, Hertfordshire: Garden City Press Ltd.

Yunus, M. (2003). Banker to the Poor: Micro-Lending and the Battle Against World Poverty; New York: Public Affairs.

Franz von Benda-Beckmann;
Keebet von Benda-Beckmann
Social Security Between Past and Future
Ambonese Networks of Care and Support
Social security is a particularly precarious issue where states hardly provide any services in periods of need and distress. The book analyses the arrangements relationships through which food, shelter and care are provided on the island of Ambon, famous spice island in Eastern Indonesia. It also shows how relations of support tie Ambonese migrants in the Netherlands to their home villages, and how normative conceptions of need and care among kinsmen and villagers change over time. Though special in their own historical setting, Ambonese networks of care and support are illustrative of poor rural populations in the Third World. Focusing on the precursors of the violent conflict that erupted in 1998, the book shows that social security is like a magnifying glass linking past, present and future.
Bd. 13, 2007, 344 S., 29,90 €, br.,
ISBN 978-3-8258-0718-4

Gerd Spittler
Founders of the Anthropology of Work
German Social Scientists of the 19th and Early 20th Centuries and the First Ethnographers
Work is vital for most individuals and for every society. Yet it leads a Cinderella-like existence within social anthropology. Even today we can learn from older social scientists like Karl Marx, Wilhelm Heinrich Riehl, Karl Bücher, Eduard Hahn, Wilhelm Ostwald, and Max Weber. Comparing industrial and non-industrial work, they were interested in the character of work as performance, play or ethical deed, and as rational action. Due to a lack of ethnographic studies, the empirical basis of their analysis remained weak. A serious ethnography of work was started by Karl Weule, Richard Thurnwald, and Bronislaw Malinowski. Having close links to the older social scientists they introduced new perspectives based on fieldwork in Africa and Melanesia.
Bd. 14, 2008, 320 S., 29,90 €, br.,
ISBN 978-3-8258-0780-1

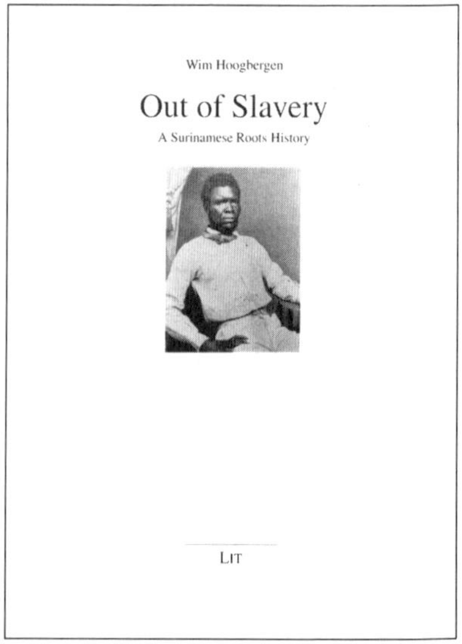

Wim Hoogbergen
Out of Slavery
A Surinamese Roots History
Bd. 6, 2008, 256 S., 19,90 €, br., ISBN 978-3-8258-8112-2